GW00865823

Se___ ___ ___y!

And again, together
we managed to get a
new book
in circulation.

Thanks for the
support!

Mollina / Spain

05.09.2022

Monika

© 2016 Monika von Borthwick
Production and publishing:
BoD – Books on Demand, Norderstedt
ISBN: 9783756221400

1. Edition (2016) German
1. Edition (2022) English

English Translation: Patricia Troncho (2022)

Carpe Diem?

If you want to explore Newfoundland and the maritime provinces of Canada, please bear in mind that you'll have to slip into a warming anorak even in summer. Every rain-free day is a gift at the edge of the Labrador Current. Rubber boots and good rain wear are also essential. You can admire icebergs from Greenland on the island in the north as late as June/July, and the small harbours are often decorated with ice floes until well into the summer.

But when the sun breaks through, this region of Canada opens up in all its diversity and drama. In the north, a former Viking settlement bears witness to the earliest community, even before the Europeans "discovered" America and later established themselves there. Small, picturesque fishing villages tell of a hard struggle for existence - in the past as well as today. Lonely stretches of land give flora and fauna the opportunity to face the harsh weather.

The capital, St. John's, impresses with colourful wooden houses and a lively pub culture. The oddball humour of the population is unique, and they all love their musical heritage. Carpe diem! Seize the day …

Monika von Borthwick belongs to the older generation and lives in culturally rich Upper Bavaria. In addition to her professional work, she looked after bus travellers as a tour guide in Europe. Even then, she wrote down her experiences with the countries and their people in as much detail as she could.

After the death of her husband, she shifted to travelling alone and explored numerous areas in Europe and North America on her own with her newly acquired motor home and her two dogs. In the process, she discovered a love of storytelling and sent detailed reports home by e-mail. These documents form the basis of her personal stories from each host country.

Monika von Borthwick

Carpe Diem!
Seize the day!
... tomorrow it could rain again.

With the motorhome through
Newfoundland and the
maritime provinces of Eastern Canada
(PEI, Nova Scotia, New Brunswick)

The entertaining diary of the
MoWuKnuffels

*I never travel without
my diary.
You should always have something
exciting to read
with you.*
(Oscar Wilde 1854 - 1900)

Every preparation is different
A little theory to start with

At the beginning of 2013, I was once again fortunate enough to unexpectedly discover a pleasant sum on my bank account, which certainly enabled me to embark on a big trip with my two dogs for the last time. After all, I already had some years of experience being sixty and who knew how long I would still have the energy and health to tackle a major project.

I had to abandon my last tour in Toronto in 2010 because I tripped over a hose while refuelling and suffered a splinter fracture in my left ankle. At that point, the tour to Newfoundland had to be cancelled. I wanted to pick up where I left off and fulfil my next travel dream.

In the meantime, our "family" situation had changed a little: my travel-experienced Wuschel unfortunately had to leave us for health reasons, instead the bright Pomeranian Wurschtel joined our pack. He had been a home-bred dog and was now gaining his first travel experiences with his new globetrotting family. To train for this varied life, we spent the winter with the camper in Spain on a camping site. This time was already tremendously exciting and new for the little dog. (see "Chorizo & Co", BoD Verlag Norderstedt!)

Great undertakings cast their shadows ahead and so I went into the first planning phase as early as spring 2013. I tracked the internet daily for hours, looking for a cheap used Canadian motor home. In the process, I discovered the largest platform for this at "Kijiji.com".

Why Canada as a starting point? One of the main reasons was the chronological order and planning of the trip and my temporary general visa for the USA which expired in autumn 2015. The second decisive reason was the matter of the driver's licence. Canada rewrote the German document into a Canadian one without a hitch, a prerequisite for taking out national car insurance.

International driving licences were accepted by the Canadian Traffic Act for six months, but not by insurance companies. My plans still amounted to eighteen months. The rules in the USA did not require a practical test in most states for transcription, but one had to pass a theoretical exam. At the age of 63 and with forty years of unpunished driving, that was too silly for me.

The third reason was my friends between Toronto and Montreal, experienced in motor homes, who would help me, buy a used one and whose address I could give as my Canadian base. A valid permanent address is essential for such an endeavour. How important and helpful this was – as we would see later.

Very well! After an extensive search, a few vehicles came into view in the summer of 2013. My friend Richard and his wife visited and took a look at their general condition. Again and again, I had to hear: "Leave it alone!" Then suddenly a call via Skype: "I have bought an RV for you!" He had chosen a vehicle on the net, for about 8500.- CAD. Richard had negotiated the supplier down to 7500.- CAD. The car had a few years under its belt, was in good condition after inspection and supposedly had only 76,000 kilometres on its speedometer. This could be interesting...

I booked a flight to Montreal for October (which again took quite some time on the PC) to inspect my new vehicle and take care of all administrative matters on the spot and in person.

Before that I had to find a suitable insurance company at a reasonable price. Easier said than done … I contacted more than twenty-five insurance companies via the internet to get an acceptable fee. Many were not interested at all and did not reply, some had outrageously high price levels. Only one "broker" was able to make me an acceptable offer. It was thanks to his commitment that we finally did business. Phase two began.

**Open your wallet! Purse closed!
Surprises guaranteed!**

My ten-day stay in the province of Ontario was almost over-flowing with activities. In between, there were several – to me unnecessary – holidays, such as Thanksgiving, when our hands were tied because no office was working.

To get any papers at all, we first had to pay the sales tax. Since we secretly cut the purchase price for the office to 4500.- CAD, it was accordingly low ("only" about 600.-CAD). In return, we received the so-called "history" of the vehicle. It listed all the previous owners and the mileage of the car. When I studied it in detail, I was astonished to discover that the 76,000 kilometres advertised had suddenly become 125,000 kilometres. Had the previous owner cheated us? Had the speedometer been manipulated? We asked him for a talk. It turned out that he had told us miles instead of kilometres in the advertisement so he had made a mistake in the designation. Because of the resulting depreciation, we bargained down an-other thousand dollars. I was still happy about that.

The next step was the safety and emissions tests which have to be done every time a vehicle is bought or sold – either by the previous owner or by the buyer. So off to the garage! After a short check, we were told that more extensive repairs would be necessary than we had expected. The cost was 2,500.- CAD! Plus, the emissions test with.... I had no choice! Gritting my teeth, I signed the garage order.

The profit from the two reductions was therefore completely lost. From a traffic point of view, however, my new rolling home was now absolutely safe. As a small consideration, we wanted confirmation from the dealer that the gas test would be OK. We hoped to be able to save at least a little here. This was noted on the invoice as requested. The gas safety test was only required by the insurance company.

So we marched again with the available documents to the state traffic office, to acquire the sticker for the vehicle tax. The lady at the counter was not on the engaging side but still pointed out to us that the motor home's tax was still paid until the end of the year. Since the vehicle would be in the barn until May 15th anyway, we could save ourselves the expense and settle the debt when I returned to Canada. Thank you very much!

Finally, I was able to move my motor home into its walled winter quarters and was about 450.-CAD lighter for its six-month sleeping place.
Without the driving help of my friends, I would have been totally lost in this constant back and forth and would still be travelling from office to office today. For insurance reasons, I was not allowed to drive my own vehicle, as I did not yet have a Canadian driver's licence. But I needed my German driving licence for the winter trip to Spain, so I did not want to have it rewritten yet. Thus, although I was listed as the owner of the car with all rights and obligations at the agency, Richard had to be my driver with a Canadian licence.
I found this arrangement grotesque, because with the international driver's licence I could drive around anywhere in Canada for half a year and take any rental car. But not with my own Canadian vehicle! Long live bureaucracy!

We thought we finally had everything in place for the big trip. Satisfied, I climbed back on my plane to Munich, not without having taken a canoe trip on the lake in front of Richard's house – on a beautiful day of the beginning Indian summer.
Shock on my return: my insurance broker informed me by email that the insurance company wanted an official gas test and that the workshop's note on the repair certificate was not sufficient. However, the deadline for the provisional insurance would expire in the next few days. Richard had to bring the vehicle out of hibernation, make an appointment with a me-

chanic and forward the confirmation of the successful inspection to the agent – all in a rush! Further cost 64.- CAD that I could pay thanks to the technical possibilities of the internet, otherwise I would have been completely lost. Could I finally lean back and enjoy the Spanish winter? I still didn't trust the peace but when I saw on the visa receipt that the insurance company had debited the sum of around 500.-CAD (350.-Euro) for the first year, I concluded the activities of phase two for myself!

Arrival mid May 2014
Canadian driving licence
Not as simple as assumed

May 2014 – we arrived in Toronto after an eight-hour flight to the neighbouring continent! Knuffi survived the flight calmly and without protest. For Wurschtel, my liberty-loving companion, it was more strenuous. Being locked up was tantamount to prison for him. Richard was already standing at the exit ready to pick us up. This time, all the logistics were easier than the previous times because I could count on help.

Entering Canada was absolutely hassle-free. I got my stamp in the passport and many good wishes on the way. For the dogs I had to pay about 40.- CAD entry fee. The European dog passport was accepted without any problems, although it came from Spain. I had "disposed" of my old passports somewhere, but had the dogs vaccinated on time. So there was only one vaccination in the passport. To be on the safe side, however, I had the copies of the former passports close at hand.

Toronto welcomed us with rush hour traffic. We had landed at an extremely inconvenient time. There were two hundred and eighty kilometres ahead of us and we had to pass through the city and the heavily populated outskirts. "Stop and go" was therefore the order of the day and there were no stopping places to finally let the dogs out. They kept their bladders bravely tied shut and were happy to finally have their mistress near them again. Getting out of the car was also out of the question because of the rain. It wasn't just raining, it was pissing down! Pardon me!

Halfway there, we were finally able to stop at a "Tim Hortons" snack bar, give the dogs something to drink and provide ourselves with a snack. You wouldn't believe how elastic dog bladders could be! Around half past eight we finally reached our destination, in the middle of the Canadian bush, at Bob's Lake. All three of us fell asleep as soon as we could, because I had been up for twenty-three hours today due to the time difference. Tomorrow we would take a look at my new rolling home and bring it here.

The motor home started without any problems! It had survived the Canadian winter in its permanent quarters well. We took it to my friends' place by the lake, in the middle of the forest, careful not to let the police see that we hadn't put a tax stamp on it yet. That would come later. For the time being, we still needed a valid driving licence to set off on our adventure. Nothing easier than that – we thought.

We went to the driving licence office the next day, armed with the necessary papers: the passport, the driving licence and (as we thought) the international document. After all, the latter paper included the necessary translation in several languages. The lady at the counter told us that this was not accepted and that we had to show an authorised translation. So we got a phone number and an address in Kingston. We called the Immigration Service and were told that it would take a week to get the necessary translation. The cost was eighty dollars – but with an additional certified copy! Even if I had been able to produce an authorised translation from Germany, it would not have been accepted and the money would have gone down the drain.

Richard was so upset about this illogical regulation that he almost lost his cool. Only slowly could I calm him down again. It was what it was, I needed the paper and had no other choice. If we had asked for a provisional document, the waiting time would have been extended by another eight days. We hoped that by the end of this week the document would be in our hands (delayed by Labour Day, a public holiday) and we would finally have cleared all the bureaucratic hurdles.

The "new" motor home found its place for the next few days in the middle of the forest, next to Richard's boat. After he had towed his watercraft over the bumpy forest path, my doubts about the size of the camper vanished. If we could get through here, I could venture into the wilds of Canada with it!

In the meantime, I wanted to devote myself to the internal organisation of our third home. All the suitcases from the first trip and several oversized plastic bags lay decoratively scattered on the bed – chaos to the power of three! Where to start? One container after the other, nice and neat! Finally, I relived the experiences of the past weeks when I had polished up my own camper in Germany.

It was now sorted, sifted, cleaned and scrubbed. The previous owners had left many appliances on board upon request. In addition to a toaster and a small hot-air fan, there was also a hoover, a coffee machine and an electric plate. The kitchen had to be stocked up with some utensils. The predecessors did not seem to have been particularly active cooks. Long live the microwave and no-wash fast food!

Karen's cupboards emptied, mine filled up! Despite everything, intensive shopping was the order of the day, first at the "Dollar Store" for mass-produced goods, later at "Walmart" for specials. Hurray for the credit card! We had to think of everything, from safety waistcoats to screwdrivers, from pot-holders to spice jars and from clothes pegs to throw blankets. The list was endless, and we spent almost nine hours shopping from shop to shop the day after for this reason. The sorting work started all over again but in the end, we came up with a respectable motor home for our needs. Survival guaranteed!

Topic driving licence:
Faster than expected we got the call from the immigration office: we could pick up the translation, after paying 62.21 CAD with taxes, for the same content as in the international driving licence, but on DIN A4 and with an embossed stamp for the certification. Don't be angry, just surprised! Now quickly to the driving licence office… This time it went like clockwork: 80.- CAD, passport, German driving licence, translation, eye test and photo on the spot – and I got my provisional licence, valid for ninety days. In three weeks, the real driving licence would show up at Richard's place. Valid for five years! My German driving licence was confiscated and supposedly sent back to Germany. Let's see what solution I come up with at the end of our adventure.

The very next day I contacted the insurance agent, gave him the driving licence number and from that moment on I was the person responsible for my BSLA-920 (mnemonic: Bull-shit/Los Angeles - 920) Nothing easier than that!

The tax stamp was still missing. Cost for two years: 180.- CAD. Important: a duplicate of the tax stamp had to be glued into the vehicle registration. Where did I have this important paper? Panic! At home, I searched through my documents a hundred times, texted my neighbour to please look in the pho-tocopier, drove my two hosts slightly crazy ... and finally dis-covered the green piece of paper in an envelope with collected old and new bills! My God! Alzheimer's said hello!

Actually, we could have left then, if the bed hadn't been so miserable. You could feel every spring. So I decided to dig into my pocket once more and get myself a good foam pad. Easy to say! Delivery times of up to ten days everywhere and problems with price and sizes. Karen got on the phone and the internet. I'm sure we could cut the thing ourselves. Thanks to her patience and persistence, we drove back to Kingston the next morning and bought an alternative for 212.- CAD. Not just a cushion, no, it was neatly covered with solid fabric. With the truck, transport was easy, because the thing measured 1.40m x 1.90m, and the weight was easily manageable as well.

At home, we slipped the cover down and cut the foam to fit the camper. The more difficult work began afterwards: we had to patch the solid cover back together. This with my handicraft talents! Thank goodness Karen had sufficient skills for both of us. Fortunately, the kitchen was big enough for us to do the job. I will have to think carefully about whom I will pass my motorhome on to after my tour, judging by the bent fingers and pinpricks from this sh... work!

Our rolling home for
the next 18 months:
Year 1991
125,000 km,
petrol engine
8 m length
... and very thirsty

17

Knuffi (f) and Wurschtel (m), my two travelling
companions - each ten years old.

I had the feeling that we would be saying "goodbye" in the next few days. I was beginning to get impatient. Firstly, as a long-time single person, I was no longer used to fitting so absolutely into a familial community. There was not one minute of free space left for me that week – except for report writing. Both hosts meant all too well and mothered me like an infant, stuffed me full of advice and overwhelmed me with countless questions. Dog-tired from the day's events and the ever-present foreign language, I often took up the cooking spoon in the evening to be able to repay my hosts' helpfulness a little.

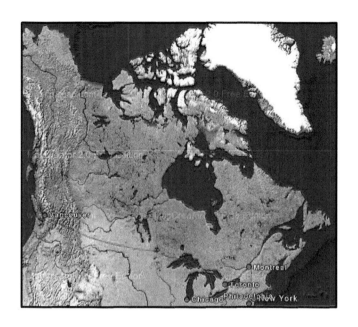

Total Canada

Direct route to Newfoundland

Kingston (ON) - Sidney (NS)

1,800 km - 10 days

Private remarks

End of May - the mood to leave!

Once again, our departure was delayed by another day. We had discovered during an all-round check that neither the heating nor the fridge worked on propane. Richard tried all the possibilities to get the two devices going. Probably just a small repair, but did he know how? All his attempts were crowned with failure. Instead, he achieved more success as a driving instructor. He had me drive the narrow forest road to his cottage, nagged me with reversing and turning, had me start the generator in the wilderness and tested all the levers and switches with me. I had to get used to the different dimensions of the vehicle, in length as well as in width and height. The automatic transmission also took some getting used to. At junctions I tried to shift gears all the time. False alarm! There was nothing there! I hid my left leg under the seat as a precaution so that the other would not be disturbed. You wouldn't believe how automated some actions are. After about an hour, my teacher was satisfied with me, and I had to squeeze back into the hole in front of the hut as the last test. I had done it! I had passed!

My poochies once again enjoyed the extra day in absolute freedom. There was no leash requirement here in the bush. They were free to chase squirrels, chip monkeys and wild turkeys as they pleased. They always came back to the hut sooner or later when I whistled. Knuffi occasionally took a refreshing bath in the forest stream, looked like a piglet afterwards and had to wait outside the door to dry off. Wet dogs were not welcome in Karen's tidy household.

We tested our bed in the forest for two nights, as Karen's son came to visit and claimed my accommodation. I didn't mind sleeping a little upside down because of the incline. In return, I had a certain retreat for our trio and a taste of our future freedom.

Finally, we were ready to go. We drove only one hundred and fifty kilometres on this first day and left all the sightseeing points behind us. In **Gananoque**, we tried an RV dealer for repairs with 50% success. The fridge could be started (as suspected only a small repair!), but the heating would need a longer check – and we would have to wait one week for an appointment! That was too long for me. Secretly, I decided to save the money for the time being, as I was heading for summer. Nicely naive! By autumn, the heater might have broken down again if I didn't need it, so I postponed the workshop until later. Besides, if it got colder, I still had my two live hot water bottles to wrap around me.

Bulk shopping at Walmart in **Brockville**. I had my fridge to fill and needed various other things for more amenities in my new home. Good thing the chain store had large shopping carts. Prices for groceries and other daily consumables in Canada were high! I estimated they were a good third higher than here in Germany, if not half. My budget certainly needed some top-ups, as petrol was no longer as cheap as on the previous trip in 2010 – the equivalent of "only" 1,00 Euro per litre.

The municipal campsite in **Iroquois** was quickly found with a few minor detours and turns. Normally, the municipal sites were cheaper than the commercial ones. For this night, I needed the pitch, because I had to dispose of waste and free my pipes from the remaining antifreeze: 30.- CAD (a good 21.- €) with strong electricity. As so often in North America, with my eight metres I was a pipsqueak among the big trailers. Never-

theless, there was no envy, because I was the most agile sister among the big brothers! We stayed in a green area, with adjacent parkland and a glider airfield. Ideal for dog owners! But that evening, it only came to a small disposal round, because the shopping had to be stowed away. Besides, I finally wanted a snack, because I hadn't had anything since breakfast and without a *siesta*, I was usually exhausted by nine o'clock in the evening.

We took it easy on the second day of the trip. I wanted to benefit from the electricity connection and type the travel report of the previous day into the PC, as well as briefly dart through our small flat with the hoover. The evening before had gone too fast for me. As a rule, departure time at campsites in North America is not set until early afternoon so this gave free space for various activities. We started at noon.

Three hundred kilometres laid ahead of us. I calculated more than four hours for this, as Montreal was located halfway. The time in between would be enough for a short *siesta* – I thought. Shortly before Montreal, we crossed the "border" into the French-speaking province of Quebec. At the welcome centre, I was provided with more than enough information about the entire province. It wasn't easy to switch my brain to French after all the English! It worked surprisingly well and armed with two plastic bags I marched to the camper. A little bit before this point, I quickly took advantage of the free Wi-Fi service of "Tim Horton" and had a little nap. At 3.30 pm I was ready for new surprises.

These were not long in coming. We drove at walking pace along four lanes through the city of Montreal (four million inhabitants including the outlying areas and the second largest city in Canada after Toronto). New motorway junctions came up all the time. The GPS was a real help to me in finding my way through the urban jungle to the other end. It took me more than two hours to cross the city, I was fed up with the concentrated driving and, exhausted, I headed for a Walmart in Trois Rivères. To make matters worse, water started pouring out of all the floodgates and defensive driving was the order of the day. The big trucks showed little consideration and roared past me like a water slingshot. How might one feel in a passenger car?

Around 7pm I was standing in front of the market and was done: three and a half hours for almost two hundred kilometres. Now there was food for all the occupants, a very short walk and a quick purchase from the host. Wow, the wind was icy! I was already regretting my decision not to repair the heating. I had my comrades in my sights and got by with a hot tea. Wurschtel felt most comfortable in my bed anyway. If I had to, Knuffi could join me around midnight or early in the morning. When that happened I lay squeezed between the two friends: I under the covers, both on top. This was an advantage in cool weather but had a disadvantage when the temperature becomes hotter than twenty degrees.

We change sides

In order to get a little closer to our destination Newfoundland, we managed three hundred and twenty kilometres on this day – without stress. We continued leisurely at 80 km/h on the TC #20 towards the northeast. Why so slow? I had noticed with dismay over the past few days that my "baby" was suffering from enormous thirst. 24 litres of regular petrol per hundred kilometres... I couldn't remember my previous old vehicle drinking so much. Was it the petrol engine instead of the diesel one I had before? No idea! Now I would try to test at which average speed I would save the most.

To ease my conscience, I came up with the following little calculation experiment (called "milkmaid calculation" in German). Up to now, I had been driving at an average speed of about 100 km/h. I had to calculate the cost of petrol. Petrol costs: 74 litres of normal petrol cost an average of €68 at that time (visa bill), so "π times thumb" (German "calculation system") one litre/1.-CAD (Diesel is a lot more expensive). This gave me 300 kilometres, so one hundred kilometres with my big carriage cost me just under €23.

Comparison to the camper at home: 80 litres fit into the tank. Assuming a price of about 1.35 € per litre of diesel at that time, that's about 110 €. I drive a good 500 kilometres with that. Therefore 100 kilometres at home cost me about 22.00 €. If you take the higher price of petrol in Germany as a basis, the difference will probably be even greater. With this evening comparison calculation, my shock had subsided somewhat. After all, I was a lot heavier and bigger than my *Wuschelmobil* in Germany, which in turn would drive up the kilometre price at home. So I accepted the thirst of my "baby" as it was. I had no choice anyway!

The bad weather had subsided in the meantime. The temperatures, however, were not above ten degrees, so heating was the order of the day, even in the camper. The sun rose higher and higher and from **Quebec** the sky was bright. After the big city, which we bypassed without any problems this time, we switched to the south side of the **St. Lawrence River**, as there were only ferry connections further north. The water became wider and wider, apparently making bridge construction too costly or even impossible. (Total length with estuary 2,900 is kilometres – largest estuary in the world).

There was a lot of farming along the route and again and again the small farmhouses disappeared behind the mighty silos, whose round towers rose over everything like the fingers of a hand. Sometimes the **TC #1** led directly along the water; sometimes it went more inland and apart from fields or forest there was little variety to see.

We were well on schedule and so I decided to take a day's rest at the urban campsite in **Rivière-du-Loup**. Not least because our direct route to the ferry to NF would then take us inland from here. The prices were acceptable, with all the "trimmings" 65.- CAD for two nights (44.-€) and very nicely situated with a view of the river. What I loved about North American campsites was their infrastructure: water connection to the municipal drinking water system, your own sewage right behind the house and a current of 30 to 50 amps. That was the power needed for the four retractable walls of the big trailers and their top-class air-conditioning systems. There were many of those vehicles here. In addition, just about every site had a picnic bench and a fire ring.

According to the weather forecast, the sun was supposed to shine tomorrow, but rain was expected for the day after. Carpe diem! I combined dinner, lunch and coffee into one meal in the late afternoon and enjoyed my ham noodles with salad outside. After the evening walk, duty called and I sat down on my two buttocks to type the last two days into the laptop as well as send-off necessary emails. The next thousand kilometres would take us almost to the end of the world!

Relaxing day in Rivière-du-Loup

We had a fantastically restful and quiet night and crawled out of our wide senior bed together at eight o'clock. When I write together, I mean together. Wurschtel kept me warm all night and Knuffi had become too bored alone by six in the morning. The second mattress topper has created a comfortable height for my old bones and almost reminds me of my bed at home. There were quite a few things to do and try out in the morning. With extensive personal hygiene and household chores, it quickly turned into lunchtime. Now out for a long walk with my gang! The spring sun was still shining.

It had only just become spring here at the end of May and the green of the deciduous trees was decidedly fresh, with many now unfurling their leaves. The forest gave a Nordic impression with many slender and tall conifers.

Our municipal campsite was three kilometres away from the centre of town, near the ferry to **Saint-Siméon** on the other shore. We walked a little along the water's edge. We discovered another campsite on the plain, a little higher in price and not nearly as cosy as our park. But it was opposite a small copy of *Neuschwanstein* Castle in Bavaria with a permanent Christmas exhibition, like *Käthe Wohlfahrt* in *Oberammergau* (Upper Bavaria).

I would have a quick look at the town centre tomorrow when we stopped for shopping at Walmart. None of my guidebooks reported much about this little town, seemingly a normal ordinary "nest". The walk didn't help calming me down. Wurschtel in particular was beside himself. My two companions had to get used to the leash again. The ten days of absolute liberty in the wilderness with Karen and Richard had made them totally forget obedience. Well, now and then a different wind had to blow!

Who stole an hour from us?

We were up early today! The first brightness lured us out of bed at around half past five. No wonder when you close the shutters at ten o'clock the night before. I felt well rested. Why kill precious time? At eight o'clock we were already standing in front of the still-locked doors of our favourite supermarket called WALMART. As usual, I had thought of a few things I could use to improve or beautify my household.

At half past nine we set off inland. The forecast rain held off mightily although threatening dark clouds could be seen in the hills – I don't want to talk about mountains – but there was little wet on the road. We passed through a friendly landscape,

where the eye could admire countless green hilltops. Amused, I watched the moose collision warning signs at the roadside again and again, especially at dusk. Unfortunately, these mighty primordial beasts kept themselves hidden in their safe forests in the morning. Up to the Quebec provincial border, the #185 was mostly single-lane due to construction work, but they were busy working on the four-lane expansion of this connection to the neighbouring province of New Brunswick.

A spacious information centre welcomed us, and I was given a lot of information material. They kindly pointed out to me that we had now changed to Atlantic Time and had thus lost an hour of the day. This cost me my beloved siesta.

Edmunston was the next, for the moment, featureless town. Where was the next major WALMART for free overnight? My GPS gave me satisfactory information for **Woodstock**. That was further than originally planned, but within reason.

From the provincial border of "New Brunswick" we got back on TC #2 and were able to drive along four lanes, interrupted by an obligatory fuel stop for my boozy baby. Judging by the distances of the petrol stations, I guess I had to get back into the habit of topping up as soon as possible after using half a tank, because you never knew... The situation was not as dangerous as in the Yukon, but with this thirst, caution was the mother of the porcelain box – as we say in German!

Several stops would have appealed to me, such as **Florence-ville**, the self-proclaimed capital of French fries in potato country, or **Hartland** with the longest covered bridge in the world. Certainly, the Scenic Route through the *Appalachian Mountains* would not have been too bad, or the road along the *St. John River*. But I refrained and put off my curiosity until early autumn, when my plan was to retrace our route back. My immediate destination was still Newfoundland, and I didn't want to get bogged down.

The WALMART in **Woodstock** welcomed us after two hundred and ninety kilometres; we found a quiet place to sleep and quite a few green spaces for my two "rabbits". I could even receive Wi-Fi in the camper, but I had to spare the home laptop power. I was able to work with my netbook, however, as I had 2 x 5 hours of battery with the tiny thing. That would be enough until the next campsite. If it came to it, I'd have to start the generator, but it made too much noise in a public car park.

A little further towards the goal

Little to report from today. We motored almost three hundred kilometres, in glorious sunshine, on four lanes and constantly surrounded by forest. Boring, because all the traffic was reduced to two cars in the front, one car behind and every now and then a truck coming along to overtake.

Wurschtel was happy about my "cruise controller" and the vehicle's automatic transmission. This left my right hand free for patting. The little guy took advantage of this at the appropriate time and pressed himself with all his might against my driver's seat on the right-hand side. He didn't get any further because I had secured both dogs well. Knuffi was more content. She spent most of her time sleeping on the passenger seat: sometimes curled up, sometimes with her head on the door handle so that it wouldn't fall off, sometimes with her head on the armrest. One gradually noticed her (nearly) ten years of life. All three of us were no longer young.

I postponed filling up my propane gas until the next major town, but my gut feeling sent me to an exit where I saw a large petrol station and an RV dealer opposite. The latter, at least, had to know where I could get hold of what I was looking for. And lo and behold! He had a propane tank on site! Forty litres of space! So not badly calculated at all… That gave me supplies for more than two weeks!

We arrived at the WALMART car park in **Moncton** tired and bored. No, I didn't really feel like driving any further. We would need two more days to Sydney (Nova Scotia) for the ferry. So, I spent the late afternoon doing some beautification work. The evening belonged to literature studies and travel reports. Not exactly idyllic, but inexpensive...

Month of June
Red nose, red head

Heavens! It was cold this morning when we crawled out of bed! Not even eleven degrees Celsius in the camper and outside; that's why my nose got red. Everything else was toasty warm on me, as I was lying tightly wrapped under my warm blanket, shielded from the cold on both sides by Knuffi and Wurschtel. I hated being cooped up like in a sleeping bag, but it was OK for today, so it took quite a bit of effort to crawl out of my warm nest at around seven o'clock, but the dogs had to go out ... Praise be to those who work hard and are on the go this early! After a big hot cup of tea, things started to get slightly better – with me and the temperatures.

I remembered an insulation trick my previous owner had used on the first American motorhome. I needed a hardware store for that, though. Today, on Sunday, only WALMART was open. Isolation material would help against the cold *and* the heat. When I asked WM about a suitable radiator, they told me that they had already modified all the shelves and only had fans for the summer. Well, not then!

Once again, we had a stowaway on board and for the second time, a mouse had taken up residence in my four walls. After all, it was warmer than outside! Torn toilet paper was a giveaway! I tried my luck with a "mousetrap" and precious mozzarella. Sometime during the night there was a click, the cheese had disappeared, but there was no mouse corpse to be seen. The mouse must have had quite a fright. Hopefully, it had escaped! I, however, received several blows when I tried to set the mousetrap again without my glasses. I couldn't imagine that the creature hadn't been hit at all. Or was I dumber than a mouse? The bait for the coming night was prepared anyway.

My two companions always smelt mouse holes in the meadow but in the camper van, this hunting instinct apparently failed...

In the early afternoon, during the siesta, an undesirable side effect occurred. As usual, Wurschtel snuggled close to me during the siesta, causing me to break out in a sweat this time. With a red head, I finished my breather. In the meantime it had become pleasantly warm outside again. The weather was very kind to us. Bright blue...

After about sixty kilometres we crossed the "border" to the next Canadian province: **Nova Scotia**. A very friendly visitor's centre in a green area welcomed us. Of course, as usual, we got the free maps and information brochures about the region. They even had a departure schedule for the ferry to Newfoundland.

One hundred and seventy kilometres now to **New Glasgow** – with bad road conditions in some sections, many frost heaves. In the WM there, we took a delayed lunch break with pancakes and breakfast sausages. I decided to drive another sixty kilometres to **Antigonish**: they would benefit us tomorrow. We had enough electricity, water and tank capacity, so our WM had to and could hold out for the third night. I preferred to save my money for the National Parks in Newfoundland.

At some point, the four-lane TC Highway ended and became a two-lane road. It was immediately relaxing to be able to drive "properly" again, to "experience" curves and to vary the speed. Basically, I was already on my long-term project for the summer of 2015. The Trans-Canada Highway stretches from St. John in Newfoundland across the entire continent to Vancouver but keeps changing its number. I would travel this current section in detail –according to the rough planning – in about five weeks with many side trips on my way back.

Shortly before the destination - North Sydney ferry port

It was frosty this morning too, but within a short time the sun warmed us up pleasantly. Two options were available to us in this weather.
Option 1: We harden ourselves and don't shy away from getting up.
Option 2: We stay in bed until eight o'clock, when the temperatures will be over 10 degrees.

I opted for Option 1 because moving forward was more important to me. On average, I had to calculate two and a half hours until all three of us were ready to go. As a single person, you were responsible for all the work yourself, from cleaning the windows to feeding the dogs and tidying up. That simply took time. Today we had the last 200 km ahead of us. In total, we had been on the road for about 1800 km since Kingston, ON. Well, Canada is vast...

It was a varied drive this time, as we came into contact with the island and fjord world of Nova Scotia. As always, a blanketed sky and spring-like temperatures. The place names were either Indian or Gaelic/Scottish. From Aberdeen to Inverness, Iona and Inverary, many typical place names were imported from the Scottish Highlands. This time there were even some viewpoints and I pulled out my camera for the first time to play tourist. We enjoyed the first view of the fabulous Cape Breton and its spectacular national park!

The highway led us directly to the ferry. No chance of getting a seat tomorrow or the day after. Thursday would be the next opportunity for 214.- CAD and a six hours crossing. The dogs were free if they stayed in the camper: they would certainly manage that!

It didn't matter, we just stayed on this side of the "channel" for the time being and we would rest now, which I had planned for Newfoundland. I could also make my further plans here. We found accommodation at a very quiet campsite for 30.- CAD a night with all services, free internet access and a view of the water. Here we would take it easy until departure time.

 Private remarks

Nova Scotia – View to Cape Breton, NS

Campsite „Arm of Gold" near Sydney, NS

 Private remarks

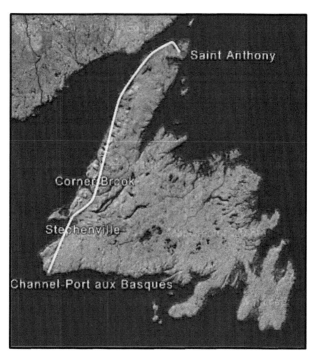

Canadian province
Newfoundland and
Labrador (NL)

Newfoundland: 111,390 square kilometres -
500,000 inhabitants - almost 10,000 km
coastline - capital St. John's - oldest city in
North America
in former times the poorhouse of Canada
today: fishing, tourism and oil production

 Private remarks

First route with partial sections
Channel-Port aux Basques to the
Viking settlement L'Anse aux Meadows – 700 km

We actually made it! After six hours of crossing, we were able to set foot on Newfoundland soil. I say it again and again: Don't give up on your dreams! Stay true to your resolutions!

After my accident near Toronto in 2010, I never thought I would be able to continue my journey to this remote corner of our world. At that time, the eastern part of Canada and the Maritime Provinces were already dead to me for financial reasons. After all, I was also four years older!

And now this! I just couldn't quite grasp it yet when our ferry arrived in *Channel-Port-au-Basque*. We were over an hour late because the ship could not leave the harbour in North Sydney until much later, due to the tide being too low. The Canadian mainland wept tears for us and covered itself in mourning, i.e., fog. The veil only lifted on departure. For the dogs, it was another long period of absence, but they could move freely in the camping car, had food and drink, as well as enough warmth and air. In any case, they were not locked up like in the flight cage. Nevertheless, they were happy to see me again after this second long separation! Such love and loyalty are simply wonderful!

We made it through our two days of waiting at the golden-armed campsite. The first day was crowned with lazing after the long journey, a long walk around the campsite and planning for NF. On the second day, I sat at the PC all morning and booked one Provincial Park after the other for our round trip. I did that just in time to be able to book most of the campgrounds as I had already missed out on some at the end of June! I looked for WALMARTS and checked commercial sites on the internet. Gros Morne NP also required advance booking.

With all my research, I became more and more aware that I absolutely could not make ends meet over a month's stay -

except with stress. I did not understand that. So, I let the planning run until the end of July. I wanted to take my time, because I certainly wouldn't come here again in this lifetime to catch up on what I had missed.

Channel-Port aux Basques greeted us as Newfoundland should: freezing cold and in fog, with residual snow on the low hills. Mind you, it was the beginning of June! By now it was eight o'clock (four and a half hours' time difference from Bavaria) and the dogs urgently needed to go out. We stopped briefly at the information centre at TCH #1 on the way to the "Cheeseman PP". I stocked up on groceries as a precaution, took the dogs for an invigorating walk - as did some other ferry guests - and headed for the overnight spot. Here I could even get electricity, which was not the case everywhere.

After being fed, my two companions lay contented and full on various armchairs and carpets. If only they could guess that they were among the most well-travelled dogs in Bavaria! I tried to use the electricity for a short while longer to write my reports. Basically, I was as sleepy as my two mice and, after uploading the pictures, soon fell into the trap as well. Good night!

Ferries in Sydney NS with a view of the city behind

Arrival at Newfoundland (NL)
Channel-Port aux Basques

Private remarks

Newfoundland is not Spain!

That was clear to me this morning when I opened my eyes! I could already hear the rain pattering on our roof tonight, but when I looked out of the window at around seven o'clock, I couldn't see anything at all – only the densest fog. On top of that there was an icy and strong wind. You know this kind of thing from Scotland, don't you? I could forget about any sightseeing tour. Anyway, there was a lot of organising to do. Three hours of "morning exercises" and we were ready to go at eleven o'clock.

This was followed by a bold leap by me into yesterday's visitor centre so as not to get soaked in one fell swoop. I wanted to check my emails there, as contrary to expectations there was no reception in the Provincial Park, and at the same time I also wanted to check my reservation confirmations for the next few days, as I was still waiting for two night confirmations in my plans.

Oh, horror! I had accidentally deleted the confirmations and neatly emptied the recycle bin... How to get the missing data now? With so many reservations, I didn't even know which park I had missed, let alone the date or its reservation number. That's why I could only be helped by the centre's crew with their cross-connections.

The friendly ladies moved heaven and hell to find a superior place in the programme. Their efforts were successful and after some time a fax arrived at the office with all my lost data. In the meantime, we had a nice and detailed chat. In return, I promised to pay them a visit on my return trip after my extended journey and tell them about my experience. I had the feeling that they would be happy to have something to do besides the daily monotony!

Next stop was the harbour to secure my return trip to the mainland. The end of July was high-season, and I didn't fancy being stuck in an endless queue. My final plans definitely gave me seven weeks to conquer the island. If Labrador was cancelled, I would have some resting time before returning to the mainland.

I could save myself the trip to **Rose Blanche** to the east today. That would be casting pearls before swine – as they say in my language ... or carrying owls to Athens! Thick threatening clouds hung over the island and the wind whipped the rain mercilessly. The smartest thing to do was to drive the planned hundred and fifty kilometres to the next overnight stop immediately, because that way we would at least be warm and dry in our snail shell.

We saw absolutely nothing of the mountain ranges on either side of the road, because the clouds hung down into the valley, but the dangerous gusts of wind near the **"Wreckhouse"** spared us, thank God. All we saw of the supposedly impressive **Codroy Valley** was the sign. I put it on our "to do list". We drove sixty kilometres through a wooded valley, bordered by the *Anguille Mountains* in the west and the *Long Range Mountains* in the east.

The TCH was maintained "*so la la*" in this section. Considering the harsh and long winters, the frost heaves were justified. Sometimes you could see the markings of previous vehicles breaking through under the second or third layer of tar. I drove with great concentration, but every now and then there was still a major hop when I couldn't avoid one of these "potholes" or simply overlooked it. Wurschtel was suspicious of the many water noises under the landing gear, and more than once he checked the floor under the side chair to see if an enemy might not break out from underneath.

Where was the next WALMART? I urgently needed weatherproof shoes, i.e., rubber boots and a water-repellent jacket. My various anoraks had been tested as a precaution, but they were soaked through in no time with the masses of water. Now, three of them were hanging out to dry in the camper. A lucky coincidence made me pack my half-winter boots, but they simply could not withstand the torrents on the road.

The next opportunity was in **Stephenville**, not too far from my evening destination. For just under 25.- CAD, I got nice boots and a supposedly waterproof jacket in my size in the men's department. Women apparently didn't need such outdoor clothing, they stayed at home in such bad weather!

Yay! Shortly before our *Provincial Park Barachois Pond* it finally cleared up and the rain stopped for a while. We got a pitch on the lakeshore, hidden behind trees – very private! Unfortunately, there were no pitches with electricity in this park. But it only cost 15.- CAD. There was a dumping station and plenty of good drinking water, but we would have to keep each other warm tonight if necessary, should the temperatures drop further. After seeing so many patches of snow along the road and in the mountains I couldn't believe that last week (according to the staff at the visitor centre) it was close to 25°C on the thermometer. Writing was done on my little netbook and later there was an overall transfer of pictures to the laptop. One just had to know how to help oneself! As a last resort, I could always use the loud generator!

After my *siesta* had been cancelled today and all the four-legged friends around me were snoring, I soon turned out the lights for myself as well, hoping for nicer weather! Carpe diem!

Blow me down!

The name of today's PP (Blow me down) suited our day very well. It had finally stopped raining during the night, but there was no sign of the sun that had been forecast! Well, at least it was dry, and the thick fog had lifted, so we set off on our first adventure route as planned. We had to put yesterday on the lost list.

Once again, we headed for **Stephenville** close to the small airport, over the pothole road for the third time. I wondered if it was still in operation but the whole place didn't seem very trustworthy to me. Yesterday we already drove this route in search of the much sought-after WALMART. Today I already knew the potholes and approached them more carefully. The route looked relatively short on the map, but by this evening we had covered more than three hundred kilometres.

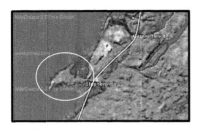 For today I had set my sights on the small ***Port-au-Port*-Peninsula**, an enclave of French settlers. All the villages around this small stretch of coast are of French origin, and the traditions of the Arcadians are still honoured here today. The French spoken here is still somewhat antiquated. The Arcadians were cruelly expelled by the English at the beginning of the 18th century, partly abandoned in boats and irresponsibly left to their fate. The British claimed the fish-rich sea areas for themselves in a warlike confrontation. Many of the displaced later built a new home in the south of the USA (Louisiana among other places) – and they became the Cajun culture. Besides the small fishing villages, the coast also had natural beauties to offer. An impressive cliff alternated with flat beach accesses. I had received a small bro-

chure with insider tips from the tourist office and I picked out a few of the 101 suggestions.

First was the wooden church "Our Lady of Mercy", the largest wooden Catholic church in Newfoundland. It seemed to be under restoration and was closed. The adjacent museum and former rectory,  now with tearoom, did not open until July. Perhaps the church hall then too? Anyhow there was enough time for a short walk around the impressive building.

We passed an alpaca farm and reached a small idyllic harbour with two fishing boats, an outhouse and bizarre rocks. I gritted my teeth a little, because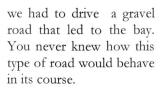

we had to drive a gravel road that led to the bay. You never knew how this type of road would behave in its course.

But there was no problem and we parked between two fishermen's cottages. Nobody was there. Accordingly my two companions could once again run and roam without a leash and there was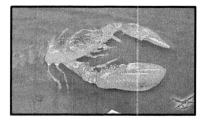

plenty for their noses to discover. In the meantime, mistress took some pretty photos.

We made a short stop in the **harbour of Cape George**. Here, of course, I had to take pictures of the many lobster baskets, the catch of which provided a livelihood for many fishermen.

I then went in search of the monument to the displaced Arcadians, the old French oven where bread is still baked twice a week in the old tradition, and the rock with the rare Kittiwake birds. All three of the destinations I was looking for were at the tip of the cape in *Boutte du Cap*. I wanted to get some exercise with my two friends, so we set off on foot to the first vantage point for the breeding colonies. Jesus! It was so cold! The wind whistled around our ears so the leashes flew horizontally. No headband could help! I even had to hold the hood of my anorak with one hand to prevent the wind from blowing it off my head. With the other hand I held my two companions on the leash. Otherwise, their hunting instincts would have run away with them. I puffed my way up to the first vantage point

of the smaller colony. As a precaution, I tied both companions to a bench so that I wouldn't get tangled in the leashes and tumble over the precipice while taking pictures – a necessary precaution on this steep coast.

On the way back, at least we had the wind at our backs. Nevertheless, I missed my warm gloves. Unbelievable! In this weather I saw Newfoundlanders in shorts, sandals and light T-shirts working in the garden. Were we Europeans such pampered wimps? Hard to believe! There were still remnants of snow hanging in the mountains and it was already summer for the population. Maybe there really were only two seasons here?

After a hot soup, off we went to the other side of the peninsula. No sooner had we taken the bend than we were overcome by the thickest fog. Visibility was less than thirty metres ahead of us. As far as I could make out, there was only stony desert: no one had settled here. We had to cross a small pass and then the haunting was almost over again at the seashore. At least we could see a few metres away, although wisps of fog hung in the air. For this reason, the driving was very strenuous, because in addition to the low visibility, we had to watch out for potholes.

Newfoundlanders seem to take pleasure in decorating their gardens. I saw remarkable attempts (not always particularly charming) ranging from lighthouses to colourful cairns with cannonballs and on to a variety of flags. Only the garden gnome was missing ... Of course, I couldn't just stop and take pictures: decency and respect for privacy forbade me to do so. But it would have been funny.

Now, for the fourth time, we crossed the bumpy road near the airport. One hundred and seventy kilometres laid ahead of us until our evening destination. The last sixty kilometres were village roads. What a village road! I could hardly catch a glimpse of the fjord, because the #450 took up so much of my time on the road that it demanded full concentration. Here on the deeply cut *Humber Arm*, one small village followed the next, the houses tightly packed together, not as spacious as on the last coast. I was glad when we reached the small but nice PP "Blow me down" at half past six. Walk round, dinner, homework, last pee-pee tour and it was half past nine again without a midday *siesta*! What did I need a TV for? Tonight, it would also probably get cool, because the remaining snow fields hung unpleasantly near into the valley. Would the promised sun finally come tomorrow?

I'm slowly getting fed up!

This morning at seven o'clock it was 10°C in the camper and 7°C outside. That's what my outdoor thermometer said to me! Wurschtel was on my right in bed and Knuffi on my left. They were two constant-temperature hot-water bottles – as their body temperature was one degree higher than in humans! Very pleasant in the cold. Dog in bed? You can nod your head to that! In our predicament, a dog heating pad is better than cold or freezing feet.

We struggled to get out of bed. Two pairs of trousers on top of each other for the first morning tour… Hot water on the stove to rinse off: that warmed my hands! A hearty breakfast with lots of hot tea… That awakened the spirits. The warm tea even made it down to the feet! The flames on the gas cooker helped raise the indoor temperature by two degrees. So our triple body heat added another two degrees. And lo and behold, we had almost bearable temperatures of 14°C in the snail shell. I was craving a hot shower. Since the sanitary facilities – called "Comfort station" – were off our pitch, I immediately packed up all the stuff and parked in front of the place. Today was also a day for waste disposal. One of my favourite things to do…

The fridge had to be filled up. After all, we were going into the wilderness for several days, far away from big shopping opportunities. Dog food was getting scarce too. Thus, our first major destination was **Corner Brook** WALMART. I was curious about the small **Larke Harbour** at the other end of the bay. A typical little Newfoundland fishing nest. There was only a slight diversion and only a photo stop due to the cold wind.

Same with **Frenchman's Cove**. Friendly people! Everyone waved at us as they came towards us on foot – tightly wrapped in winter clothes.

We filled up the tank and did some bulk shopping at the supermarket. At "Canadian Tires" I found out that my propane request could only be fulfilled in *Port au Choix*. Almost four hundred kilometres away on the Peninsula, the big index finger pointing north! My jaw dropped! I had no idea how long my forty-odd litres would last. Compared to home, with the heating on all the time and the fridge running, I could get by for a fortnight on an eleven-litre bottle. But my hungry baby here? Heating was not the order of the day anyway. I didn't feel like standing in the wilderness without gas and maybe not even being able to cook. No, thanks! The consumption had to be sampled first. Of course, that messed up my overall planning. But later I came up with a workable solution so that I didn't have to cancel my plans completely.

Now enough of the everyday problems! We sat down on the TCH for a few kilometres and then turned at the right time onto #430 (Viking Trail) and later onto #431. At an exit I bought the Canadian National Park Pass, which is obligatory for all campsites in the parks. Included were several other "national shrines". It was valid for a full year. I could even use it when I re-entered the country next year. I got into conversation with the nice lady at the counter and saw on the weather list another 7°C for tonight and then three days of sunshine with temperatures up to 24°C. Should I really believe that? My later internet research dampened my hopes enormously.

At around five o'clock we reached our destination, drove backwards into our pitch and had a large meadow to ourselves. Beautiful, if it hadn't been for… weren't we just talking about the weather? We drove through a fabulous area that we saw absolutely nothing of! Guidebooks are full of superlatives, but the clouds hung almost to the road and covered all the peaks in dense cotton wool. Over one pass we were even stuck in the middle of the soup and were glad when we could see the headlights of the oncoming traffic just before we met them. All that remained was to hope for tomorrow. The National Park Camping is located at **Trout River Pond**, a long lake that was cut off from the sea by nature in a fjord at some point. With a price of 25.- CAD, it is not one of the cheapest, but the pitches are spacious, and the recreational possibilities varied.

By now it was ten o'clock, although I had wanted to be in bed by eight. We recorded a meagre 14°C inside, 8°C outside. A warm blanket and a pot of hot tea helped me get through the evening homework.

Fog, mist, white touch…

I would like to add… "cold breeze!" At half past six in the morning, it was seven degrees – inside and outside! No, my friends! All three of us hit the hay once more and snuggled up to stay warm! We actually slept another round together until eight o'clock. Later we recorded three degrees more… Where was the sun promised by the weather forecast for today? My internet had been right! So the usual warm-up round was announced.

Shortly after ten o'clock we were ready to start, because at least we could see the mountains clearly up to their halfway point. Besides, the car quickly heated up considerably while driving.

Our first destination was the small harbour at the **East Pond** of *Trout River*. From there, a hiking trail led along the coast with a beautiful view of the small bay. Of course, we didn't follow the path all the way, just until we had everything in view, as far as the clouds allowed. Wasn't there a thin blue stripe of hope on the horizon? The cold wind died down a little and a feeling of warmth came over us. Afterwards, we took a walk along the boardwalk on the beach and discovered some useful handicrafts that were being sold in front of some of the cottages.

Well, when it cleared up, we headed for the trailhead of the **Tablelands** – the starting point into the desert of the *Table Mountains*. This strange rock looks like a lunar landscape, with little vegetation. As soon as we reached the ridge, everything was covered again: thick in clouds. It was unbelievable how quickly the weather situation changed from metre to metre. You really couldn't foresee what was going to happen around the next bend. Only the patches of snow showed a persistent presence. There was absolutely no reason to stay so we drove on to **Woody Point**.

This small town was once important to the economy of this stretch of coast and many wealthy merchants built larger-than-usual houses here. The inhabitants even had their own theatre. Unfortunately, a major fire in 1922 destroyed many of the original dwellings. However, efforts were made to rebuild at least a few important buildings true to the original – probably also because of tourism.

This time I left my gang at home and set out alone to take pictures. At the inlet it was clear and cold; at altitude, foggy. Let's try the Tablelands again! I wanted to lie down for a bit at the car park there and later conquer part of the hiking trail with my poochies. God, I was tired! The cold was exhausting!

That wasn't the worst idea, because while we were napping, the clouds cleared and a hint of sunshine came through the haze so we set off again for another hour. Once more, I saw clouds coming from the sea into the mountains. I headed for the camper, because I didn't feel like stumbling over the rocks in the fog with two four-legged friends on a long leash.

We had breathed enough fresh air for today and used the camera diligently. I now wanted to go home and charge all my devices with the help of the generator. The PCs were in dire need of it, the mobile phone was mute, and the camera battery could do with some juice so we were ready for the next few days. The infernal machine was only allowed to run here between 5pm and 7pm. I had to take full advantage of that. Our stomachs had to manage without food for a while, so that I could also use that electricity to write the report. Pictures would be added sometime later as in three days, we were back in touch with civilization.

 Private remarks

Bay of East Pond

Typical colourful Newfoundland outport

Gloves and socks: warming side job

 Private remarks

In the inhospitable "Tablelands"

 Private remarks

Heading north on the Viking Trail

As usual, the three of us peeled ourselves out of bed. This time we had a pleasing eleven degrees for getting up. I was grateful for every degree higher on the thermometer. At half past nine we were ready to go and first had to dive under the cloud of the Tablelands. At least we had a clear view today. Two cheeky moose even jumped across my path, but by the time I stopped and rummaged for the camera they had disappeared into the protective thicket. Hopefully they won't be the last!

We returned to #430, the so-called *Viking Trail*, which led to the far north of these Fingers (officially: Peninsula). Our destination was the campground of the National Park at Shallow Bay near Cow Head. We changed from the mountains to the plains. Almost one hundred and forty kilometres should not be a problem for us.

Our first stop was at a monument of a national great. Mattie Mitchell belonged to the *Mi'kmaq* tribe. He was a successful hunter, guide and prospector, who made useful contributions to the cartography and exploration of the Northern Peninsula, as well as in forestry and mining. Then we took a small path that led to an idyllic stream. Wurschtel and Knuffi thus had their second outlet.

The detour to **Norris Point** didn't bring much, except for a few beautiful views of the Tablelands and the south branch of the St. Lawrence River.

While looking for the lighthouse at Salmon Point, I came across a fish shop in Rocky Harbour. It looked delicious! For this reason I quickly decided to revise my menu for today and tomorrow as two different kinds of fish appeared on my table. Please don't ask me for their names, I have forgotten them again. There were also some nice lobsters on display. I didn't dare to try these huge specimens because I didn't have the necessary cooking pot. Nevertheless, I quickly had the preparation explained to me and disappeared in the direction of Salmon Point.

A nice little lighthouse overlooked the whole of **Bonne Bay**. Unfortunately, the exhibition and the tower were being renovated and the pictures from bygone days had been temporarily moved to an outbuilding. While looking at various photos, I got into conversation with the ranger (National Park), and she told me a lot about the past and the winter that had just passed. People had to pay up to 20% more in maintenance costs this year than in previous winters. Smiling, she said that this was probably due to the increased amount of alcohol they had to drink to keep warm inside.

We now moved to the coast, which with its storms and dangerous swells has caused many a ship to go to its doom. At a special stop, we could descend to one of the many remaining wrecks. There is even a folk song about the misfortune of this freighter and the rescue of all 92 people.

Broom Point with its old fishing hut was disappointing, probably because we had arrived at the wrong time. There would have been a guided tour every hour, but we didn't get there early enough. Consequently there was only a walk and some photos.

For the next two nights we sat almost alone on a sprawling National Park campsite at **Shallow Bay**. The fine grey sandy beach was within walking distance, there were hot showers and proper toilets for once and the pitch was spacious. With my annual pass, I even got a discount on camping fees at Trout River and here. Tomorrow would be the moment of truth, because I had to get my propane gas: that would definitely be exciting.

The date of my death!
Wednesday, 11th June – frozen to death in the Newfoundland summer!

When I woke up at around eight o'clock with a red nose and cold feet, I realised that there was still some life left in me thanks to my dogs. The night had lowered the temperature to a scant 2°C above freezing. However, the back and front of my body were surprisingly warm thanks to my two bedfellows. 20°C! Not bad when you add the 7°C outside temperature at 8.00 am to the 13°C in the camper! We had to hurry so that we could drive. That's when the engine started to heat up. Besides, the prospect of a full tank of propane gas was weighing me down.

One hundred and twenty kilometres to **Port au Choix**! We sat that one out on the right a...cheek. I inwardly said goodbye to the campsite and gave up the following night! I wanted to finally have electricity again and not freeze! A gift! Hooray! We found the aforementioned petrol station with the filling station in **Port Saunders**! It was indeed the only propane source for motorhomes with built-in tanks on the entire Peninsula! (300 km south to Corner Brook and 200 km north to the last end of the Peninsula!) I was only thirteen litres short from the past eleven days, despite constant use, so the panic had been unfounded. From now on, however, I could calculate and knew that I would not need a refill before the end of the month. That was more than reassuring. If I added the commercial camping days, my supply would be almost enough to last until departure. My spirits rose considerably.

Port au Choix was closed with its excavations and thus the visitor centre too. I amused myself with the dogs a little in the fog on the arctic-looking beach which was desolate and hostile to life. A few pitiful plants eked out an existence in the gravel. It was unbelievable that they could still find food here. Small and low, they protected themselves from the incoming winds. No wonder that the Vikings left the entire north coast again relatively quickly, although they too were used to a harsh climate in their homeland.

The monotonous landscape and the fog made me think twice but now I was already up here, far away from so-called civilisation. Should I turn back now, as planned, or develop new plans? For the time being, I decided to continue to **St. Barbe**. I wanted to make enquiries about the ferry and the outports of Labrador. It was only ninety kilometres northwards. The road was well-maintained, but the fog continued to weigh on the landscape and on our minds.

We stopped there for lunch at around two o'clock and I then discovered some unpleasant things: the ferry sections along the east coast were very long. Add to that the omnipresent fog, and the outlook was rather bleak. Dogs yes, but in cages, not in the cabin, village-hopping not possible. One had to stay on the ferry for the entire two days, little time for a shore excursion. Then there was the price! I had to pay eight hundred dollars for a single cabin there and back. What would I do with the camper in the meantime? I decided to call off the venture. I didn't want to do that to myself and my dogs. Only to say I had been to Labrador? I would invest the time saved in visiting more places in Newfoundland. There was a picture of the ferry leaving and the project was sensibly dead. This time, reason really did prevail.

Iceberg Festival in **St. Anthony** until 15 June! That was a call! However, there were another two hundred kilometres between the current starting  point and two commercial campsites at the northern tip. It was too early to stop here in St. Barbe; therefore we saddled up the horses. The advantage was we would make progress and would stay warm and dry. The prospect of a warm shack tonight and enough electricity was tempting though. I was also able to add the Viking settlement at *L'Anse aux Meadows* to my programme but the reservation for another PP in the south was cancelled, giving me more room to manoeuvre.

A few kilometres further on, it cleared up. That's when I saw the first one swimming! Ten percent visible, ninety percent under water... The St. Lawrence River was releasing its ice. Some distance away I saw larger ones bobbing around!

MOUNTAINS OF ICE! I now understood the goose bumps in this part of the country. The cold Labrador current was making its impact felt. How else could the white giants from Greenland keep themselves alive for so long. After a hard and long winter this year, the prospect of an iceberg tour was within reach. For the time being, I was content with the small hills.

Road #430 now swung inland. It became more mountainous and with the hills the fog came again! The road went dead straight through tundra-like landscape. As in the Yukon, the highway was elevated on a dam, probably because of the frost. I had to find out whether there was permafrost in the ground. It was possible, given the current weather conditions and the short summers.

The **Viking RV Park** was not far from the site. It was simple and not particularly well equipped, but I had enough electricity and Wi-Fi was also available. In the cold, I refrained from using the hot but unheated shower! The woman is herself, was the motto this time. I started my own hot water pot and enjoyed the warm drink! I worked up all my travel notes until almost midnight and wallowed in the pictures. It was wonderful not having to go to bed at dawn because the cold forced me to. My little heater ran intermittently through the night but didn't manage to bring more than 14°C of warmth into the place, but with the threat of freezing outside, that was quite a feat for the little thing.

At any rate, we finally had it warm again for days and tomorrow we would visit the ancient Roman – no Vikings! – site. The winter anorak and gloves were already prepared! Besides, the weather forecast was satisfactory.

Europe allegedly closer than Toronto

Indeed! I found this info in a travel guide. I checked it out and it wasn't true… but it sounds cool anyway!

Today we took it easy and warm. It was just above freezing outside during the night but it was bearable in our castle. Today I got an email from home saying that it was over 34°C with sunshine in Berlin! We had the other June extreme here…

In the morning I continued working on the travel reports, because I wanted to be up to date again. At around noon we started for the nearby historical sightseeing part of the National Park - **L'Anse aux Meadows**. Here, at this headland, "opposite" Europe, the Vikings had settled for a short time. This has been historically proven by excavations. Newfoundland is probably the "Vinland" described in their saga. Unfortunately, it was not possible to find out why the first Europeans on the island disappeared again so quickly. Was the climate too strenuous and harsh for them? Very few artefacts have been found that would allow a more accurate historical interpretation. The tour was informative and the visitor centre instructive. In addition to a video presentation, one could also get an idea of the living situation of the visitors at that time thanks to a good 3D display. A boardwalk led up to a reconstruction of housing units. Of course, guides dressed in historical costumes were not to be missed. However, the whole presentation was based on facts and less on "Punch and Judy" as in the nearby Viking Land, which would be more recommended for children. From many points you had a good view of the whole bay and looking at the many ice floes you felt the cold rising inside you again.

Speaking of the cold, a friendly ranger at the reception made it possible for me to book a place on a boat tour to the icebergs in St. Anthony for tomorrow. As my mobile phone had no network reception, he put his service phone at my disposal. Thank you!

The subsequent tour with my two dogs turned out to be pleasant. Since I couldn't take them into the park, we walked a little way out into the moor, which had been made accessible to visitors by a boardwalk. Looking at the vegetation, one could well imagine that the rough fellows were reminded of home here.

Want a little *siesta*? We had plenty of time, because I didn't want to drive another hundred kilometres around the bay. I preferred to drive around a bit more, following my gut feeling and trying to take a few typical pictures. So, we were back at the RV park at around five o'clock and I had enough time to take care of my second fish. It tasted just as delicious as the variety from the day before. The meat of yesterday's fish was strong and tasty, whereas this one was tender and melted in your mouth. I think I'll stop by the fish shop again on our way back.

Reconstructed settlement of L'Anse aux Meadows

 Private remarks

Iceberg Avenue

It was hard to believe. At six o'clock in the morning, the sun was already fighting its way through the fog, and we decided to get up. At breakfast it laughed in the window. Had it lost its way? How much more beautiful the world looked under the sun. I even broke into a sweat while cleaning up. As we didn't have a long journey to make today, I used the free time for more important tasks, like vacuuming and cleaning the house.

Since we were up so early, we were able to leave at ten o'clock despite the additional chores. It was just under an hour to **St. Anthony** on the east side of the coast. The small town (measured with Newfoundland scale) is the supply centre of the entire "fingertip" of the Peninsula. Until July the attraction are the icebergs, which move from Greenland far into the south. They are carried by the cold Labrador Current: sometimes faster, sometimes slower, depending on their shape and weight. As the winter was hard and snowy this year, the pack ice did not break up until mid-May, delaying the migration well into June. The entire harbour of St. Anthony was still frozen over last month and relics of the pack ice could be seen everywhere.

Following the nose, we reached the end point of the bay with its small lighthouse. There were some nice walkways, which we followed for over an hour. It was wonderful to walk in the sunshine again. But one should not be deceived: an icy wind was blowing, and the temperatures did not move beyond single digits – and that in the middle of June. Besides, my dogs had to take a walk because during the boat trip they would have to take care of the camper.

Afterwards I prepared myself for the boat trip. I still remembered Alaska with the glacier tour in Valdez Bay. My God, I was freezing then! I didn't want that to happen again. So, two pairs of thick socks and the winter boots, double jumper layer and winter anorak, as well as sturdy gloves, ear warmers and emergency hat but it wasn't overkill, as it turned out later. We were offered nearby icebergs and we circled the giant in the bay, but could not see any whales. As far as I could guess from the explanations in impeccable Newfoundland English, the peak season for this would not be until July. Not so tragic, I had already come face to face with a whale with a baby in Baja California. Besides, the locals still have to keep tourist money tinkling in the till after the icebergs. Far out in the Atlantic, one could still see many of the giants swimming, with about 7/8 of them hidden under the surface of the water. Unimaginable!

On the way here, I had already spotted the RV park I was planning to visit tonight. It was located a little outside the small town and required the payment of an appropriate fee. However, its facilities were much better maintained than at the previous place. I could even manage another "out-of-town" shower tomorrow. It was the only one in the area and therefore probably in demand. Besides, it was the weekend and on top of that we would have nice weather, supposedly, in the next few days... so we showed up there early to get a spot. Indeed, caution was in order, because about an hour after me, one camper after the other came looking for a place to stay. I'd probably fight for a pitch tomorrow too. For the next three days, the retreat to the "palm" of Newfoundland was on the agenda. Maybe then I would be able to see more of the coast than on the way here... I hadn't seen a weather report yet, as the internet here was terribly shaky.

St. Anthony – Iceberg Tour I

 Private remarks

Newfoundland can also be different…

The weather forecast was right! We woke up to sunshine at around seven o'clock and I was able to take a cosy shower in the outhouse. At half past nine we set off!

Back to the west coast! I wanted to take an alternative route today, which was not marked on my software. It was more inland and only a few kilometres further – **#432, Grenfell Drive**. If you like trees and solitude, this is the right place: 116 kilometres of nature, mostly coniferous forest, broken up with just-blossoming birch trees. Now and then a car – when it was busy we saw a maximum of ten. I didn't count the many cars parked by the side of the road in the middle of the wilderness though, but there were some. I observed a lot of people tending to their roadside gardens in the beautiful weather.

Roadside gardens? To the left and right of both roads #430 and #432, in the midst of apparent wilderness and completely away from villages, you could always see small areas marked out with posts, sometimes with ribbons or scarecrows. These small privately cultivated gardens play a significant role in providing for the population. In addition to potatoes, cabbage, carrots, broccoli, lettuce, onions and turnips were also grown. After the construction of the two previously named roads, the families of the fishing villages began to use what were now easily accessible small plots along the way. Their enemies were game (which did not despise the titbits) and the short growing season, especially this year. These small private gardens were the only diversion on the relatively new and well-built road.

Again, I noticed that most of the road ran on an embankment, where even traffic signs had their own "throne". The shoulders were wide, but carelessness could quickly become a deadly trap if you fell down the steep embankment. Despite the soporific single track, I didn't get bored, because I hoped to spot one or two "moos" on this stretch. And I got lucky! Twice, frightened ladies took to their heels in front of my monster. I couldn't blame them. The gentlemen were nowhere to be seen, so I had to rely solely on the meaningful signpost.

We were happily back on the west side of the peninsula, south of the Labrador ferry. I was tempted by the odd spur road to the coast in the beautiful weather, because between the Viking Trail and the Gulf of St. Lawrence there were always wooden strips that blocked the view. I found the mini harbour of **Barr'd Harbour** particularly charming, so we stopped for a while, and I watched a lobster fisherman sorting his catch. He wasn't very talkative, but then he showed me the size of the lobsters they catch. Smaller ones that didn't fit the scale were returned to the sea to grow further (they still had a little grace period).

Let's try our luck again in good weather with ***Port au Choix***! I knew the info centre was closed until Monday, but today I wanted to drive the gravel road out to the lighthouse. It was worth it! A photogenic tower, two inviting chairs (which weren't particularly pleasant in the cold wind) and the deep blue water. The three of us all alone in the world on this patch of earth... It was wonderful. I therefore decided to take our lunch break here (half past two).

It wasn't far to the first camping stop on the way. Maybe even the second? I had an eye on last night's accommodation situation and didn't want to risk having to stand somewhere without electricity during the cold nights in the pampas. I gave up my *siesta*, quickly refuelled for tomorrow and bought a few things I had run out of. When I got there I felt exhausted from the concentrated driving. After all, it had been more than two hundred and fifty kilometres again today. I opted for the first, cheaper place for 21.- CAD with electricity and water connection. The *"River of Ponds"* park was on a lake whose water was as brown and boggy as whisky water is for the Scots. It had only a few pitches with electricity, but beautiful and large areas for camping in the middle of the forest. We went for a walk and explored the surroundings. On the service pitches we were the only guests and, in the woods, a single family with several children was having a good time. That was all!

It was half past nine again by the time I had finished typing my report. A peaceful atmosphere inside and outside! The lake was ours alone, the other guests were well hidden. My two companions were snoozing in various corners. But woe betide me if I got up to lie in my bed! Immediately, Wurschtel took up his "beware position" in order to be able to jump in time.

 Private remarks

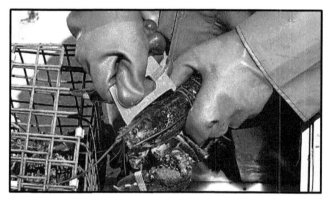

Lobster Fishing in Little Barr'd Harbour

 Private remarks

At the Port au Choix lighthouse

Private remarks

A day of relaxation

After all, that's what Sunday is for! We made it one hundred and seventy kilometres further south. My intention was to perhaps be able to squeeze in the boat trip at *"Western Brook Pond"* in Gros Morne National Park today, weather permitting. The conditions would have been ideal but it was not meant to be. Maybe I would have reached the boat in time. However, since three kilometres on foot had been advertised beforehand, the time was too short for my age and my bones. In the end, I was standing at the jetty almost on time (ok, I was five minutes late) and could only wave. Too unsafe for me – so off to Rocky Harbour to a more select campsite.

But wait! Now I had forgotten to mention the short stop at the rocks in *Arches Provincial Park*. It probably cost us the time we needed. Anyway, as a trio, we were the sensation with a tour group from Quebec, which had also made a small stop and had a picnic with the magnificent view.

Two things had to be done in **Rocky Harbour**: the reservation for the boat tomorrow (even though the outlook was rainy) and maybe visit the fish shop. Would it be open on Sunday?. It was… that's why this time we had a nice slice of salmon and once again a good piece of fresh halibut. Too bad I couldn't cook the dark "Scissors Animals" because of their size. I didn't have a suitable pot on board. Fortunately, this emergency could be remedied. They had already cooked lobsters on offer. The friendly fish seller also cracked the thing for me and explained what was edible and what was not! I therefore knew what a treat would be in store for me in the next hour.

I had chosen the *"Good Sam"* campsite in **Rocky Harbour** because of its proximity to the lake and its better offers. I wanted to finally use the free afternoon to do laundry! What has to be done, has to be done – after three weeks of wandering around. What? Only three weeks? That's right! Yes! We arrived in Toronto exactly one month ago today, took a week of preparation and had been on the road since the end of May.

We got a nice screened-in spot and could sit outside, barefoot and wearing a T-shirt! It was an unfamiliar feeling after so many cold days. As there were three washing machines available, the washing was quickly done.

As I've told you before, I'm not at all happy with the commercial machines here at the campsites. For one thing, they often only work with cold water; and for another, I always have the feeling that they only spread the dirt more evenly. At least you have the illusion of washed clothes, especially if you throw in a scented cloth or two in the dryer. I know why I only buy cheap outfits for such trips, because after a year all the items are disposable. The alternative is using a bleaching agent against stains, then you'll have absolutely homogeneous pastel colours after a while.

Too bad about the beautiful lobster! It looked so appetising in its red colour in the shop! Now it had been picked out, disassembled into individual parts and was no longer attractive at all! It tasted great with a little mayonnaise and buttered toast. I replaced the usual white wine with a non-alcoholic beer. The only thing that bothered me was how much of it went to waste. Afterwards, there was finally a midday nap. The world could be peaceful too!

200 kilometres from west to east

Yesterday it rained cats and dogs since early morning. It was hopeless to explore Western Brook Pond. I didn't want to walk through the countryside for three quarters of an hour in the pouring rain and then not even see the mountains because of all the clouds! It didn't want our visit, so the pond could stay away from us! So I said to myself and turned over and went back to sleep for a little longer.

Later, ten minutes of disposal were enough for me, during which I almost got soaked, despite my rubber boots and anorak. That drop in temperature again! My heater was running at full blast. I devoted the whole morning to my long overdue office work. There were bills to print out – I couldn't pay them because the mobile phone didn't identify any network – health insurance applications to write and my logbook to bring up to scratch. I had been sloppy with my entries over the last few days. As a result, I was busy until early afternoon. My poochies also hid in various corners as it was too damp outside for them too. Only in the late afternoon the mood calmed down and after a long *siesta* I walked with the dogs through the village and to the bay. The clouds were still hanging down to the treetops. We just had to air out before we started growing mould from sheer laziness. The walk, however, was not much fun because the wind was whistling around everyone's nose.

This morning it cleared up a bit, as described in the forecast, and the sun showed itself in places. However, I did not want to change my plan to leave, as it still looked gloomy in the mountains. So we now ventured east: maybe it would be milder in the interior of the island…

I intended to cover the four hundred and thirty kilometres to Twillingate in two stages. I would save a day and maybe add a night at the Dildo Run PP. I had studied a lot yesterday and had dug up quite a few sights. One more day would do me good.

Sixty kilometres of Viking Trail remained to the TCH in **Deer Lake**. I didn't bother with the insectarium there. There was nothing else to marvel at in this small town. I postponed my urgently needed shopping to Springdale in South Brook. The mood of the landscape was unique, sometimes even threatening, with the sun breaking through, the battling fogs and the deep blue waters surrounded by the delicate green of the birch leaves and the strong darkness of the coniferous forest.

A little morning walk couldn't hurt, so I was tempted by a sign pointing to waterfalls to make a quick stop. The *Southeast Brook Falls* plunge picturesquely several metres into the abyss, surrounded by primeval forest and wilderness. A small, safe footpath led through this forest and ended at the edge of the cascades. It was just enough to stretch our feet. The three of us enjoyed this short walk of half an hour and the dogs couldn't keep up with all the sniffing.

Afterwards we had one hundred and twenty kilometres of TCH #1 and forest, forest and forest again, interspersed with beautiful lakes, such as the elongated *Deer Lake, Sandy Lake, Birchy Lake or Sheffield Lake*. The highway was well built, mostly three lanes and with surprisingly few potholes.

84

Our location today was near **Halls Bay**, but I believe it was an offshore lake, not a bay. We were accommodated at *Kona Beach Park*, for 27.- CAD. It was still well priced with electricity and water. We had a wonderful view of the lake and a huge area for me and my dogs to run around. There were still few guests on the site. But that would change abruptly from 27th June, when the summer holidays began (the owner assured me of this). From then on, I had no more reservations. Let's see in which gravel pits I will then set up my camper. It was not much different in the Yukon in 2007. At that time, however, it was not because of overcrowded campsites, but because of limited possibilities for overnight accommodations.

The intended shopping was further off, because Springdale was off our route and South Brook turned out to be a village with three houses and a petrol station. All right, we can postpone the matter until tomorrow, when we pass Windsor/Grand Falls. Here I had already scouted out a Walmart. We still had so much on board that none of us would starve.

Private remarks

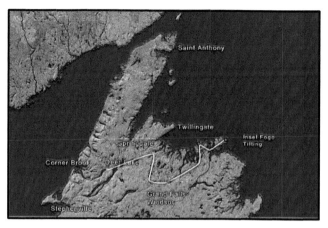

From West to East
Twillingate and Fogo Island (520 km)

Private remarks

Dress warmly! It's getting cool again.

Not a cloud in the sky! A shame not to get up, even though it was only six in the morning. Every one of us felt rested! So what? Why waste precious time? Consequently, we were on the road shortly before nine o'clock, heading for **Windsor/Grand Falls** – a twin city at the centre of the region. I happened to glance at my fuel gauge. Oh God, I should get a refill as soon as possible! I had to endure fifty kilometres to the next "village" **(Badger).** A town was an exaggeration; you'd better call it a garage with a petrol pump at the TCH. Saved! My "baby" was very thirsty. Our tank had a capacity of almost exactly a hundred litres so I wouldn't have got very far! We encountered a little more traffic than the last few days; otherwise we only found isolation, forests, deep blue lakes and rivers. Beautiful!

The next longer stop was the aforementioned centre with a Walmart, but without vegetables or fruit. Well, I got dog food, bread and drinking water too, apart from all sorts of other things. For the rest, I went across the road to the more expensive competition. They had hefty prices: one kilo of grapes for 10.- CAD (7.00 €) or a shabby iceberg lettuce for 4.- CAD (2.80 €), a bag of grated cheese almost 8.- CAD (3.20 €) and a plain Camembert cheese also 8.- CAD. You could only cry for our ALDI or LIDL. A few examples of the Canadian-Newfoundland cost of living (summer 2014).

Shortly before we left the TCH, an information centre fell into my hands. Couldn't hurt! Yes, there would still be boats leaving today for an iceberg tour at 4pm. The weather forecast for tomorrow: probably rain! Carpe diem! Why procrastinate? I wanted to get out on the water again! Another hour and a half to go! We would manage that well, albeit with a growling stomach.

We spent an hour and a half in a patchwork of potholes, sometimes so deep that you could cook spaghetti standing or lying in them. It was a serpentine drive (traffic permitting) and therefore exhausting. There were beautiful views of the individual fjords with their archipelagos and I had to stop once because I was simply captivated by the view. Otherwise, I didn't want to get bogged down and drove through to the final destination.

We were lucky as there were enough registrations for the four o'clock boat in **Twillingate**. So, now the dogs had to be walked, because they couldn't go on the small boat for the next two hours. I had already packed my warm clothes in my rucksack as a precaution. For survival I ate two bananas and an apple! From then on, there were plenty of icebergs! In comparison, you could forget the icebergs of St. Anthony!

Of course, with the excellent weather I had to go to the *Long Point lighthouse* afterwards and photograph the whole scene from above. It could be gone by tomorrow.

I ended up at the local community centre. There, from June until the end of the summer season, a so-called "Dinner Theatre" takes place. It is performed by local actors and musicians. They had strongly recommended this at the tourist office and I had also got this tip from my friends in Vancouver. So I signed up for tomorrow evening. It wouldn't be too bad with the onset of darkness and I was familiar with the neighbourhood.

Impressions around Twillingate

 Private remarks

Icebergs in large numbers!

 Private remarks

An imposed day of rest

I was so tired last night that I forgot to tell you about our location. We had ended up in a lovely little Provincial Park again, twenty-two kilometres south of **Twillingate** on **Notre Dame Bay**, near #340 and got an electric pitch near the sanitary facilities. As mentioned, we had arrived a day early. "Dildo Run" – the name of the park – was too pretty to be chosen only as an overnight location. ("Dildo Run"– sorry, the campsite was really called that! – A rather unfortunate name in British English – I know!) Yesterday I was still thinking about how I could manage to enjoy the surroundings here a little more extensively. Today, fate was with me.

Ready groomed and fed, I wanted to start at half past eight. The neighbouring *island of Fogo* was on my agenda with the ferry passing Change Islands. The weather had indeed changed: it was cloudy, but still dry. Ideal for a sightseeing tour, so to speak, in Newfoundland.

First take off attempt – a brief flare-up, the end!
Second take off attempt – a short click, end!
Third take off attempt – nothing at all!
I could forget about Fogo for today!

Friendly neighbours helped me start the engine with the starter cable. The polite ranger in the registry sent me to a workshop just one kilometre away. Very helpful guys there… The battery was on the blink (not the youngest anymore, just like the entire staff), the alternator ok! Well, at least it was something! At around two o'clock I could pick up a new battery but as a precaution, the workshop phoned the supplier. Back to the park, then! Yes, the ranger would come by and give me another jump start at around two o'clock. In view of the situation, today would have to be reprogrammed as a hiking day. I had discovered a path just around the corner from our campsite. Two kilometres: that would be right, I thought. I put the dogs on a short leash and off we went!

At first, we took a leisurely walk through the forest along the bay. Boardwalks bridged the damp patches. Then the path became narrower, the roots became more frequent and the ground boggier and I had the feeling that these two kilometres would drag on longer than indicated. Eventually it got so boggy that I probably turned back just before the viewpoint. No, I didn't feel like it anymore! The dogs were tiring and pulling in all sorts of directions, because there was more than enough to sniff at and at some point I got fed up with the line dance. Towards the end I felt every single root in the ground, despite my walking shoes. After one and a half hours we arrived back at our starting point! We had done our duty and all three of us had had our fresh air run for the day. I looked forward to my castle and did some of my writing while the dogs recovered from their strenuous tour.

Shortly before two o'clock a new start attempt. With difficulty the box got going, so the ranger was relieved. Within three quarters of an hour, I had my new battery and was 220.- CAD poorer. But what a sound when starting!

Now we had to kill time until six o'clock that was when the dinner theatre was on. The weather had changed (it was raining again) and the temperature dropped seriously. If we speak of an irritable climate because of the changeable weather in Bavaria, then I would like to know what they call it here ... maybe "Darwin's climate": only the strongest will survive.

As I had my house with me, there was no need to go back into the park and I explored some smaller side arms east of Twillingate at my own pace. Sometimes I felt like I was at the end of the world – and then again in this ghostly atmosphere! At **Cobbs Arm** I spotted a sign for a lookout point. There were stairs leading up to a granite rock. It was a bit slippery in the rain, but I was careful. We got a great panoramic view of the island world of the fjords and there was a higher platform to take pictures! The dogs had no problem with the height. I hoped to be able to do the same and took a run up with some momentum. However I had not taken into account my lack of athleticism and my age. The venture failed miserably and I tripped on a stone and landed on my ass – specifically on my tailbone. Ouch! That hurt! I got up on all fours and tested my mobility. Ok! I could still walk, albeit with painful limitations. I listened to my body and gave up the rest of the way. I was lucky! I could have fallen on my back! Another lesson for me for next time...

In the camper van, I immediately dug out my ubiquitous Diclofenac ointment and first rubbed the bruised area vigorously with it. Later I swallowed one of my tried and tested decongestant pills. I was able to sit, although I had to get into the car a little carefully. There was no limit to the driving, except that I felt the potholes more intensely than before. But it was bearable: I have survived quite a few other things!

What to do in such bad weather? I didn't want to let the day pass by and do nothing. I went to see the small fishing muse-

um at the dam at Black Duck Cove. A former fisherman had
built a vivid reproduction of the former fishing conditions
from the place where his parents worked. Here, the two novels
I had read about the early immigrants of Newfoundland came
to life for me. Add to that the weather, the fog and the icebergs in the bay, as well as temperatures close to the minus
mark in June – truly not a sweet spot.

Slowly it was time to make my way to the *Crow Head community centre* for the dinner theatre. It was a treat! The food was

great, some kind of goulash soup for starters, salmon, cake and coffee or tea for dessert. Everything homemade! I had nice and well-travelled holiday guests from Ontario as table neighbours and we got into lively conversation. The whole staff of the theatre worked together in the kitchen, then served and later cleared away. After that, it was down to business! You wouldn't believe how many acting and musical talents came out. I had a great time, even if I didn't always understand everything, because they all spoke fast and with a strong accent. The limited makeshift stage set and the skilful costuming for the sketches alone were worthy of special applause. All the actors and musicians were amateur artists and often could not hold back their own laughter when a punch line was particularly successful. This was especially amazing since they were on stage six days a week with this programme in the summertime.

The time flew by and by the time I checked my watch it was after nine o'clock. Time to go home before darkness fell. We had a good half hour to drive. Ok! I think I could have spent the night outside the centre. But in this cold, my electricity connection and the possibility of enjoying the heating were more motivating to me than the fear of darkness. Everything with the necessary caution! Most of the time I only saw the potholes when the water splashed like fountains. Fog was the order of the day and the windscreen wipers were busy. Most cars stayed behind me despite my reduced speed. Apparently, it was more pleasant to follow a dawdler than to be the first in line to drive down the road. I was also probably the bigger bumper in the eventual contact with a moose!

Shortly before ten o'clock, I set off on a virtually blind run into my bay. It was a good thing that I had taken the measurements beforehand and so I was standing on my pitch like a pro, despite zero visibility. I quickly connected to the electricity supply and took the dogs out! Apart from the small fall and the incidental expenses, the day had gone quite well.

 Private remarks

Twillingate – Dinner Theatre

Private remarks

Fogo Island

It was foggy and not the best weather for an excursion. But wasting the whole day in the camper? I hadn't come to New-foundland for that. When the weather was nice, everyone could do something. I slipped into two pairs of warm trousers (leggings and 2 pairs of trousers), packed my storm jacket and put my winter boots on. Note the date wearing this outfit (last third of June)! It was sixty kilometres to the ferry to **Farewell** at **Port Albert**. Since we were already up at half past six, we made it to the midday ferry with ease. I passed the waiting time sensibly with paperwork until a clerk told us to queue.

What was I looking for in the fog on a strange island? Maybe it would be clearer out there on the Atlantic Ocean. In any case it wasn't expensive fun, because as a senior citizen I only paid 16.- CAD for the 45-minute round trip. Not much was lost! We crossed the river in a thick "pea soup". Three hours until the return trip at 4pm should be enough for a first im-pression. I didn't want to put down roots there...

According to the guidebook, **Tilting** should be seen. There-fore, we drove the thirty kilometres across the island. It was not big! Rocky and dotted with raised bogs, ponds and small lochs. On the one hand, I felt transported to Scotland on the

103

Isle of Harris; and on the other, Dartmoor with its mist and the Black Hound of the Baskervilles came to mind. It was a constant up and down. At times I was happy to see a new bend in the road, at other times I could only see oncoming traffic as I approached through the veil of mist.

The place is an early settlement of Irish immigrants, dating back to 1730, which is already ancient in North American historical thinking. The structure of the fishing village had been preserved and several historic buildings lined up along the coastline. On our walk, I was lucky enough to have a reasonably clear view, so I managed to take some typical pictures. With some delay, the ferry brought us back to the main island. I was exhausted and took a short but deep nap in the cafeteria. Around seven o'clock we reversed into our position in the park. Dinner was served to everyone as quickly as possible, because no one had had anything to eat all day. It was incredible how much my two comrades-in-arms could chow down.

 Private remarks

Fogo Island - Tilting

Private remarks

It's not getting warmer at all!

This morning I jumped out of bed at six! "Guys! Sun!" I didn't even check the outside temperature on the thermometer and I bitterly regretted this on my first walk around. Thank goodness my two mice were very quick with their morning business. Then I saw the display: 5°C and the sun disappeared behind the clouds again in shame. I did my morning chores, including vacuuming. Oh dear, what a mess we brought into the place every day in this filthy weather. No amount of floor scraping could help.

We set off for **Boyd's Cove**, not even twenty kilometres south of us. A festival was planned for today at the *Beothuk Interpretation Centre* and I hoped to learn a little more about the indigenous people of Newfoundland at first hand. The term "Redskin" was coined for this "First Nation" and was later applied to all Indians. This name came from their tradition of painting and covering their bodies with ochre-coloured earth. On the one hand it was a religious ritual, on the other hand protection against mosquitoes and sunburn. (In this weather? Really?)

The centre was modern and revealed a lot about the excavations there. There was not much in the way of events and we went to the "Spirit Garden" at the waterfront, with its many colourful little fetishes in memory of loved ones or formative events. The 1.5 km walk to the excavations was a waste of time as it was raining again. Besides, there was nothing else to see other than holes and squares in the grass.

It was eighty kilometres to our next base, the *Provincial Park "Notre Dame"*. I had planned to drive through the small bays and towns to the right and left of the "Road to the Isle". But it turned out that it would only have been a collection of a few kilometres each time, which would have been of no use.

The journey to **"Notre Dame"** suited my mood because I felt tired and drained today. Had the night been too short after all? Did my medication have any after-effects? Were the impressions enough for the moment? I decided to head for the chosen "harbour" immediately. I was lucky; they were able to offer me a pitch with electricity, as some cancellations had been received. I hadn't had a chance when I had initially booked, as it was the weekend and everything was fully occupied, despite continuous rain. The park was conveniently located on the TCH and on a pretty lake, so it was extremely popular.

I climbed into my bunk at around two o'clock and slept for over two hours. I must have needed it badly. I felt better afterwards, and Wurschtel probably did too, because he also slept soundly by my side. Lunch at four, a short walk around the campsite with exactly one hundred pitches… Light drizzle and a maximum of 10°C … The whole scene reminded me so much of my trip to Scotland in 2011 when it rained for six weeks – even in June and July! I could well understand that the Irish and Scots were reminded of home here (not only because of the landscape) – so they thought it was a perfect place to settle down.

Tomorrow the weather could be whatever it wanted! I wasn't going to take the wheel! For the moment, I would stay for as long as I thought necessary and could be guaranteed space. I desperately needed some rest. The spirit of enterprise was sure to return when I was relaxed enough.

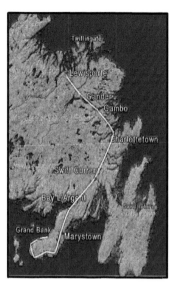

Burin
Peninsula
600 km

 Private remarks

We are back to normal!

It is 8pm at the moment when I write the short report for today. The park has become quiet. Most of the visitors have left because work is calling again tomorrow. A few permanent parking spaces are still used by huge trailers, but unoccupied. The thermometer shows an outside temperature of 13°C and it is overcast. The humidity is high, but fortunately it hasn't rained all day today.

We slept longer than usual, Wurschtel snoring stretched out along my front and Knuffi snuggled curled up in the back of my knees. There was not much freedom of movement left for me. This was drastically limited anyway because of my still damaged backside; but it was nice and warm, I have to say.

We spent the day comfortably "computing", reading, walking and cooking. It was warm in our snail shell as the little heater was running continuously. I enjoyed turning the video clips from the dinner theatre into a little film. That takes a lot of time, if you've ever tried it… Well, now the decision was made to leave tomorrow after all, because there were quite a few kilometres ahead of us.

The "tragedy" of Newfoundland is that you can't put together a round trip in the true sense of the word; because of the many peninsulas you are always forced to return to the TCH somehow. Over time, this adds up on the mileage indicator and that slows down your planning to a great extent. Two hundred and forty kilometres look so short on the map! Yet this is the only stopover to the end of the Burin Peninsula, my next but only destination. So, let's do it!

111

It was to be expected

Bright blue sky! I got out of bed at seven o'clock. That suited our purpose well: we had a few kilometres to cover today. We were drawn further into the east of Newfoundland. Yesterday's rest day had paid off and I was curious again about what was to come. As planned, I got the motorhome ready for take-off, then to the shower, to dispose of the waste and to the Wi-Fi hotspot for long overdue emails.

As we were driving up the small hill to the sanitary facilities I heard a strange metallic noise. All-round check … and no, nothing was on the ground. Restart! The steering wheel was hard to turn, the brakes hardly reacted. This had happened to me before, several years ago, at the border between the USA and Canada. A passer-by lifted the cover! The fan belt had died. I had suspected it! No wonder, given the age of the vehicle.

Once again, friendly rangers had to take action on my behalf. They phoned for a tow truck, as I couldn't drive another metre. Not every garage had the equipment to tow a motorhome. Someone had to be called from Grand Fall, an hour and a half away. That was going to be expensive! I phoned the CAA, the partner organisation of the ADAC in Germany . Motorhomes were not covered, I was told. I didn't understand this, because at least the towing costs had been covered. Be that as it may! I needed a working vehicle again and for that purpose I had my

deposit account just in case.

Finally, after two hours, the rescuing angel came, put support shoes on my camper and we drove together to a workshop in **Lewisport**. This is probably where all the unfortunates of the Provincial Park were served. They found the time to look at my vehicle. The mechanic found out that something else had broken, which had probably triggered the loss of the fan belt. I didn't know what he was talking about. I don't even understand the technical context in German, let alone in English. Either the car worked, or an expert had to make it work! For this reason, fixing my vehicle took longer than intended. But let bygones be bygones. Let's reschedule! Having been through the situation before, this incident did not upset me in the slightest. I was only happy that it had not happened to me on the deserted TCH or in the wilderness.

At home I had packed all the guardian angels and lucky charms for this trip that I had received as gifts over the years. I have now used up two of them: the unexpected fall and now the fan belt. For the time being, they should be able to get restored soon!

At around half past three I drove back to the Provincial Park 500.- CAD lighter (towing costs 300.- CAD, rest work and repair costs). I didn't feel like going on another long trip. I was in good hands here. They gave me my old place and were childishly happy about the chocolate biscuits I had brought for the ranger team as a thank you for their help.

After lunch had been replaced again by only two bananas, we had proper supper and a walk with my in-house crew. I wonder what they were thinking when the car went off course and started driving without their mistress.

The first "gravel pit"

This time we had a trouble-free start in the morning at Notre Dame PP. As a precaution, I filled up with water and emptied my tanks after several days. As a result, we would be self-sufficient, come what may. We got back on the TCH towards **Gander** and **Gambo**. This part of the road was in excellent condition. Sometimes the road was only two lanes, but on the right side we could already see the future additional road. Bright blue sky! Dark blue lakes – or fjord arms not recognisable as such! Again: lots of forest and very few clusters of houses. It was a wonderful ride and I just let myself get carried away, no matter how far we got today and where we settled down for the night. We could make the total distance of four hundred kilometres to **Marystown** in one go, but we didn't have to. The reservation for the next park was for tomorrow.

Our first stop was just before the exit to Gambo. First, I wanted to drive into the small town from the lookout, but I saw in the guidebook that the information centre about *Joe Smallwood* was not open until June 25th. We would visit it on the way back.

Joe Smallwood? In this area almost every third person was called "Smallwood". Said personality was an extremely popular and long-ruling Newfoundland politician who was born in this small town. He brought the railway to the island and boosted the economy through extensive timber trading. There is an interesting story about him by a Newfoundland writer who combines biographical fiction in novel form with the history of Newfoundland's development. Highly interesting to read, if you are keen on this world... The book also exists in German, but only in second-hand bookshops. For me, at least, the name had taken shape. The river landscape with its many small is-

lands was enchanting and I was also impressed by the view of the small, spacious town.

114

We entered a totally different scenic area as we passed through the *"Terra Nova" National Park*. Perhaps our Black Forest high road could be used as a comparison. It was constantly uphill and downhill, with wide views of two deeply cut fjords glistening in the sunlight. This national park was on my agenda for later.

Again, the picture changed as we turned onto #210, the **"Heritage Run"** into the **Burin Peninsula**. This peninsula stretches some two hundred kilometres southwest from the turnoff of TCH. We moved through a bare plateau, interspersed with a few unkempt trees and many dark blue to brown pools. The vegetation on the ground was sparse, almost a tundra-like arctic landscape. Then another major bend and birch forest prevailed.

It was early afternoon or late noon – whatever you want. We needed a break, maybe even a stop. One hundred and forty kilometres still separated us from the main goal. We had managed two hundred and fifty kilometres so far without any problems and without much effort. Why, actually? If we could get a place to stay in **Swift Current**, that would be fine with us. It was a small resort with only ten pitches and unfortunately full. What a pity! On the next stretch to **Marystown** (150 kilometres) I couldn't find any other place.

The woman in the office gave me the tip to try a wild camping site a few kilometres further on. I couldn't miss the dirt road before the bridge. I recognised the turn-off, saw the mogul track and didn't really trust the place. Therefore dogs to the rescue! A little run was due anyway. I parked the camper and set off to explore on foot. A trailer "overtook" us at walking pace, it was a lot bigger and longer than me. What they could do, I could do too! Let's have a look at the place! Several colleagues were standing in the pampa on a large, somewhat bumpy gravel surface! Ok! Here I would be able to save 23.-

CAD of my last expenses. Better and greener than at the Walmart in Marystown! I had the feeling that the "colleagues" here all knew each other. I had probably ended up in an unofficial fishing camp because many boots and trousers were lying around to dry.

They followed the motorhome with the foreign number plate with attention, probably dropping their jaws apart as to how someone like me had found my way here, and tolerantly left me alone. I really missed the usual and innate curiosity of North Americans here. Lunch and a cosy *siesta* happened with the doors and gates open. It had become warm in the meantime (an unusual 26°C) and fresh air did us good in the snail shell.

We kept following the further course of the gravel road on a walk. Some 4x4 trucks followed us. So there had to be an end, a destination somewhere. We ended up at an old bridge over the *Pipers Hole River* which had a real Canadian river picture with an angler in front of our eyes (see epic film: "Life is a river") and several high-spirited youths in swimwear (!) cavorting on the rocky river bank. One of the boys climbed onto the bridge arch and jumped into the hopefully sufficiently deep pool below. That left me speechless: firstly because of the height and secondly because of the water temperature! Wurschtel was also absolutely amazed at where the man on the wall had suddenly disappeared to. Unbelievably, he saw him reappear at the bottom! He completely forgot to bark.

In the meantime, it turned 6pm, the heat had died down and clouds were gathering. A gusty wind came up, which drove away the mosquitoes and black

116

flies, but hopefully would not herald worse weather. Let's be surprised!

Carpe diem! – Seize the day!

… It might rain again tomorrow! Everyone who travels to Newfoundland should be urgently aware of this. Or do I always have this bad luck with the weather? I'm thinking of the rainy six weeks in Scotland in 2011 or the wet winter in Portugal in 2008/2009 or … no more self-pity please! There are enough other tourists on the road who would have to put on the same shoe. It can't be helped!

So, the introduction to today's weather was already written. In the morning there was a small glimmer of hope in the sky, but in the course of the morning it clouded over considerably. Later it showered heavily…

Despite everything, I enjoyed the long drive southwest into the "boot" of the Peninsula. I had never seen a stranger landscape. If you spread out a natural sponge in front of you and fill its hollows with water, you can roughly imagine the landscape for the first eighty kilometres. One pond and a smaller lake followed another, sometimes connected by a narrow channel. Tiny islands tried to divide the evenness of the water surface. The shores were rocky, barely covered by taller plants. There were only a few spindly conifers, bent and dishevelled by the wind. The white marsh grass trembled in the wind. No human habitation was visible and the hilly landscape in the background rose stony and bare.

I made a short detour to **Bay L'Argent**. From here, a passenger ferry departed for two outport villages, which were not connected by any road. This would appeal to me for a day trip. I turned off #210 and after a few kilometres ended up in the high mountains and at a fantastic bay with a cliff. The information was not very exhaustive. I had to turn to the internet to find out more. The undertaking stood and fell a) because of the weather and b) because of having my two dogs with me. If it didn't work from here, then maybe it would work later from the coast around Harbour Breton. In any case, the plan was postponed for the time being.

We drove back to the starting point and made our shopping stop in **Marystown**. At the local Walmart there was no sign prohibiting overnight stays. When in a tight corner! With a heavy heart, I dished out some money at another supermarket. I was really in the mood for non-alcoholic beer. That might have been an expensive venture: A six-pack of "Beck's alcohol-free" at 0.33l for 10.- CAD without tax! (7.- €) Those were almost Oktoberfest prices! I quickly stocked up on several kinds of fruit tea, which was not exactly cheap either …We have already talked about the high prices.

A few more kilometres and we had reached today's destination. The PP *"Frenchman's Cove"* is in the middle of the forest, on a very wide bay, near a golf course. This made it particularly desirable. Negotiations with the ranger revealed that they could give me a pitch with electricity for the next two nights. Otherwise, only a simple pitch would be available. This weekend would be a long weekend because of the upcoming 1st July (Canada Day) and therefore very "busy". Besides, the summer holidays start on Friday. Although 1st July was a Tuesday, in Canada the closest Monday is always treated as a holiday. That's why I was so unlucky. Accordingly I hoped for a cancellation of an electricity pitch for Friday or else I would look for the nearest gravel pit. What's the point of paying for a place without service? I could have it cheaper. When the weather calmed down, I wouldn't need electricity for heating. My two furry hot water bottles would work well again tonight...but relying on them could not be a permanent condition.

Burin Peninsula

Like Italy, Newfoundland has its "boot". This one juts far out into the Atlantic Ocean. We tackled this boot today and were on the road for one hundred and eighty kilometres. The starting point was the Provincial Park in **Frenchman's Cove**. The rain had eased overnight, and the visibility was relatively clear. Carpe Diem!

If we managed to complete the tour today, we would win another day. Last night I was still working on the new planning for the month of July and realised how little time I had left and what I still wanted to see.

Frenchman's Cove itself is a tiny nest with a single grocery shop. It also benefits from a small golf course and camping. The cove is wide and full of roughly polished pebbles. Across **Fortune Bay**, you can get a glimpse of the next stretch of coastline. Shortly after setting off we came to the first stop. From time to time, along the coast, small parking areas with information were set up at prominent vantage points, ideal for free overnight stays. This is only mentioned in passing.

My next destination was the larger town of **Grand Bank** with its glorious past at the turn of the century. It takes its name from the Grand Banks off Newfoundland, blessed in earlier times with unfathomable fish wealth.

Here, nations fought about fishing rights and from here cod was transported all over the world. An ingenious system of remuneration ensured the entrepreneurs' prosperity and made the fishermen dependent on their employers. In the modern fishing museum the past came alive and a large mural transported the viewer to the time around 1920. Many good explanations accompanied the depictions.

The merchant ships brought the dried and salted fish to markets in Spain, Portugal, France and as far as the West Indies. On the return journey they were loaded with rum, sugar and syrup from the south, as well as goods from Europe and the United States. If there was enough fish and the price was high, the traders and ship owners made their fortune. In return, they paid the ordinary fishermen and dockworkers with credit, not money. This system was a complicated method of accounting for debt and credit. The merchants provided their fishermen and their families with tools and food supplies – on credit. At the end of the season, the catch of fish and the number of cod supplied were tallied. After the existing debts had been deducted, the remaining wages were again given in the form of credits for purchases from the employer. These could be redeemed for food, clothing or other goods. If the catch was bad, there was no credit, only debts.

Processing the catch on land was backbreaking work. When a schooner arrived at its home port, the cargo of salted fish (as far as preservation on the ship was concerned) had to be further processed for preservation during transport. It was dried in the sun for this purpose. Good and careful processing guaranteed a high price on the market. Drying the cod required good weather and arduous work.

First the fish was washed to remove the salt. The cut fish was placed on wooden racks called "flakes". In Grand Banks and other places where the French first fished, the fish were dried directly on the pebbles on the beach. When necessary, everyone was involved in the process. However, women were primarily in charge, while children and older family members shared the household. The women worked from dawn to dusk to lay out the fish, turning it over to keep it from mould and rotting. The workers wore extra-long bonnets with neck protectors to protect themselves from the sun.

Of course, the wealth of the merchants also left its mark on the city's architecture. On a tour you can still find mansions from that time. Particularly interesting were the balconies on top to keep an eye out for the ships.

Grand Bank or the Labrador Current impressed me so much because these names had always stood for something far away, something inaccessible, just like the Yukon or Alaska. The fact, that I could now actually travel to these places excited me enormously. Even the cold and wet weather didn't bother me anymore.

The journey continued: we wanted to drive around the cape, but the road got worse and worse from **Fortune** onwards. Fortune is the excursion port for the two offshore islands, which are still French territory and for which Canadian needs a passport to cross the border. A not very inviting settlement, I felt.

Once around the bend the fog spread! Slow driving was the order of the day, as the patchwork of roads did not allow for high speeds. It was the purest bumpy road. Vast wasteland, low vegetation, scrawny trees, desolation, especially in this atmosphere … I wondered more than once what made people persevere in such godforsaken villages, in the middle of nowhere. Water! Bare mountains! Catastrophic roads! Three neighbours and NOTHING else!

Only in **St. Lawrence** did some life stir again. The small town owed its existence to its mining past. A small mining museum bore witness to this. But more than that, I had the impression that this settlement lived and still lives from fishing, because several mighty schooners lay at anchor. It was interesting to observe the rising fog banks along the entire route. I had only experienced such movements on the Pacific coast of the USA.

Slowly, my stomach started to tell me something. It was almost half past two and I started to be on the lookout for a suitable stopping point for a short break. Again, we found a cute little car park with signs and a fantastic view of *St. Lawrence Bay*. We had warm soup and a refreshing *siesta*. We had time; our next landing place was not too far.

Shortly before reaching our final destination, I had the glorious idea of letting my dogs run a little off-leash on the deserted beach of Frenchman's Cove. It worked like a charm! Suddenly they were both gone, down the pebble slope. They came back when I called them and I took the precaution of putting them back on the leash. Then I noticed with horror the awful smell of rotten fish on both four-legged friends! Ugh! They must have caught a carcass and rolled around in it, hidden from my view! That's why they looked so happy! But not for long!

I gave them their first wet rubdown in the camper. The second one with soap and brush followed at the campsite. Afterwards, I looked just as wet as my lady and gentleman, but I didn't care! In any case, they were not getting into my car like that. I held their leashes with one hand and tried to give them a soap treatment with the other. Being offended was not an option at all! No one was coming into my bed today, even if I had to build a fence around it! No, thanks! Both now smelt something like lavender and that probably bothered them more than me. Let's see if I can get the vile smell out of my nose overnight. Even when it rained again, one window would stay slightly open. And when the heating goes nuts, the "perfume" settles in whether you like it or not! We would drive up the boot again tomorrow and probably spend the night in the gravel pit from last time.

 Private remarks

CODFISH CURRENCY

MAKING FISH WHILE THE SUN SHINES

Grand Banks / Centre of cod fishing around 1900/1920

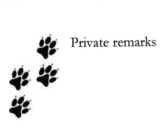 Private remarks

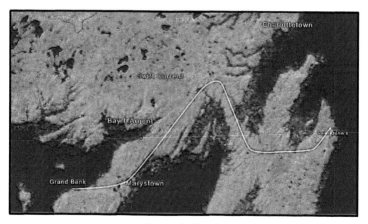

Grand Bank
Island capital St. John's
360 km

Private remarks

St. John's (end of June)

We did not have a dry night on Friday. It came out of the clouds in buckets and in the morning, there was also thick fog. We got up relatively early and I consulted my map! If things went well we could make the three hundred and thirty kilometres to St. John's in one go today. So off we went on the road! That way we would save another day. Everyone can imagine that disposing of waste and drawing water in this rain was no joy, but I wanted to be prepared for all eventualities. Absolutely soaked, I got behind the wheel. Anyway, inside the camper we were dry and warm.

I calculated five hours driving time, if I included the first two hundred kilometres with pothole hurdles. The calculation worked out. Up to the "Isthmus" we were on the road for almost three hours in continuous rain and fog banks. With the TCH back under the wheels, I stopped for a short fuel break, hoping for a little better visibility. As we left the "mountain masses" of the Peninsula behind us, there was suddenly some visibility. Two kilometres further on, this hope was dashed until St. John's. Flying absolutely blind! I saw nothing at all of the landscape. I only noticed that it was constantly going up and then down again, that's why I didn't risk going more than 80km/h. Although it was still pouring with rain there was a lot of holiday traffic. Here, suddenly, the TCH was more than busy when compared to the previous sections.

Of course, I decided not to make a multiple WALMART overnight stay in this weather. I wasn't tired of life after all! Not yet! Even though the campsite at Pippy Park was in the higher price category we could afford it! I wanted to be warm and dry. On the way, I sent one prayer after the other to heaven asking for an electric place for us there. We were heard! Perhaps the dogs had also thrown their connections up into the balance. As there had been several cancellations (due to the weather!) we were offered a place near the heated sanitary facilities. It was a little sloping, but I was happy to accept this small shortcoming. I would cook a little uphill during the next few days but I would not fall out of bed! I quickly connected to the electricity; I could take care of everything else later.

Here, in the middle of town, they charge 45.- CAD per night, but we had electricity, water and sewage disposal available. Supposedly, the bus drove right below the entrance to the city centre. Therefore, I could leave my mice at home for once and enjoy myself alone.

Now, there was absolutely no hurry. First came a thorough body care, later the fight with the internet. In a secluded corner of the park they had Wi-Fi. I urgently needed to get on the net because I had several bills to pay. But that only worked if I had mobile phone coverage at the same time. However, it had been sh… for the last few weeks. On the island, only the corner around Cornerbrook in the west and St. John's area in the east has international service. I sat down in an anorak and hood (end of June!) in the morning at 7°C in a draughty shelter and almost despaired of the speed of the transmission. For the sake of documentation I wanted to take a picture with the video camera, but some defect prevented this. It would have been too beautiful! Finally, I had everything done and shivering I retreated to my den. For today, my dogs were used as watch-dogs.

I would have had to wait almost an hour for the bus. I didn't feel like it, because I wanted to take advantage of the sun, which had suddenly fought its way through the fog and won the day. I tried to find the centre with a not exactly optimal city map. Just under three kilometres on foot! But not in a straight line, as in the promotional photo… No! Up and down hills, just like in San Francisco!

My first destination was the modern museum "The Room". From the futuristic building, one should have a fantastic view of the entire harbour and the old town of St. John's. After about an hour and several failed attempts due to the inaccurate map, I had made it. That should have been enough for me, but for 5.- CAD senior fare I could also visit the adjacent museums. I wouldn't have had to pay anything for the main hall alone and the panorama terrace. But I found out about that afterwards…

A few pictures of the former life and importance of the cod had particularly appealed to me. Now I also knew what the many long wooden poles were for; I had seen them set up everywhere in the fishing villages.

How did I get to Signal Hill and Cabot Tower in this fantastic weather? It was too far to walk… By chance, I got hold of the brochure of the city trolley. For five dollars you can "hop on, hop off" the whole day! It was a bit late for today, but the only way to get up the hill. I saw a few daring campers, but with the excursion traffic? No, thanks! I better let the bus driver do the work… motto: "Carpe diem! Seize the day!" I let myself be driven!

Unfortunately, Marconi's tower, from which the first overseas telegraphic transmission had come about, had been closed for renovation work. No problem! Instead, I was surprised by the view of another iceberg and fog clouds coming into St. John's Bay. But as soon as they passed the narrows, they disappeared. Out on the Atlantic, thick wads of cotton wool billowed and the foghorn from the small lighthouse tolled incessantly as a warning. In the harbour itself, the sun was shining.

A short walk led me down to the former Queen's Battery defences. Here, some real military men were busy explaining their First World War service to the tourists. It was real because, as training, they really lived as they did in wartime. They used to train them on this hill for their mission in Europe. The gentlemen were having lunch, served from various tin cans. I was starving, as my stomach had not been fed since morning, but at the sight of such food I lost my appetite.

Thank you! My feet and I had had enough for one day. In front of the Visitor Centre, I waited for my bus and drove downhill again towards the "Rooms". There I hoped to catch a taxi for the return to the campsite. Not even five minutes later someone picked me up. What a relief! Only now did I realise the distance I had walked this morning – no wonder I was exhausted. But that was not enough as when I got home my two mice were waiting patiently for me. They also needed their run now…

I spent the next hour walking with my entourage along one of the park's many well-developed hiking trails. Then I finally had my main meal for the day and a ravenous appetite. I took no time to cook properly. Quickly a little bacon in the pan, some eggs over and fresh salad then I warmed up some leftover roast potatoes that were still in the fridge. Enjoy your meal!

While I was writing, it had become dark. I had done my daily share of recording my adventures and for sure I was going to lie down for the next half hour! Carpe diem!

Cabot Tower, Signal Hill and Queen's
Battery

Private remarks

 Private remarks

St. John's - Part 2

After hearing the foghorn every ten seconds all night – until I fell asleep, of course – I came to the logical conclusion that there was still thick pea soup out at sea well into the early morning. Would a visit to **Quidi Vidi**, the hidden fishing village, make sense? After all, it was behind the Narrows, on the open Atlantic. Here at the campsite, it was already sunny at half past nine.

I let fate decide: "First come, first served" – taxi or public bus? – depending on which one came first I would shape my day's programme. A white taxi with a nice talkative driver won the race and for 15.- CAD he drove me to the small fishing village.

I was right, the fog was still over the lake and the small harbour. Of course, the atmosphere varied accordingly, as the haze floated through the strait in different consistencies and fought its battle with the sun, sometimes more, sometimes less successfully. A pretty little place, right next to the big city and not overrun with tourists… Was it the hour of the morning? I found some nice motifs, including a local microbrewery. Unfortunately, I was denied a taste.

I found my way to the lake. It was a lovely walk along the southern shore. Many people were with me, of course, the young and older people like me, dogs (... and cats, I almost said!) with their masters and mistresses, all kinds of leisure-seekers. It was pleasantly warm, even if you could see the fog coming through the bay. I especially liked the colourful houses on the opposite side.

It should be briefly mentioned in this context that in 1892 a major fire reduced over 1,500 houses to rubble and left 1,900 people homeless, and that therefore only a few relics from its past remain in one of the oldest cities in North America.

I had reached St. John's again after barely three kilometres and now wanted to walk the two oldest streets in the city – *Water Street* and *Duckworth Street*. As the turnover of the harbour had decreased more and more, shops, pubs and restaurants moved into the colourful houses. Here, everyone found something to their taste; especially in the evening, when the pubs with live music were well attended.

Also I found something to suit my taste: by chance, I came across the Newfoundland Chocolate Company with handmade chocolates. I just couldn't resist and focused on "Icebergs" and "Canada Day" in original colours at a sinful price. I'd better not tell you how much I paid, or some people will think I'm crazy! But these delicacies were delicious! It's not as if I treat myself to anything else…

Since I was already spending money today, I went back for a second time. In a somewhat upmarket souvenir shop, I saw a beautiful little double sculpture carved from the antlers of an elk. I really wanted something small and fine to remember Newfoundland by. The price was ok (the equivalent of a tank of gas) and was made by a local artist! That was acceptable and the noble work of art changed hands. After all, I couldn't bring complete "horns" on the plane later!

In the meantime, I got hungry again and was drawn back to one of the pubs. There I discovered a small brewery, probably old. I tried it and was not disappointed, either with the food (seafood chowder) or the ambience. It was well attended, which was always a good sign.

Quidi Vidi

 Private remarks

Private remarks

St. John's well established pub culture.

 Private remarks

145

 Private remarks

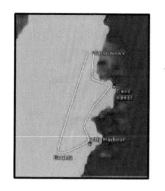 

Two trips around St. John's

Private remarks

Petty Harbour and Cape Spear

Take it easy! Today we already had the third beautiful day in a row when we woke up. A record result in the last four weeks! As we had extended our stay at the campsite by two nights, today we would go on the first excursion. The total tour was no longer than fifty kilometres, so we had plenty of time in the morning and I could even check my mails. Unfortunately, they did not all bring good news.

We started at around half past ten and drove first to **Petty Harbour**, with some detours due to wrong GPS programming. A nice little fishing harbour... I liked it here a lot so I grabbed my two gypsies and strolled around in the sunshine for over an hour. Somehow each of these little harbours is the same and yet different: each has its own character. This one had squeezed itself into a protective strait and entrenched itself behind a dyke wall after a flood or storm surge almost destroyed the whole site several years ago. From our parking spot, we could once again make out a beautiful iceberg glistening in the sun against a wall of fog.

Well, we were still in the sphere of influence of the Labrador Current. The fog bank was getting closer by the minute. You could see it heading straight for us. After a good hour's walk, it had almost reached the coast and engulfed the iceberg. This didn't look good for our next destination, but we set our sights on it anyway. **Cape Spear** is a National Park project and at home in the easternmost corner of North America (not just Canada!). That was as far as it went…

The approach around noon was still clear, but the fog was already wafting around the Cape. Good! What the North Cape could do in Europe, it could also do in the American continent. We parked in the haze, hiked in the fog to the "easternmost" point of the continent, climbed up to the modern, spooky-looking lighthouse and looked around a bit in the former dwelling of the lighthouse keeper. We could only guess at the depth of the abyss because of the poor visibility. Both my dogs were suspicious of the sound of the foghorn and Knuffi, with her tail between her legs, moved forward in flight.

After an hour, my legs were aching and I thought that a lunch break was just what I needed. Eventually, the clouds cleared, and the sun shone through at times. I found a decidedly cosy little restaurant with just one table and a view of St John's Bay with a view of Cabot Tower. The food was simple but tasty (ham noodles with salad and top-class chocolate for dessert). The landlady had even prepared a little cot for me to take a *siesta*. What more did I want? My dogs were also welcome guests... I can only recommend this pub!

After my recovery period, all the fog had cleared, and the sea lay deep blue and glistening in front of me. Next thing I know it was late afternoon thus I harnessed my dogs to the leash once more and tramped with them along the cliffs for another hour. In the company of other tourists I saw water fountains rising from the sea for the first time on this trip.

The whales had returned from their winter quarters in the south, probably accompanied with offspring. At least that's how I had seen them in Baja California. Sometimes you saw a shiny black back briefly emerge; then again, the famous tail fin came out in a sweeping turn. Or one playfully showed off its sparkling white belly during a somersault. It always happened in a fraction of a second, and as a layman I could only wonder how animal photographers often managed to take such fantastic pictures. I did not succeed in taking one. Time and again the animals were already submerged when the shutter clicked. But that's what professionals are for...

That was enough for today! We had been out in the fresh and cold air for more than three hours in total. The clock struck six and I shifted into reverse. We had briefly to stock up on our supplies and were home dead tired at around seven-thirty. My two companions were also exhausted from the many impressions and now lay scattered and snoring quietly around me with my legs up. I had finished my homework and was now planning another tour for tomorrow. Good night!

Canada Day - Holiday
Only a hundred kilometres and still broken

The fourth beautiful day in a row! It had to be an accident. I closed my eyes again suspiciously at half past six and slept until half past eight. The sun was still smiling…

Therefore Plan B came into play, the trip to the north of St. John's, the **Killick Coast Scenic Drive**. Despite some daw-dling, we made it to the road by eleven. Once again, we passed through a variety of bays. Our first stop was at **Middle Cove**. In this picturesque bay, quite a few Sunday-trippers were ca-vorting on the pebbly beach. A few daredevils could even be seen in the water. The children especially seemed to have no sense of cold here! For them, summer had started today!

Our next stop was **Flat Rock**. Anyone looking at the rock formations could guess why the little place was given this name. Here we had our first long walk along the East Coast Trail. At the moment it is still more a project than an attraction, but it is in the process of being developed more and more for tourism and hikers. A short stretch was enough for us, as the rest of the trail seemed unsuitable for two dogs.

Addendum

Yesterday evening, I was still so exhausted that I interrupted my diary entry and was only able to return to it this morning with some distance.

So where were we? Oh yes, **Flat Rock**! The next settlement was a little bigger than the previous ones. From the car park of the small pilgrimage site in **Pouche Cove** (... which was even worthy of Paul II Pope's visit in 1984) we had an excellent view of the whole bay. Here, too, the big friends (i.e. whales) were cavorting and enjoying their lives, just like us, even entertaining us with some acrobatic leaps in the air.

When I wanted to follow the road further to the headland of **Biscayan Cove**, I was warned by a sign (after the tarred road had suddenly ended) that the following stretch was only to be driven on with 4x4s. But I was already stuck uphill. I reversed and with all due caution steered the long carriage back down the narrow path with a few drops of sweat. Everything went well! I was able to turn around in a driveway…

Then I followed the tarred pothole road across the peninsula to **Bauline**. The road descended steeply into the small coastal village with only a few houses and a tiny harbour for lobster fishing – see above! We stopped between two fishermen's huts and went for a short walk – for an overview – to a gravel pit above the settlement. Yes, there really weren't many large flat parking spaces for a vehicle like mine!

Man, it was warm today! There was not a breath of air in this bay. The dogs gratefully accepted the gift of a small fresh-water stream. Even Wurschtel, the water-shy fellow, took a refreshing dip, not to mention Knuffi. When I had a look at the nearly empty fridge I had only bananas and yoghurt for lunch. With the temporarily strict diet, it's surprising that I haven't lost a single gram of weight lately (a long-term goal on this trip).

Slowly we puffed our way back up to the heights after this break. The motorhome had a lot of work to do with its weight and the incline. Another bumpy road to **Portugal Cove**. This settlement with its harbour belonged to a populated part of the headland. Contrary to all the information in books and maps, the *ferry to Bell Island* was in operation until the evening, and it was "two-lane". The crossing took twenty minutes (five kilo-metres) and cost only eight dollars with a reverse guarantee. Of course, we were there on the next departure… My first im-pression when I saw the steep coast of the island was that I was admiring the "Cliffs of Dover" of Newfoundland.

A lighthouse was always a good choice! I steered the car in the direction of the sign. The small tower stood decoratively in the middle of a huge meadow, overlooking a magnificent rock monolith that housed a colony of birds. The water around it was turquoise blue and it was drilled with a few grottos… beautiful!

Wabana was the only widely dispersed settlement on this island. Otherwise, there was only a ring road around it. I had read in my guidebook that there would be some major murals of the history of the island as it had been economically important in the past for the mining of iron ore. An old mine had been restored and now led through the old tunnels underground. The mine interested me less; I was looking for the murals. I saw one in passing and wanted to turn around at the next junction. An oncoming driver drew my attention to the one-way street and I overlooked the sign.

That's when it happened! I was paying attention to the traffic, scraped the turn and heard a terrible noise! Something went berserk (not me, for the moment). Stunned, I saw the mess! Three wheels were on the tarmac, one was hanging loose in a ditch, supported by the rear stout bumper! Nice sh ...! I was stuck in a "ditch" and could already see myself spending the night on the island. Had I been too scatter-brained? Had the tyre slipped? Why were all the other three still on solid ground? Why didn't the rear end come around the bend with me? Pointless questions…

Once again, I had to rely on my "guardian angels". They flew by in the form of three local gentlemen on a holiday outing and promised to send a truck to rescue me. By now we had become the sensation of the road section. The ambulance service stopped and asked if I was okay, several sympathetic souls asked me how my mishap had happened, the postal worker coming out of her office. This shortened my wait for definite help.

It came down the road in the form of an all-around digger. With an expert's eye, the driver checked out the situation. Provided he could attach his heavy chain to the back of my vehicle, he would try to carefully lift me, move me, and put the wheel back on the road. All I could do was pray and watch. A second helper came along and shouted directions to the excavator driver.

The chain was thrown over the heavy vehicle, the lateral joint supports were extended for balance and inch by inch he moved my big vehicle upwards, again and again paired with short sideways movements to turn it slightly. The excitement was probably written all over my face. At first, the excavator operator scoffed a little, "Women at the wheel…" But when he saw my number plate, he said appreciatively: "… driven all the way from Ontario?"

Finally, I too was able to help a little from behind the steering wheel. As with parking, foot on the brake until I got command… It jerked horribly a few times, the steering wheel moved, swung out and I got my balance back! All four wheels had solid ground under them! No one can imagine what a weight was lifted from my heart. I would have loved to hug and kiss my helpers! But I remembered my age and held back. Instead, I took the photo showing the ditch and the excavator.

I was also lucky that absolutely everything important was in order, nothing was broken and only a small edge on the right rear was damaged. It could be patched up with silicone. Apparently, the weighty bumper had absorbed the crash and protected the linkages. The entrance step was slightly bent, but with a few strong hammer blows one of the helpers got it working again. The excavator operator charged a hundred dollars for his services (... a fair price, I think), the other also got a small tip for... me being able to drive again!

A friendly observer of the action took me to one of the murals. They were widely scattered around the community, and you really had to know where to look for them. Despite my mishap, I let my curiosity get the better of me and took several more pictures.

We reached our ferry at six o'clock and I still had twenty kilometres to go to the campsite. We turned in hungry. Understandably, I didn't feel like writing much that evening. Besides, it was so humid that I was sweating profusely, even with the window open. The dogs were hiding in corners, as there were a lot of fireworks in the area because of the holiday. Today I managed to summon the nerve to write down our last story before breakfast.

Irish Loop

Probably due to yesterday's experiences, I didn't feel as fit today as I would have liked. Our check-out wasn't until 1pm, so I did all sorts of things besides cleaning up. I didn't know what I would do that day. It got cloudier and sultrier. After the shower I could have jumped under the water again. That's why I didn't plan too much for that moment. If I could get a serviced pitch at **La Manche PP**, it would be a comfortable afternoon. I needed a little rest for myself and the dogs. The park had been in such demand over the long weekend that I hadn't had a chance to use the internet. Not even for unserved pitches.

Today it worked out! The first part of the Irish Loop was not particularly exciting so I only had one photo stop with a view of the offshore islands at **Tors Cove**. The cloud cover didn't particularly invite me to go on a whale watching tour. I also wanted to cut expenses down, after I settled the balance of June in the logbook a few days ago. That's when I hit the skids. Certainly, there were several expenses that would not be repeated, such as the ferry back to the mainland or the various park passes and reservation fees, as well as equipment for the motorhome. But still! The most expensive thing was the fuel: almost 1,200 €! That was twice as much as I had estimated. The distances in Newfoundland had a huge impact but I couldn't save on that –or I wouldn't see anything!

THE WABANA MINES

The existence of iron ore on Bell Island was known as early as 1610 when Sir Percival Willoughby, whose family controlled extensive iron ore mines in England, petitioned that the Island be included in his grant so that he might exploit its potential.

Mining operations did not begin, however, until nearly three centuries later when the full extent of the ore deposits became known. In 1895, the first cargo of ore was shipped from here to Nova Scotia by the Nova Scotia Steel & Coal Company. The two independent companies initially involved in mining on Bell Island – the Nova Scotia Steel & Coal Company and the Dominion Iron & Steel Company – merged in 1921 to form the Dominion Steel Company which continued to manage the mines until their complete shutdown in 1966.

ERECTED TO COMMEMORATE THE 25TH ANNIVERSARY OF NEWFOUNDLAND'S CONFEDERATION WITH CANADA DEPARTMENT OF TOURISM GOVERNMENT OF NEWFOUNDLAND AND LABRADOR

Private remarks

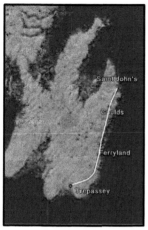

Irish Loop
Avalon Wilderness
Cape Shore
150 km

 Private remarks

The route around the **Avalon Wilderness** is called the **Irish Loop** because an extremely large number of Irish people established themselves on the local coast during the settlement period, and even today the population is very attached to Irish tradition, even in the accent of the language. The wilderness itself is not accessible and is an absolutely protected area where, among others, the caribou retreat and roam the coastal region in summer and autumn. I left the number of days we would need for the two "fingers" to chance, as I did not want to put myself under any more stress after yesterday's event.

Ferryland

Yesterday's rest day had built me up again: we could go on. We were out of bed quickly and on the road early. For us, that meant departure shortly before half past eight. The weather was double-edged, very cloudy with a few small sun holes and a strong wind blowing. It had already made the camper rock during the night. Maybe it would blow the clouds away?

And indeed, on the way to **Ferryland** the clouds disappeared, and it became sunny again. Steadily it went uphill and downhill. The coastal road #10 dipped from hundreds of metres down to various small towns and then went back up high into the forest. I felt like I was on a roller coaster.

Our first destination for today was Ferryland with its excavations of the 17th century settlement of **Avalon**, probably one of the oldest permanent settlements in North America anywhere. But for the time being, I was more interested in the lighthouse, which could be seen from afar on the road. The road there was not particularly suitable for my vehicle and so I took my two companions on the leash, and we set off on foot to cover the two kilometres. For normal walkers this would be a short hike of a good half hour, for the three of us about twice as long, because every second flower had to be sniffed or a marker set down. But that didn't matter, because the landscape scene was overwhelming and the weather great, although the strong wind was a little annoying.

A lot of birds were nesting on the offshore islands, and the many small fish (capelines) were gathering around the shore, attracting the halibut and the whales. At some point, the road turned into a normal hiking trail, and we had wonderful views to the picturesque lighthouse and backwards to the coast.

The lighthouse crew set up a freshly packed lunch for walkers, like at a snack bar. Nice idea! But we had just come from breakfast and didn't feel hungry. So my dogs and I sat down on the bench in front of the tower and watched the sea. One by one, several whales cavorted in the water right in front of us. This time I managed to prove that I had really seen them. Not perfectly, but at least they weren't completely under water. Meanwhile the Wuffis waited patiently in the shade of the bench.

After half an hour I had seen enough, and the whales disappeared into the open sea again. So, time for us to start on the way back. This time the wind was blowing in our faces and it was exhausting to stand up against it, but we made it anyway. I quickly put my two companions in the camper because I wanted to see the excavations of the settlement. They are still digging there today, and you can look over the shoulders of the restorers in the main building. A connection to Germany has also opened up. You wouldn't believe how "small" the world was around 1600. Artefacts have been found there from Portugal to Spain to Germany, France and England. And all because of a fish called Cod!

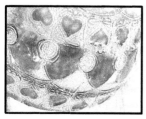

sprig-moulded jug from the Westerwald region of Germany

After my tour, I treated myself to a small lunch and a nap. I really had to keep up this habit, so I felt better in the afternoon. I think the self-imposed stress of the day before yesterday was partly to blame for my misery.

Now I continued south. I wanted to check out the unsupervised and therefore free **Chance Cove Provincial Park** for a free overnight stay. It was getting foggier, and we drove through a ghostly landscape. The picture around us had absolutely changed: I felt like I was in the tundra. No more trees, hardly any bushes, plants low to the ground, bog lakes, boulders and now and then a lonely house. Together with the fog and the strong wind, the impression was more than spooky. When I read that the way to the park was six kilometres on gravel road, I thankfully gave it up and drove to the next village, **Portugal Cove South**. There was a visitor centre near the town entrance and I wanted to find out if the road to **Cape Race** and the fossils was passable for my vehicle.

I was strongly advised against it, partly because the lighthouse would be closed. The Cape still appealed to me so I considered the possibility of joining an expert guided tour tomorrow. I could park my camper with the dogs and be chauffeured there in a van with a ranger. That would be something special, wouldn't it? There was enough space so I booked and changed my schedule a little.

I got an overnight tip for **Trepassey** and a short time later I was sitting on a campsite that was no longer in use (gravel pit 2). All around me there was a little buzzing, crashing and bumping because the generator was not running smoothly, but it was doing its job. Thank God it hadn't been damaged the day before yesterday. After all, I needed juice for my batteries again tomorrow and at the same time the text and the pictures had to go into the PC.

Mistaken Point

This was the name of the place where fossils from a geological period of 550 million years ago had been discovered. The fishermen in the area knew of their existence long before this discovery but could not interpret their historical sensation. It was not until two biologists eager to hike saw the huge significance of these "petroglyphs" that the site made the list for the first ten next additions to UNESCO's World Heritage List. Until they are added, the point is absolutely protected and visitors are guided to another site that was discovered a little later, lying outside the relevant area. You are allowed to hike there with a guided tour, so I wanted to join this one today.

The start was at 1pm at the information centre in **Portugal Cove South**. We had enough time until then and first explored a little in the surroundings of Trepassey. The sun was shining in the bay, fog was moving in from the sea and the horn was blowing its warnings in the air; it looked as if the sea was beginning to boil. The path to the lighthouse was heavy gravel so I gave it up: it was too far to walk this time. I wasted the waiting time in the information centre, read all kinds of explanations in great detail and became more and more curious about the sight. How could it be otherwise? The fog was again thick and impenetrable over the whole area. Two kilometres further and…

We were ten participants in total for this little expedition, all with our own cars. I had the privilege of getting in with the two friendly guides. We drove seventeen kilometres along a gravel road that I really wouldn't have wanted to drive with the camper.

From the trail head, it was a good half hour into the wilderness until we reached our destination. Arctic loneliness all around us. As already described, hardly any trees, low vegetation, many berry plants, several dirt holes and ferns in all variations. If a small tree did manage to survive, it stood alone in the landscape or was torn apart by the wind. The wind blew strongly around our ears today and it was several degrees cooler than in the information centre. Headband and anorak were once again the order of the day at the beginning of July.

My God, what a pace the youth could set! I was no longer able to keep up, even though I was kindly given a walking stick right at the beginning. However, since there were always stops for various explanations, even the slow snail Monika was able to keep up.

When we arrived at our destination, we had to split into two groups, because otherwise there were too many people for the sightseeing spot. A steep cliff rose out of the sea and bore witness to the fact that Newfoundland was connected to Africa and South America in the distant past. The sporty participants climbed down, of course. I was able to deny myself that

167

with my wobbly joints. Even from the hill, the fossils were easy to see, and I could easily capture them with my telephoto.

Before even the last ones turned around, I made my way back, because I wanted to have a little time advantage for my walking rhythm. Otherwise, it was too depressing to be the last one to follow a whole group. It also gave me a little more time to catch my breath and take pictures.

I couldn't get lost. There was only one path, which used to be taken by fishermen to fish for cod in this bay. I enjoyed the silence around me in these moments, had time to absorb the solitude and let nature take its effect on me. No conversation, no matter how kindly meant, threw me off balance. It was a lonely but impressive hike, which was only stopped at the very end by the stragglers. All in all, a wonderful afternoon, even if a little foggy.

I could have spent the night at the information centre without any problems. But I was hoping that the fog would have disappeared in Trepassey. Besides, I had more room to run around on my pitch. We quickly had dinner, because contrary to my intention, lunch had again been replaced by only two bananas. The obligatory walk was shortened to two rounds and the foot care took priority next to the diary entry. I could already hear the end of the bed calling my name... See you tomorrow! Carpe diem! The way was the goal.

To the fossils at Mistaken Point

Private remarks

 Private remarks

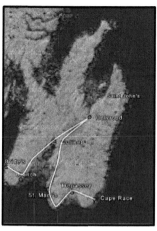

Cape Race
St. Mary's
Holyrood

Bird Sanctuary
- Cape St Mary
260 km

 Private remarks

Pothole Crescendo and Symphony of Fog
From the Irish Loop to Cape Shore Drive

We had another good and quiet night at our chosen campsite. In the morning we were totally surrounded by white cotton wool. We couldn't even see the railing of the sports field twenty metres away. This was going to be fun! But let's wait for the next bend!

The next bend didn't bring anything, nor did the next one or the one after that. Everything was completely covered. You could see the edge of the road, but the area beyond that remained invisible. I still had hopes for **St. Vincent's**, further away from the battle of the two opposing ocean currents.

Whale watching! I laughed so hard! You could barely see the next house on the beach or even the Atlantic Ocean or a hint of St. Mary's Bay.

Besides, we had to be incredibly careful with the potholed road. Even a distant shadow on the road meant stopping, because you couldn't guess whether it was a patchwork or an open "bathtub" and both were to be avoided. If the road was clear, you could do a bit of swerving to avoid the holes, paying attention to oncoming traffic or the rear-view mirror. If the road was not perfect you had to brake sharply and bump over the frost heaps at walking speed. Sighted too late and the fridge would open. The third time I bolted it shut! The fog did its bit to make visibility worse. Wurschtel grumbled every time the fridge rumbled again.

And that went on for two hundred kilometres! No fun at all, and I decided to spend the night in a more civilised way at the only campsite south of the next finger. Besides, I was short of water. I had to heat up again, because the high humidity made everything clammy and damp, with the paper like laundry. How did the locals deal with it? They were probably used to it or heated their homes like the devil because everyone has enough wood lying in front of their hut.

175

A little stretching of the feet was called for at **St. Mary's**. The beach of the small village of **Gulch** would also be great for a free overnight stay. Picnic huts, outhouse, tables and benches and an everlasting grey pebble beach. I soon had the beasts inside my sandals so I had to laboriously trudge back to the camper. Finally, I had to take a photo of the lonely wild irises. The dogs were whizzing around freely in the area, because no one was out in this fog...

We continued our blind flight towards **Holyrood**. About twenty kilometres before the junction of the #90 with the TC#1 there was a sanctuary for injured wild animals *(Salmonier Nature Park)*. They were kept "captive" in enclosures, but they were embedded in their actual wild environment. A three-kilometre-long boardwalk led through these enclosures, so it did not destroy nature when walking around and the animals could move freely. The night owls among them, such as arctic fox or weasel, kept hidden around noon, but I got a good shot of caribou and moose. Of course, there were a lot of people out and about on Saturday. Understandably, the dogs were not allowed into the park but I was free to move around and take pictures. Once the wind blew, then it looked like a thunderstorm, in between it got cool and again stiflingly humid, or the sun came piercing through and it was time for the mosquitoes to have their fun! All this within two hours of walking around. The only things left were snow and rain...

176

As planned, after the two-hour tour I took my lunch break with a small siesta. Wurschtel was surprisingly calm despite the car park environment and so I was able to start fresh again for new ventures at 3pm. For my next loop I had to go back another twenty kilometres to get on the #91 to **Colinet**. There was a salmon ladder to visit at the *Rocky River*. It started to drizzle lightly and then rain came. Not a jumping salmon in sight! Neither up nor down. Apparently, it was also too rainy for the animals to be out of their element…

Now I am sitting here in **St. Bride's**, at the turn-off to the Cape St. Mary's bird sanctuary (an absolute highlight in this corner) and the world is coming to an end at 9.13pm! It's getting dusky, the wind is howling around the motorhome, the dampness of the fog is seeping through all the cracks, and you can't see ten metres out of the window. Once again, I turn on my little heater. My snail shell sways like a desert ship, although it is standing between two very large brothers. Not even the dogs want to go out anymore!

The pitch is expensive for its facilities (30.- CAD), but as it is the only one on the whole Cape, the owner knows its value. Nevertheless, I am happy to have found shelter here. I think I would be scared alone in the wilderness today – which is not the case under normal circumstances. There is a small restaurant attached and out of curiosity I treated myself to a "moos" burger with fries tonight! The muddy bun was returned with a thank you. Moose or no moose, it tasted something like beef with a bit of seaweed flavour. Well, I tried it and am going back to my real beef steak. By the way, moose meat is not served everywhere: only in special places that needed and got a licence for it. Whether it will work out tomorrow with the birds is written in the fog. First, we have to spend the night. That's how it is in Newfoundland: at least one third of the planned programme had to be crossed off the list due to the weather.

Private remarks

Private remarks

Gannets

The night was terrible. There was whistling and howling all around our mobile. Understandably, I didn't sleep a wink during the rocking. It wasn't until well after midnight that the atmosphere calmed down and I slumbered fitfully until half past six.

A quick glance out of the window: nature grey in grey, visibility as usual… So, dogs cuddling with me in bed and another round of sleep. We didn't miss a thing! At half past seven another look out the window… No way! A clear view of the vast barren landscape and a blue stripe in the background.

But now the usual morning programme was quickly reeled off! For the price, I took advantage of all the "amenities" and treated myself to a hot, long shower. Disposing of waste and taking on water were the order of the day to ensure our independence: I quickly asked a departing guest about the road quality to Cape St. Mary's – no problem! But better safe than sorry! Then, in blustery winds and full sunshine, we were on our way to **Bird Rock**. This road was narrower than usual, but excellently built – hardly a pothole and only three bumps in thirteen kilometres.

Dogs forbidden! Understandable! Consequently my two comrades looked after the car and I disappeared in the direction of bird rock. It was about half an hour's walk along the cliff – at a normal pace. I staggered along the path like a drunk, because the wind was blowing very hard from the sea. Of course, it took me longer and I ran out of breath from time to time.

Cape St. Mary's Ecological Reserve is home to one of the largest breeding colonies of gannets on the North American continent, which have found a safe place on a large solitary rock close to the coast – up to 11,000 breeding pairs. You can get almost up close to these huge birds with a wingspan of up to 1.8 m and observe them perfectly. Even from a distance, you can hear their insistent cries, which enliven the eighty-metre-high cliff. Of course, other seabirds also join this community, but they are in the minority.

An impressive spectacle was offered to the spectators here. An eternal back and forth and a constant up and down with the wind; the birds seemed to have come to terms with the strong gusts and glided lightly and easily through the air. Not one – unlike me – was blown off its path. You'd have to be a gannet...

At around half past one, I arrived back home with my two companions, completely out of breath. But now they had to get out quickly. Knuffi made herself as flat and wind-slippery as possible and Wurschtel tried, like me, to keep the direction to some extent. The two of them soon had enough and all three of us were glad to land in the wind-protected harbour again.

Our next destination was now sixty kilometres further north, the former capital of Newfoundland, **Placentia**. My God, was road #100 miserable! Did they have a "ten-year plan" for road renewal here, come what may? Only after ten years would a section be resurfaced or patched up in a bungling manner? Did the few inhabitants of this area have to pay for the renewal themselves? Did the government have so little money, or did it need no effort for the few inhabitants in the villages? I found no answer. In our country, the population would kick up a storm to get reasonably well-maintained conditions for their taxes. Was that why most car types were 4x4s, because then you didn't feel the holes so much? In any case, I rumbled along this potholed road more badly than I could manage, smashed my thermos bottle with its contents when it fell out of the cupboard, and of course took my time. Nevertheless, I was able to see some beautiful stretches of coastline. Due to the weather conditions, the sea was deep green this time and swooshed mightily against the coast with high waves. Unfortunately, there was no direct access to most of the bays. The locals probably had their sneaky ways.

Placentia impressively and vividly documents its chequered history in the struggle between the French and the English for fishing privileges in the former fort high above the town. The relics are now a National Historic Site and with my pass I got in for free. Even the dogs were allowed to tramp through the fortifications on a leash. But before we started our visit, we had lunch (again at three o'clock) and a snooze until four. The sky began to be overcast again, and it looked like rain.

I had planned free camping tonight for financial reasons, but I found absolutely nothing suitable. Either the possibilities were too close to the road, or the access was too narrow for my motorhome. A campsite on the #100 didn't appeal to me at all, so I headed straight for our route for the next few days, the **Baccalieu Trail**. However, we only drove a few kilometres up to **Green's Harbour**. That was an alternative for 25.- CAD. If it didn't rain tomorrow, maybe I could do my laundry. It was about time, otherwise I would suddenly be out of clean underwear…

Private remarks

Cape St. Mary's Gannets

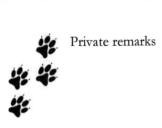 Private remarks

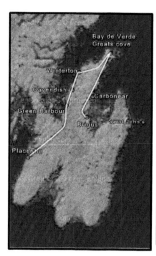

Baccalieu Trail - 300 km

 Private remarks

On the trail of the cod
Baccalieu Trail

I left the campsite late yesterday by our standards, but had three machines' of clean (?) laundry in the cabinets again. As was to be expected, the wash had to be done in cold water again but hopefully the remaining bacteria would have been killed in the hot dryer. We said goodbye at around one o'clock.

That was just the right time, because the bad weather was subsiding, and the sun was slowly breaking through. We set off on the cod trip, the **Baccalieu Trail** (*Bacalao* in Portuguese, Cod fish in English and *Kabeljau* in German). The route was marked by Highway #80.

It went constantly along the coast with partly beautiful views of the water. The first photo stop was in **Whiteway** with its striking trident rocks (Shag Rock) out in the bay and under a beautiful blue sky! Newfoundland! Always different from expectations…

I slammed on the brakes at **Cavendish**. Out of the corner of my eye I saw the cover of my planned Eastern Canada book! I think that will be it, at least for now! Once with and once without my camper perhaps! What does the reader think? For the sake of completeness, the intended title was "Carpe diem – before it rains again! Or something similar… In any case, I was enraptured by the colourfulness of the three houses, with their reflections in the pond! Simply classic!

We drove on: **Heart's Delight**, through **Heart's Desire**, to **Heart's Content**.   Romantic place names, aren't they? The first working transatlantic telephone cables reached Canadian shores at this small town in 1866. The original cables, laid from Valentia Island on the west coast of Ireland to here, still exist on the seashore. Some of the original equipment was on display at the refurbished Cable Station. I am not much of a tech-

189

nology freak, but I was greatly impressed by the news revolution of the time. The people who were employed here belonged to Newfoundland's elite, had special schools for their children, were highly paid and lived in their own houses with servants. At that time, a two-class society emerged in this former fishing village due to development. This difference was equalised later at the beginning of the First World War, when more and more people were employed to cope with the flood of information and tasks.

The girl at the ticket office persuaded me to buy the reduced ticket for the boat museum in Winterton. Ok! If I didn't make it today, four dollars wouldn't be that much of a loss. After the rest break, it was a little late and the planned round to the northern tip was too long. What to do? My empty fridge and the water shortage were burning under my nails. Comrade squirrel/hamster was getting nervous! Why not drive the eighteen kilometres to **Carbonear**, visit the Walmart and other supermarkets and do some unrushed shopping? Then we would have our place to sleep for the night. Tomorrow, we would make the leisurely northern turn of a good hundred kilometres. This decision turned out to be a sensible one, because it was already half past seven and I had stowed away all the shopping. All right, cook something now? Not in the mood! At the most, a couple of pancakes (ready-made) with maple syrup! That was quick and didn't make much mess…

The night's rest was not quite as ideal as usual, because there was a constant back and forth of cars and motorbikes. It got quieter around midnight, but as early as four in the morning a truck started to torment its generator. The noise woke me up. I felt hungry because of the meagre dinner and with the first movement I had both "children" in bed. It took a little while until the next snooze. For tomorrow I would look for something quieter.

Nevertheless, I started at around ten o'clock today and drove (or rather rumbled!) the east coast #70 northwards. I encountered all the existing landscapes of Newfoundland, from the impression of high mountains, to swamps and bogs, coniferous forests, reddish dunes, arctic vegetation, to sandy beaches. One cove followed the other, one bay the next. The advantage for me was that in all the fishing villages the speed was reduced to 50 km/h, so no one behind me could get upset because of my slowness. There was a lot to look at.

Shortly before **Bay de Verde** we came into contact with icebergs again. This time they had already shrunk on their long journey here. In addition, the warm weather of the past few days caused them to thaw and break apart into smaller pieces. The bird island in front of the village could not be visited because of its shelter, but there was the home of a former whole-saler in the active fishing village, where a museum was set up and where vivid and personal on-site stories were told about the living conditions sixty years ago. The entrance fee of five dollars included a personal guide for the tour and a cup of tea with the guides at the end. I got to talk at length with a lady my age and was able to find out about several other details of life in Newfoundland then and now.

In the meantime, fog had crept into the bay, obscuring everything and causing rain. Not exactly the weather to go to Red Head Cove, even if it was only a few kilometres away. The "Red Head" was directly in the fog bank according to the assessment of the situation, so we tried around the next bend at **Grates Cove** with its listed stone walls.

Once again, we ended up at the end of the world... In the centre of the village all three roads led to nowhere. The stone walls turned out to be ordinary

192

stone ramparts, like the hundreds or thousands of them you see in England and Ireland. There they were nothing special, but here they were listed. We found a great campsite, which could be an insider's tip for free overnight stays. Level, with a wonderful view of the water and the small lighthouse, some picnic benches and rubbish bins… Too bad we had other plans and the weather didn't cooperate. Maybe I would have changed my mind. Next time then!

During the lunch break at the viewpoint, it started to rain again. I tried to make my way back, as I still had the boat museum in **Winterton** on my agenda, if they would let me in with yesterday's ticket. They allowed it! A young lady personally guided me through the interesting exhibition. After half an hour I was tired, despite my knowledge of English. The young lady spoke fluent Newfoundland and even with several attempts to get her to slow down, I only understood half. Half an hour could be exhausting when you can't make out what they say!

I was drawn to **Carbonear** to a pitch at a distance from yesterday's market activity. On the way here, I had spotted a large sports complex with parking spaces. We would try it there for the night. We were not far from a road with little traffic, but it was quiet around us. Across the street there was a large, abandoned school because the holidays had begun. Who was going to exercise outdoors in this bad weather? At night there should be almost nothing going on! Well, then…

210 km backwards

Indeed, it was a quiet night with some rain and wind, otherwise unspectacular. My two companions got me out of bed at seven o'clock so we were able to start around nine. Our first destination was only five kilometres away. **Harbour Grace** played a doubly important role in Newfoundland's past. Today, this place has shrunk to a small market town, but can still boast some impressive buildings despite numerous fires.

The small town was once the pirate's nest of *Peter Easton*, a privateer who spread fear and terror in the early 1600s. He amassed immense wealth through plunder and eventually retired to Savoy as a marquis.

Three centuries later, in 1932, Harbour Grace became famous when *Amelia Earhart* set out from the airfield to become the first woman to cross the Atlantic solo.

We drove irreverently through England's first official colony of **Cupid**s without visiting the excavations there (much is simply repetitive) and ended up in **Brigus**, a pretty but cramped little village. I was able to savour this with my box until I found the house of *Captain Bob Bartlett*, now NHS. Who was this little-known personality?

Robert Bartlett lived at the turn of the century until 1946 and made a significant contribution to Arctic exploration. He had

gained experience in ship handling and navigation under the most difficult conditions of drift and pack ice, storm and fog during seal hunts off Labrador. He thus joined the

194

team of polar explorer Robert E. Peary in 1909 and gained fame as navigator of the expedition ship and during the sledge tour towards the Pole. Especially in the USA, he became known and celebrated through lecture tours. He was an all-round talent and scientist, filmmaker and collector at the same time. During World War II, he supported the Allied forces in establishing military bases in the far north – for me a fascinating personality.

As a side note, the current house was actually built ten kilometres away and only later moved in its entirety on rollers to its current location. I have already read about this practice among the settlers and seen impressive pictures of an entire village moving its buildings across the ice in single file.

Twelve kilometres to go to the lifeline of Newfoundland. I was happy to be able to drive on a paved road again and to switch the autopilot on. I almost fell into a kind of speed frenzy. TCH back to the West! The drive through the Newfoundland Isthmus was like the drive here: fog, fog, fog in its densest consistency. At least it wasn't raining as dreadfully as on the way here. Again, I saw nothing but forest and the roadside, now and then a few lakes in the landscape.

My intended destination behind **Clarenville (Thorburn Lake)** turned out to be a flop, because there was not a single place with electricity for the night. Well, I'll find something cheaper! I wasn't going to pay 20.- CAD just for a place to stay because my on-board water was still enough for at least one night, maybe even two. I took the next exit to the **Discovery Trail** on the *Bonavista Peninsula*. Somewhere we would find a "gravel pit" for us!

After fourteen kilometres our search was crowned with success and sure enough, we were sitting in a gravel pit with a ten-minute walk to a small lake. Two locals drove past us but none

195

grumbled. We stayed the night and further reduced the month-ly travel costs! I could even run the generator to make my own electricity without disturbing others and maybe for a short time for the microwave… the work on the pictures in the big PC could wait. Writing was done on my battery-powered little device.

Private remarks

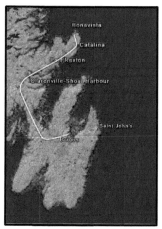

Bonavista Peninsula
Cabot Trail
Random Passage
250 km

Private remarks

Random Passage

What is behind the strange headline of the day? It refers to a Canadian TV series that was extremely popular in North America. They were based on two books by Newfoundlander *Bernice Morgan* and are available only through second-hand bookshops online: "The Colour of the Sea" and "At the End of the Sea". Before I started my journey, I almost devoured the books, because the fictional story vividly describes the situation of the first European settlers on Newfoundland at the beginning of the 18th century. This successful story was filmed and broadcast as a 4-part mini-series that had many viewers.

About eighteen kilometres from **Port Rexton**, a settlement from the period has been faithfully reconstructed for this purpose and furnished in keeping with the times with the help of museums. The settings are now open to visitors with guided tours and are maintained by a non-profit organisation. This fictitious village is situated in a landscape untouched by civilisation and has such a deep seabed that the schooner could navigate it even in draught schooner times. It should be added that much earlier a small group of people, a big family so to speak, lived on this ground.

For me, the tour was fascinating even though I had not seen the series. Every detail of the explanations found the right place in the book in my mind. The filmmakers had gone to great lengths to recreate the living conditions of the time down to the smallest detail. Of course, I don't presume that even one of my readers knows the books, but the pictures alone should give an impression of the harsh conditions at that time.

I wanted to risk it, because I was just keen to see the film with all the background knowledge I have now. The guide confirmed that my laptop would accept the foreign Canadian system. I bought the DVD and was curious to see what result would await me at home.

We drove back along the decidedly miserable #239 to the junction for Port Rexton. If I could get a pitch with electricity in the small RV park along the road, I would stay. I needed to recharge various devices and wanted to take my time reworking my reports and testing the DVD.

It worked out and I checked in immediately. It was early afternoon so I went for another walk to **Trinity** (Port Rexton), an extremely picturesque village in the bay of the same name. Should I now join the historical tour tomorrow, or continue on my way? I thought I would let the weather situation decide. Unfortunately, at this point in time, my electronic weather prophet on the internet could not pinpoint my exact location! Lost in Newfoundland… Finally, the DVD test was positive, and all readers can now easily guess what I did after I had written my report.

 Private remarks

Bonavista
Terra Nova NP

„Road to the
Beaches"

East Port

200 km

 Private remarks

"What a beautiful view!"

I had not yet heard John Cabot's enthusiastic remark. I first had to do all sorts of things that required electricity, including printing many past travelogues and much-needed use of the hoover.

Yes, you probably shouldn't watch "Random Passage" on video until midnight after an exhausting day! The sleep was not restful at all. After all the chores, including loading and unloading, I felt tired again around noon.

Today's plan had not yet been decided. However, the direction was determined when the campsite operator advised me not to take the camper to the lighthouse. Why do all these pretty little towers on the picturesque headlands only have to be accessible via narrow gravel roads? Five kilometres on foot seemed a bit far for my old bones.

We followed the trail of *John Cabot*, who was actually Italian and originally called *Giovanni Caboto*. He set foot ashore on Newfoundland's coast at **Bonavista Bay** in 1497 and is said to have exclaimed, "What a beautiful view!" I wanted to see that  exclamation confirmed. I didn't really care how the day would go.

Our route took us north along road #230. But soon I needed a break. As tired as I felt, I didn't want to go two kilometres further. Fortunately, a picnic area soon appeared and there I first lay down for an hour. This is the great advantage of having your own snail shell with you. Afterwards I had a snack and was reasonably fit again. Therefore, I immediately headed for the cape of Bonavista to pay my respects to the discoverer. For its remote location, Bonavista is a bustling harbour town of 4,000 people and still has buildings from the 19th century.

Afterwards we headed for **Cape North** with its pretty red and white checkerboard lighthouse. It was wonderful to walk here with the dogs. Lots of green areas, well-trodden or laid-out footpaths and an unmissable number of stones to mark for Wurschtel. It really was an impressive coastal landscape and I had to agree with John Cabot.

What fascinated me far more, however, was that I finally got to see my beloved *Atlantic puffins* in the wilderness. I love these droll birds more than anything. There was a small colony of these funny fluttering animals right off the coast: puffins, whales, icebergs, moose, caribou… my list became more and more complete.

After a long period of observation, I was finally able to detach myself from the cute show and turn our attention to the conqueror. He was standing freely on his hill, visible for all to see, smiling contentedly at his discovery of "Terra Nova". His ship was anchored in the safe harbour of Bonavista, a replica, but completely intact. His caravel had been faithfully reproduced for the 500th anniversary of the land seizure by the English and surrounded with a protective cover (i.e., museum). A two-month voyage of discovery across the oceans at that time would not have been to my taste. Romanticism, my arse! Privation, darkness and confinement were the order of the day. The people slept where there was a free place on the floor. The Queen of England herself was present at the inauguration of the ship in Bonavista almost twenty years ago. A video in the exhibition showed her speech. She looked young then – like all of us!

In the haste of writing, I forgot to tell you about the "dungeon". This is the name given to a washed-out rock which, due to the force of the water, basically spreads out in a meadow and forms a deep crater with two entrances to the sea. This natural feature is accessible via a wide, two-kilometre-long gravel path. As I saw several cars taking it, I also tried it with my car. Yes, the track seemed passable. We approached the "dungeon" at walking pace, leaving a cloud of dust behind us. I left my friends in the car as a precaution, because you never know with the rocks… The sea seemed to move a bit but there were no whales! No, there was a group of dolphins in the bay! Super! Up and down, again and again, in pairs! Wonderful! Let's tick that off from my to-do list as well!

In the village of **Bonavista** there is a cluster of buildings called Ryan's Premises (NHS), which was part of the overall complex of a wholesaler of the time in the 1800s. For the festivities, the houses were renovated and had exhibitions. Unfortunately, one did not get to see much of the real working world, as the respective large rooms were dedicated to certain themes of the region and the fishing industry. There would have been a lot to read and several videos to watch – all a bit much for the remaining hour of the tour. I also realised that I had already learned a lot in the meantime from my other visits and that much was repetitive. Since it didn't cost me anything because of my annual pass, I quickly roamed the localities to at least get an overall impression.

Gratefully, I accepted the museum's large car park as a place to spend the night, with a direct view of the small harbour and the frigate's ship building. Here we would spend a quiet and inexpensive night.

Road to the Beaches

Today we had a longer stretch ahead of us – about two hundred kilometres. I wanted to get to **Terra Nova National Park** in any case. Finding a campsite that provided electricity in the brilliant weather and on Saturday seemed hopeless, so I decided to take a chance. For the time being, I had to drive a good hundred kilometres on a rough track. It was nerve-racking when I couldn't get any further. … potholes galore until **Port Blandford**. It really shook up all my innards. Would they go back into place again?

I had read in one of the smart books that an accordion festival would be opening in **Eastport**, on #310 that weekend. That was bound to be a magnet. But first I had to take a long rest at the entrance to the national park at the info-parking. I was more than stressed from the driving. Three hours for one hundred and twenty kilometres! You wouldn't consider that average excellent, I know. It reminded me a lot of Mexico. If you also include the constant braking and rumbling…

The ride through the national park was just as scenic as on the way here. At the northern end, I turned east onto the **"Road to the Beaches".** It was only a few more kilometres to my destination. The road was a colourful mixture of all the shades I had already been through. Everything had been there before! I passed two RV parks with enormous prices and a facility that looked like a chicken coop! No, I would surely find better places to stay!

At the Heritage Centre, they still had a ticket for me for the opening night and they allowed me to stay in front of the centre after the show. Well, what do you know?

We spent the rest of the time visiting the charming fishing village of **Salvage**, couldn't find a suitable place to park my box, marvelled at the hustle and bustle on the small sandy beach and escaped back to Eastport, because it was the end of the world here too.

We had four hours until the evening programme. On the way here, seven kilometres before Eastport, I had discovered a deserted picnic spot on an arm of the fjord. In this beautiful weather, it was just made for us. We went there, got the camping chair out, dipped Knuffi into the water and lazed around. I was at the end of my rope: I was fidgety, nervous and unfocused. The last few days had been exhausting and were now making themselves known. I therefore decided to take an absolute rest day after tonight and bring my nerves back up to speed. Perhaps the extreme temperature fluctuations and the partly high humidity were also getting to me. At times I couldn't stop sweating, even though the temperatures weren't particularly high.

My nose had already reacted to this stress (nosebleeds) and for me that meant: "Slow down!" We still had more than ten days before our ferry back to the mainland.

The musical evening was a success. I was delighted with the players. They seemed to come to this week of events every year and were good acquaintances with the audience. Two totally different duos came to play, each with their own style. The music was Newfoundland influenced but had unmistakable Irish roots. The audience stomped, clapped and sang along. It was a great atmosphere. This music was perfect to accompany my lectures and picture shows. I struck it rich with three CDs...

The Newfoundland Health System

Sunday, an absolute day of rest! Slept, ate, read, did little rounds with the dogs, sweated in the shade of the camper… We passed the day excellently. Every now and then a few locals came by and launched their boats, a few small friendly conversations, that was all and did good. The only problem was my nose as it was not completely under control: again and again it bled a little and that worried me. Maybe I had eaten something I couldn't tolerate? I went through my list of medications and stopped using the blood thinner for a short time until I would visit a pharmacy on Monday. On Saturday I had had no luck in Eastport.

Monday took us further than planned. I was actually aiming for **Gambo** with its information centre about the outstanding politician *Joseph Smallwood* and its start of the Road to the Shore. In Gambo, all the places at the communal campsite were occupied. At the pharmacy, they couldn't help me and advised me to go to the hospital in **Gander**, which is responsible for the district. I had already received this advice in Eastport (a hundred kilometres away from here). Since I was already walking around with a cotton wad stopper in my nose again, I thought this would probably be the best thing to do. From here it was only forty kilometres. There were hardly any permanent doctors' offices in the towns like the ones we know. Every now and then there was a so-called health centre that was periodically visited by a doctor and at best had a trained nurse as permanent staff.

Which brings me to the medical care situation in NF. This can best be described by my experiences in the hospital in Gander (motto of the town: "Crossroad of the World"):

Where does one go as a walk-in seeking help? To the emergency room, of course! Waiting time for registration: half an hour. Waiting time for the medical consultation: three hours, although it was not too busy and we were accompanied by a constant broadcast of cartoons on a television. No wonder children lose touch with reality due to this permanent stream of bullshit…

An elderly woman collapses in the corridor. The lady from the registry and waiting patients try to find her a wheelchair: no doctor in sight! Nobody calling the patients either… First the patient must go to the registry – dead or alive, it seems to me. A good thing her daughter is with her.

Finally, I am called and taken to a treatment room. Two young ladies (one of whom introduces herself with a doctor's degree, the other can barely separate her teeth) ask me about my condition. I have known since my drug intoxication many years ago that constant bleeding in the nose area could be a serious warning sign. At the moment, thank God, things are at a standstill. The two "doctors" seem to be completely out of their depth and probably think I'm a hysterical old bitch. "She comes to the emergency room after a nosebleed!".

To at least do something, they order a pointless blood test in the laboratory. No comment on the medication list provided. I am not sure if they even knew the active ingredients. Blood test, of course, gets us nowhere except another hour's wait. "You'll have to consult a specialist in Grand Falls for that!" (Distance another hundred kilometres!) "But you won't get an appointment in the next ten days!"

I ask the two ladies to at least give me a prescription for a haemostatic cotton wool or something similar, to give me something for the next emergency. "We have to ask first if the hospital knows anything like that"… Out the door, back with a negative answer. In our country, every pharmacy has such a box ready! I at least ask for a copy of my blood results. Again, they have to ask if this is allowed. Always one excuse after the other! I get the results and leave the hospital completely un-nerved. If someone is pissed off at our German health system, I'll send him straight to Newfoundland or Portugal (see "Winter wings")!

I had to decide what to do: I reduced some of the medicines not exactly essential for survival for a while, reduced the caffeine in my tea, kept my head upright and in the shade as much as possible and prescribed myself another two to three days of rest at a campsite. And lo and behold, no more nosebleeds.

After the hospital experience, we found a nice campsite in the middle of the forest on a small lake **(Jonathan's Pond).** Admittedly, we had to stay in a different place every day, as the occupancy was almost complete and there was only ever something with electricity available on a nightly basis. But that didn't matter, because we had plenty of shade, the water was nearby for the poochies and I could relax.

But a hysterical ageing grouch? Was the heat of the last few days the cause? Were the big temperature fluctuations killing my circulation? Was I putting myself under too much stress? I couldn't make any sense of it...

Regarding my initial experiences on this island, I would nev er have imagined that it could get so hot in NF. The last few days were up to 30°C during the day and at night the thermometer did not go below 24°C, and as already mentioned, the humidity was extreme. My skin was constantly covered with an even film of moisture. Lazing around was really the best thing...

Private remarks

Road to the
Shores

230 km

215

Road to the Shores, Part 1

We said goodbye to the campsite at **Jonathan's Pond (Gander)** this morning. The weather was a double-edged sword yesterday and so I did all the homework, including washing the inner WoMo covers. The floor rugs and the seat covers were in dire need of it after almost two months with my two four-legged friends.

Today I wanted to tackle the **Road to the Shores** in two stages. This time the road #330 was surprisingly well built and led for thirty kilometres through an uninhabited dense forest area. We allowed ourselves a small detour at **Carmanville** in the south bay. We urgently needed a stop, because Wurschtel had been suffering from considerable diarrhoea since yesterday and he was getting restless, so nothing but out at a small stopping bay. Half an hour later, the same drama got worse: a piercing whine and my washing efforts of yesterday were in vain! We continued on to **Musgrave Harbour**. Half an hour's drive, a quarter of an hour's toilet! Ninety kilometres long…

The grey guy must have caught something at the campsite that went against his guts. With only moderate success, I gave him a dose of "Imodium acute". It could only get better! With a carpeted floor in the camper van, it was an ideal constellation. For the next mishap of the night, towels are now spread out everywhere as a precaution to catch the worst of it.

About twelve kilometres after Musgrave Harbour with its enormous sandy beach, we found our dream spot for tonight. Along the coast, there were only a few accesses from the banked road onto the offshore grass verge. We saw several camper vans and trailers parked there, but first we preferred to

check **Deadman's Cove PP** with a place for day stays. We didn't like it very much, so we turned around and drove back.

No, this place was not private, and everyone could park if and where they wanted: I was glad to hear that. We installed ourselves on a rocky spot with a view of the Atlantic and didn't let the strong wind blow us away. Behind our snail shell we found a shady spot sheltered from the wind. Wurschtel was able to attend to his needs every half hour and I had enough time to immerse myself in my detective story.

Tonight, I had planned to sleep in leggings and a T-shirt, so that I would be ready to go out the door if the overpressure should make itself felt in my dog. Here I could probably let him out on his own, because normally everyone around me was asleep. Well, have a good night!

Road to the Shore, Part 2

The night with Wurschtel was not quite as bad as I had feared. Although I had to operate the door button three times until one o'clock in the morning; his disturbed digestion then gave him peace until five o'clock and I was able to get at least a little sleep. It rained during the night, but the morning was dry later. At nine o'clock, all three of us crawled out of the bunk together. We had plenty of time, as there were only one hundred and twenty kilometres on the programme with two sightseeing points. With a heavy heart, I parted from our idyllic spot at early noon.

My first port of call was **Newton**, the *Venice of Newfoundland*, because it was built on at least seventeen islands. Even as we approached, we recognised the charm of this spot with its surrounding rocky islands. The centre of attraction was a so-called "Living Village" with guided tours and people dressed in the style of the 19th century.

The entire complex once belonged to a wealthy merchant family and was still partly inhabited by remaining heirs until the late twentieth century. Only when the last old lady died at the age of ninety were the "premises" signed over to the Heritage Association.

I was the only guest at that moment and so I was assigned a lovely old lady at my entire disposal. We got on splendidly right from the start and I was able to ask questions that were not necessarily related to the "living" museum. Right at the beginning, she took me to the small Methodist schoolhouse. The "teacher" had dutifully learned her text by heart and tried to play school with me at that time. She had just caught the right one. Sorry! With my interjections and questions, I constantly threw her off her game and she tried to return to her role again and again: improvising was probably not her thing. In the end, she was able to happily dismiss the language-illiterate and rebellious pupil for the break... I had a lot of fun. However, I found the prayers for the soldiers in the war at the beginning of the lesson a little strange. But it was worth remembering that it was the time of the First World War.

With my guide, I visited other mansions with the original furnishings. You could feel the discrepancy at that time between rich and poor, between fishermen and wholesalers, between servants and rulers. It probably wouldn't be much different today, even if today's Newfoundlander is better off on average. Again, she confirmed to me the great dependence of the common man on the favour of the wholesaler and his payment by means of credit as money was hardly adequate. I remembered that I had already described this in more detail in Grand Bank.

In the sequel, a young gentleman discreetly dressed in black crossed my path. At first, I thought it was the local priest, but then he enlightened me that he was the caretaker and assessor

218

of the delivered fish. Pardon! He had some problems with his text because the rising wind kept flicking through his pages. It seemed he could not quite memorise his role yet.

I got almost ninety minutes of the tour with interest and learned a little more about today's social structure in the "fishing industry" on the side. Many fishermen would go to a larger town for three weeks to take any manual work that was offered to them. Then they would come back to their hometown for three weeks to pursue their actual profession. No one could make a living from fishing alone anymore, even though the catch quotas for cod had been relaxed again and people had switched to lobster and crab.

Many Newfoundlanders are now employed in the oil industry. My guide told me that there was good money to be made there. She herself had worked there for a while as a dishwasher and cleaner but was now too old for that job. At that time, she was well paid.

I told her about my experience in the hospital and she regretfully confirmed the poor medical care of the local population. Her sister, she said, had died not long ago because no medicine – generally easily accessible – could be provided for her in time: that did not sound good.

Slowly it was time to look for a lunch spot for us and we found it in an extraordinary village, once again in the middle of nowhere. The entire village was built on and between boulders. A sight that was remarkable even for Newfoundland. **Pool's Island** was its name and ended, as so often before, in the backwoods of the *Labrador Sea*. Still in view. far out, were several icebergs. Here we sweated at 30°C and there thousands of years melted away just like that… It was so hot that I didn't feel like taking a midday nap with my furry beasts at my side. Besides, it was late; so, we covered the last ninety kilometres to Gambo under our wheels. This was our third attempt at the birthplace of Joe Smallwood. Would it work this time?

219

Lucky coincidence: on the way, I came across a petrol station with RV propane gas. I jumped at the chance, even if it was a bit more expensive. I thought my supply was already almost gone and I didn't want to wait until Grand Falls. But lo and behold, there were only twenty-two litres (just under half) missing from the tank. This meant that I had managed for more than a month with this amount. Not bad! Again, in purely mathematical terms, this meant I had nothing to worry about until mid-September.

Gambo offered me three options for a free overnight stay. Either we could sleep directly in front of *the information centre of Joe Smallwood* or at a nearby pub that advertised "Welcome Campers". I also spotted a park at the northern gateway to this mile-long roadside village in memory of the many woodwork-ers in the area. I gave this last place the most points. I found a sheltered corner there after visiting the centre, was able to walk the dogs along a forest path and the ball field became empty and quiet after dark.

As of writing, it was already past ten o'clock again. I there-fore hit the sack as soon as possible because I didn't know how the night would go on. Knuffi now seemed to have con-tracted the virus as well. Wurschtel has probably overcome it with the second dose of "Imodium". Now I'm curious as to whether Knuffi will have
a hard time too.

Newton – "Newfoundland's Venice" –
Road to the Shores

 Private remarks

220 kilometres further west

Today was just dedicated to driving, because we had to slowly get back to our starting point. We still had a detour to the **Baie Verte** Peninsula on the agenda and we only had five days left. After the long stretch and the heat, I didn't feel like looking for a wild place to sleep anymore, so we checked into **Kona Beach Park in South Brook**, the park we already knew from the drive here. Today, at the weekend, it looked different from a month ago. We just managed to find a place with electricity but I was just too tired to drive any further and so I preferred to pay the fee of 27.- CAD (approx. 21.-€). Besides, I had spent a lot of money in the supermarket in Grand Falls anyway, including the expensive non-alcoholic beer! Well, others drink expensive champagne … To each his own. Wurschtel and Knuffi had recovered in health and so hopefully nothing would stand in the way of a quiet and longer night.

Slowly saying goodbye

Yesterday I had studied maps and literature. I realised that I could eliminate some last day's destinations with a clear conscience. On the one hand, there were kilometre-long lonely stretches without any settlement; on the other hand, a selected part was only interesting for hikers. I decided to take another day's route towards the ferry port. After all, we still had four hundred kilometres to cover. To be honest, I was "out of steam" and intended to spend the last few days in Newfoundland in peace and quiet, stress-free and with good weather.

That's why my chosen destination was the **Barachois Pond PP**, which I had also spotted on the way here. The speedometer would then show an extra two hundred and twenty-five kilometres. It had no electricity, so it was cheap, and was situated on a beautiful deep blue to boggy brown lake, depending on the light. Today was Sunday, so I wanted to try my luck.

There was a short stop at the **Deer Lake** visitor centre, about halfway. I quickly checked my mails and got the confirmation for my reservation on the arrival day in North Sydney. There, I was finally reachable by mail. At least I was still driving around with my provisional Canadian driver's licence. It would not expire until mid-August; the official document was already waiting for its new owner at Richard and Karen's place.

Tired, I reached the Provincial Park. I was not intimidated by the "all occupied" sign at the entrance. It didn't cost anything to ask. Some places were indeed still available and so I started looking for a suitable bay. Understandably, it was more than full, as the weather prospects for the next few days were splendid.

So, here we'll stay until Wednesday and just take a holiday by the lake and in the shade under the trees. No kilometres, no sightseeing, no expenses, no stress, no potholes… it would do all three of us good. This period of rest also provided a good opportunity to reflect on the past weeks and begin the process of saying goodbye to phase 1 of my great journey. I would definitely not come back here again.

Count down 3

After two very quiet days with lovely weather, we set off today towards **Port-aux-Basques** to be close to the ferry port. It had rained during the night, but the morning was dry, although cloudy. It didn't matter, there wasn't very much on the programme. The crew took their time setting off and after three days without electricity and with water-saving measures, showers were on the agenda again.

Today we had the worst part of the TCH ahead of us. Progress was slower, but we were compensated by the weather. It had cleared up in the meantime and the mountains around us

224

were clearly visible. I took the foggy diversions from the descent into **Codroy Valley** in the sunshine this time. I also wanted to get to the westernmost point of the island of Newfoundland.

I was not to regret this detour. It was a wonderful drive along an inlet to the coast. Only the gravel road to **Cape Anguille** required some attention because of its various potholes. My clothes rail in the camper couldn't deal with that stress and gave up. From now on, all jumpers and anoraks would lie folded, waiting for professional help, because I would bend all my joints if I tried to repair it. The box with the drawers was easier to put in order. The baskets just needed to be cleared out and re-hung. Those were the little things to do at the next stop!

We enjoyed the walk along the cape and were happy about the refreshing breeze, because in the meantime it was 27°C again. There was even a freshwater stream for my thirsty souls. The rocky shore was too steep and the surf too dangerous for the dogs.

It was still too early for lunch and so I decided to continue to **Codroy Valley PP**. There was only a one day stop there, but the car park was spacious, and the shore could be reached over dunes. Here, both four-legged friends were finally allowed to take their refreshing bath. Looking out from the camper van, you could think you were at the North Sea...

Well, it would be great if the **J. T. Cheeseman PP** still had a free spot for us! Today's and tomorrow's conveniently located sleeping place would be secured. We could do the last round on Thursday and then stroll the eight kilometres to the ferry on Friday and let Newfoundland come to an end. Oh, wise foresight! We even got a place with electricity and internet access! Heart, what more could you want? With the heat, the shady spot did us good and we could sleep calmly in anticipation of Countdown 2.

Countdown 2
Closing the circle

Actually, I wanted to include the last excursion to **Rose Blanche** at this point, as it is marked on the map with a detour of fifty kilometres. This coastal region was ruined by rain and fog when I arrived in July. That was the case again today. Every few minutes I could hear the foghorn from the nearby harbour. Absolutely pointless: wasted kilometres and wasted money. I quickly went shopping, paid a fast visit to the crew at the information office and delivered some treats for coffee. Unfortunately, only one of the ladies who had helped me with my mishap with the lost Provincial Parks reservations was present. However, the rest of the crew had no issues with the cupcakes. How to make good use of the last day and beat the weather? Shortly after **Port aux Basques**, I discovered an industrial centre with a wide variety of workshops. Would I find someone to change the oil? It was long overdue, and I could save this time on the other shore. Since my start in Verona (ON), the odometer showed 8,120 kilometres more. A proud sum, which I had covered in exactly two months. Of those, 1,600 kilometres were the journey to Newfoundland. The rest belonged on the island!

Goodbye Newfoundland!

 Private remarks

Summary,
Reflection,
Conclusion of seven weeks in Newfoundland

Indeed, it is now seven weeks since we landed with our motorhome in *Port aux Basques* by ferry in the Canadian province of Newfoundland/Labrador (NL). Nine weeks had passed since our start in Kingston/Toronto, ON. We will leave this island, the easternmost bulwark of the North American continent in the Atlantic Ocean, in a few days – much more with a crying eye than a laughing one. Not for a second have I regretted choosing this destination for several years.

Newfoundland is not the holiday destination par excellence for Europeans, Canadians or Americans. New York City gets more visitors on a weekend than NL does year round. However, this is less due to its tourist infrastructure than to the prevailing weather conditions. Malicious tongues claim that it rains on the island 14 months a year. However, it is not that bad, even though we got a lot of rain from above. July, for example, was mostly on the decidedly summery side. What we froze in June, we sweated out again in the high humidity of these days.

It was not only wet and humid in June, but it was also freezing cold. At night I slept partially wrapped up between my two warming dogs and winter socks on my feet. The temperature when I woke up was often below ten degrees Celsius. Sometimes you could lose the desire to explore and when visiting this "octopus" in the Atlantic Ocean, you should expect to lose at least a third of your sightseeing programme because of fog or rain.

Not to be underestimated are the long distances and some routes must be travelled twice to get out of the various bottlenecks and back to the next arm of the octopus. In NL alone we added 5,000 kilometres to our odometer (in addition to the 1,670 kilometres journey from Toronto). The distance between the western ferry terminal *Port aux Basques* and the capital St. John's is 905 kilometres, to the northernmost tip of the Western Peninsula also about 700 kilometres.

"Newfoundland is not for timid doubters, hesitating whether or not to go. You must want Newfoundland and conquer it. Newfoundland means wind and weather, fish and birds, whales and wrecks, icebergs and Vikings, moose and caribou, Old World and New World all at once." I can fully agree with this short paragraph in one of my guidebooks and confirm every word after seven weeks of stay.

We roamed through the most diverse landscapes, from Arctic North Pole vegetation like the tundra to sandy beaches on the deep blue Atlantic or lake plains with brown moor water to gigantic cliffs. Newfoundland was always surprisingly different.

We observed floating mountains of millennium-old ice and lively whales doing somersaults in the bays, occasionally accompanied by lively dolphins. We came within a few metres of the breeding colonies of gannets on a huge rock and enjoyed the sight of puffins. We fought our way through impenetrable fog, created by the two opposing currents of the Labrador (cold) and the Gulf Stream (warm), and soaked in the rain because you had to take the dogs out at least once a day.

We looked deep into the history of the earth's development (unique fossils), learned about the cruel extermination of the indigenous people and were able to vividly understand the hard life of the first European settlers on NL through film sets (Random Passage). We spent the night in charming provincial parks and sometimes in the wild without any problems. Especially in June, it was possible to find a place everywhere at the campsites. In July it was more problematic, because the holidays had started and almost every second Newfoundlander is out on the road with their trailer, dog and family.

Daily life here is expensive, more expensive than in Europe. I had to increase my planned budget enormously. Unemployment is still high since the economic change in the fishing industry, even though many in the population have found a new livelihood in the oil industry as a substitute. Even charming outports cannot hide this fact. For this reason it amazes me how the people here still manage to survive.

We really conquered Newfoundland and didn't let ourselves be intimidated by minor and major mishaps. This Canadian province left a deep impression on me. We found friendly and helpful people everywhere and I was constantly addressed as "my love", "honey", "darling" or "sweetheart". Only the dialect of the "Newfis" took some getting used to and not only once did I have to slow down to even guess the meaning of the words.

I had taken Labrador out of the programme right at the beginning of our stay. There was simply no time to organise it. Besides, visiting the outports by ferry all the way to the northern corner would have been too much of a hassle for the dogs and very expensive to boot. I was not particularly interested in long stretches on gravel roads either. Five years ago, I had savoured it to the hilt in the Yukon up to the Arctic Circle. After all, you don't get any younger and maybe you get a little more sensible...

 Private remarks

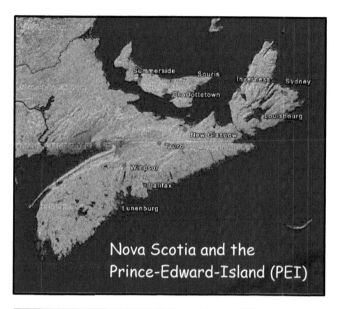

Nova Scotia and the
Prince-Edward-Island (PEI)

233

 Private remarks

End of July – First assault on Nova Scotia

In **Little Bras d'Or** we had reserved the campsite "Arm of Gold" we had discovered on the drive here. I needed a "permanent" address for my mail. It had indeed arrived and was ready for collection at the post office on Monday. I finally had my necessary Canadian driver's licence and my new credit card thanks to the help of home and my friends in Canada.

We spent the weekend more or less lazily at the campsite and I struggled with the online registration of my new Canadian mobile phone, purchased on Saturday. I was in sheer despair with all the different numbers and information required. I've been at war with filling out forms since I was a child and this had hardly changed in my professional life. And all of this in a foreign language… I had to start all over again and again because there were too many or too few tiny characters. Finally, I had filled in everything correctly and had reached the last step. The only thing left was the number of my credit card, then it was done after two hours!

Sheer horror: "Sorry, the number is invalid. We only accept Canadian credit cards…!" There I was, with a ninety-dollar mobile phone, unable to get it to work. But I really needed one, because my German contract expired in August.

There I am shopping around the globe at a million companies with VISA and the Canadian phone company refuses to accept my plastic money. No one can imagine how upset I was. Lucky that the laptop didn't get hit and end up as a projectile. Finally, the idea came to me: if I bought a prepaid card and used its number, maybe it would work…? I tried that on the following Monday, stood again for two hours in front of a Walmart with Wi-Fi service and went through the whole procedure again. We had checked out today after picking up the mail and so no more internet.

No diggity! TELUS actually registered me. I had to wait a while for the service, but after a quarter of an hour I was able to ring my Canadian mobile phone on a trial basis. Yes, indeed! It actually rang! Then I tried a quick call to my friends in Verona and I could leave my number on the answering machine. Everything was fine! Now I had to change my number at the bank so that I could access the online service.

Well, that (although a common occurrence) was a bit exciting for me. I didn't feel too much like driving a long distance anymore. The south coast with Louisburg seemed suitable for the afternoon. After resting in a quiet parking bay near the WALMART, we set off. We didn't get to see much of **Sydney**, firstly because of the rain and secondly because of the traffic. The city is home to around 26,000 inhabitants and is Nova Scotia's third largest city.

Not only did we get moving, so did the weather! It showered for all it was worth. I tried to outsmart the GPS and instead ended up at **Glace Bay** in a dead-end street by the sea! I couldn't go any further... so I had to drive the whole thing again backwards and pay attention to the GPS this time! This solo attempt had cost me almost forty nonsensical kilometres. I wasn't driving on the road I really wanted to, but the direction was correct.

I liked **Louisburg City** very much – well-kept town with restored houses from its past. The entire infrastructure with beds, restaurants and campsites was geared towards Fort Louisburg, which is very popular with tourists.

The "Play House", a reconstructed theatre from the time of William Shakespeare, came to mind. It was once built for the cinematic purposes of a Disney film and is now kept alive as a small theatre in season. For one thing, I was interested in tonight's performance and for another, the premises had a free parking space nearby! Okeydokey! Here we'll sit down! I'd rather pay 23.- CAD for the evening's entertainment before I senselessly threw it under the bus on one of the expensive campsites… The small theatre had two hundred and twenty seats, about half of which were occupied tonight.

I have to say it was a very successful evening, with lots of cheering music and a few little sketches about camping. However, the language of the sketches was so fast that I hardly understood anything. The music of the four performers was very lively. The highlight was a young lady with a fiddle and an Irish background! The drummer, the guitarist and "the man on the piano" were not to be sneezed at either. They all had good voices. The performances were a mixture of traditional songs, popped with modern rhythms and accompanied with variations. The spectators went along enthusiastically and at the end even a young girl and an older lady were carried away to accompany the fast-paced fiddling with Irish tap dancing. I had my camera in my hands all the time, but that didn't stop my feet from eagerly stomping to the beat. A nice gesture after the performance: all four said goodbye to the audience personally at the exit with a handshake!

In the meantime, the fog had moved into the bay and a clammy feeling came over the camper. Accordingly, let's hit the hay to keep warm.

Fortress Louisburg

We slept wonderfully and undisturbed until half past six. There was (still) an impenetrable fog. On a whim, I threw all the "innards" in the motorhome into a pile and with my two ladies at this early hour, I retreated to the friendly picnic spot near the lighthouse. We had discovered it yesterday and would choose it as our sleeping place this evening. It was in the National Park area, but I thought no one would put a stone on our way here. On arrival, I also found a Japanese (?) family with two children and a dog who had already spent the night in the car. All their belongings laid cleared out and covered around the car. A picturesque sight, especially when mother was the first to crawl (crumpled) out of the vehicle...

While I made breakfast and stowed our belongings in place, the fog lifted, and the sun came weakly through the haze. It was a great opportunity to take the dogs for a walk. It wasn't far to the lighthouse, and I was also interested in the Light-house Trail. We desperately needed to get moving again. There would be enough time for the fort in the afternoon. We marched along the wildly romantic rocky coast for over an hour. The trail was well maintained and doable without prob-lems even for weak joints and with eight dog legs. Neverthe-less, we were tired after our return and a nap couldn't hurt.

We were lucky! During our walk it was sunny but by lunchtime it had become cloudy and it smelt like rain. Never mind, the weather was fine for the fort.

The few kilometres there were quickly overcome. We arrived in a totally organised area far away from the actual small town. Huge car parks had been set up for the streams of visitors and a shuttle bus took the guests a few kilometres further to the reconstructed site, which had been set in the landscape accord-ing to a model by the Frenchman and fortress builder Vauban. The investment was worth it, because Canada's largest "Living Museum" attracts more than 100,000 visitors a year, despite a pricey entrance fee of 17.60 Dollars. With two children, it was easy to get rid of a fifty-dollar note, even if you paid a special price. For me it was free because I had my Canadian Explorer Pass for all National Sights.

I expected a bit of Disneyland in Canadian French, but it wasn't too bad. Even though the "residents" were all in 18th century costumes, they were unobtrusive and low-key. Of course, there were some events especially aimed at children. I really liked the many his-torical activities for the young visitors. On the one hand, a wine thief was put in the pillory and a small fairy tale theatre was staged for children. I was

239

able to capture almost all of the former on video, the latter was so funny that I couldn't stop laughing. Here I could only take a few more pictures because my battery was running low. The theme was "Little Red Riding Hood" played by men.

Since the dogs had to guard the camper, I was driven back "home" after three hours of touring. Before that, however, I stopped by the historic bakery and stocked up on healthy wholemeal bread for the next few days. It was relatively expensive, but I was simply in the mood for something hearty again and not always this flaky bread. I had switched to "Bagels" during my trip, because they had a bit of bite when toasted.

But now we were off to our sleeping place. A few walkers passed by, but soon it became quieter. With a bit of a guilty conscience (nature reserve) I ran my generator to load my equipment. We had positioned ourselves so that the (fogged) view of the sea would be oriented towards the fortress and we would be barely visible from the road behind trees. Everything was settled for that evening as well. If someone really came to scare us away, we could always resort to the parking area at the harbour.

Reconstructed Louisburg Fortress

 Private remarks

Not exactly my day

Once again dense fog in the morning. I could barely see as far as the next picnic bench. In this respect Nova Scotia (especially here on Cape Breton) was in no way behind. After an absolutely silent and dark night, we crawled out of our bunk. I had slept fitfully, with many interruptions, because this time I didn't really feel comfortable in my lonely, out-of-the-way sleeping place. For whatever reason, nightly visitors had not been announced and the dogs behaved quietly throughout the night. Be that as it may, I felt exhausted. Breakfast was at half past seven and departure was already an hour later.

I was annoyed about my lousy map material. That's why I knew neither right nor left at the turn-off. This time my gut feeling was wrong, and I ended up on a second access path to the historic fort. So back march! We came to the road to Sydney. Was that where I wanted to go? No! Another U-turn! Finally, I spotted the **Fleur de Lis trail** that would take us along the coast to **St. Peter**.

My God! What a miserable road! I can only advise everyone against it in the near future! They did build it, but it will take decades before it is satisfactorily passable. It took me almost

three hours to cover one hundred and twenty-five kilometres. Only a few places had good views (Mira River, Gabarus), the remaining seventy percent was through dense forest without any variety, except for potholes…

Accordingly, we arrived at the **canal of St. Peter** exhausted. The small town lies on the

243

charming inland **Bras d'Or Lake**, the largest inland body of water in Nova Scotia and praised as a recreational paradise. The canal created the connection between the lake and the ocean and was accordingly well frequented by sailors.

We found a shady spot, shimmied along the canal for a stroll and took a proper break first. Then we would look for a place to spend the night. By now it had become humid again and my T-shirt was all sweaty. I was grateful for every little breeze. We stocked up on supplies at the supermarket and I visited the museum (birthplace) of the photographer *Wallace MacAskill* (famous in this country) whose picture of the schooner "Blue Nose" (more about that later) is depicted on a Canadian coin.

Yes, here at the harbour area we could pitch our tents for the night. It was flat and there was plenty of room. Fortunately, I discovered in a brochure that a sailing regatta would start in the evening, followed by an "open session". No, thanks! One bad night's sleep was enough! It was still early in the day. We would surely find something suitable along the *Bras d'Or*. Besides, the breeze was more pleasant than vegetating outside in the sultriness.

Once again, I had taken the wrong direction. It was not #4 East but #4 West. I looked at my fuel gauge and started to sweat a little. Low, low, low! We were in the middle of nowhere! It was probably better to drive back to St. Peter. Once again, a U-turn! I was still able to quench my baby's thirst in time. Out of 110 litres, 108 litres had to be refilled. Oops, that was tight!

We couldn't find any spot where we could have pitched our tents in sixty-five kilometres of road. The entire stretch along the lake was firmly in private hands. In the small provincial park "Irish Cove" close to the road, overnight camping was prohibited and a huge campsite (Ben Eoin) with almost two hundred pitches was terrifying. Close together, one trailer next to the other at a price of over thirty dollars. No hard feelings! So, on we go! Hope dies last!

At the northern tip of the lake, we swung onto #216 and drove back practically parallel to the opposite shore for forty kilometres. We were now on the way to Iona, to the "Highland Village" – our destination for tomorrow. Again, the same drama! Every road to the lake was in firm private hands again. Turn-offs to the right into dirty forest clearings with logging! I was close to parking somewhere near a church or a cemetery because fatigue was slowly creeping up inside me. I also had to think about the dogs. But they endured the rocking with stoic calm. Anything would do!

Churches on this stretch? No chance! We had landed in an area with reservations for the indigenous population. The villages showed little opulence, just like I knew from the USA. Prosperity had obviously skipped the Indians here as well…

"Highland Village" – 40 kilometres, 30 kilometres, 20 kilometres, 10 kilometres, 5 kilometres! Now I didn't care anymore! Hopefully there would be a parking place there! We crossed the strait of Grand Narrows and there I saw our salvation: the small harbour of **Iona,** situated directly on the beach and behind the bridge. On the opposite side, we found a stately red church, with quite a few young people bathing and level parking spaces! A liberating sigh found its way out! By now it was quarter past six and we had two hundred and fifty kilometres of unreasonable road conditions behind us.

The dogs were allowed in the water first. Even Wurschtel bravely trudged through the water, not to mention Knuffi's attempts at diving. I felt good here! The inner feeling was always a pleasant sign! The bathers disappeared at around nine o'clock, and by half past nine I was in bed.

245

Stalling for time in a sensible way

Now it was time to plan a little because I had read that there was a festival in the Highland Village on the coming Saturday. It was a question of doing something on Thursday and Friday and limiting the driving activities a little for my own salvation. A workable plan developed: we would drive to **Baddeck** today and see *Graham Bell's National Monument*. Not too far from there I had found a relatively cheap campsite. After three "wild" nights, it was once again time to fill up with water and dispose of waste. I chose the slightly longer way to the cable ferry around the bay but I should have left that alone! The road "topped" all the options we already had.

But we survived even this wrong decision without breaking an axle and ended up at the "Little Narrows" at the cable ferry. From the other shore it was just under forty kilometres on the TCH #1, which here, however, carried the number #105. Such an unmotivated renaming had already been my undoing in Calgary years ago. Today I knew the score.

 The small town of **Baddack** was very touristy and full of visitors, probably attracted by the National Historic Site of the inventor *Graham Bell*, whose fascinating personality and inventiveness is unparalleled. We know him mainly as the creator of the first telephone, whose patent made him rich. But who knew that he also worked on aeroplanes, watercraft and iron lungs, as well as X-rays? It all started from teaching deaf-mute children.

Despite numerous setbacks, he never stopped researching and constructed the fastest water glider of the time. By the end of World War I, the development was history and this vehicle never went into series production. After his death, it was left to rot on the banks of the *Bras d'Or* until the National Committee took it on, restored it and made it accessible to the public. A saying that is on everyone's  lips, but no one knows came from the designer: "The operation succeeded, but the patient is dead!"

After this excursion into physics, I treated the three of us to a leisurely lunch break in the museum's spacious and well-maintained car park. I was still haunted by the temptation to have another wild sleepover and attend an Irish social. But then I thought of Saturday with a similar programme and started my way to the campsite.

A brief stop at a First Nation Museum of local history was not very productive, at least for my knowledge. The museum was able to pocket forty dollars from my budget, because I once again bought a music CD and a beautiful Dream Catcher.

Our night's lodging was not particularly comfortable for just under thirty dollars, but at least I had electricity and water.

Relaxing day

Hardly anything to report from today. Relaxing day was perhaps not the correct heading, because I filled the morning with all kinds of activities for which I otherwise had no time or desire or was too tired. The motorhome was thoroughly cleaned again, the bed was freshly made, the logbook was brought up to date after five days, long-overdue birthday cards were written, private emails were sent, the necessary batteries were recharged and so on. I just managed to get in the shower before it was time to check out.

From then on it was really calm. A short shopping trip to the supermarket followed, and we were already on the cable ferry again, crossing the "Little Narrows" towards Iona. It was a good twenty kilometres to the port of **Iona**. The current road was well built, and I thought with a shudder about yesterday's diversions.

It was still too hot for the harbour and so we found shelter in the small picnic park not far from the campsite. The approach was a bit bumpy for a camper, but on the hill you could make a loop and didn't have to turn around or go reverse. We looked for a shady spot, sheltered in the forest. Unfortunately, this had the disadvantage that any air movement was stopped by the trees, and although we would probably sweat more here than at the harbour; at least the dogs could lie down in the cool grass.

At about four o'clock we finally changed our campsite, because a little walk along the beach was on the agenda. Knuffi could hardly be brought out of the water and Wurschtel also enjoyed the water refreshment.

Finally, I had time to cook a proper meal. The last few days I was simply too tired or too late to cook anything. Looking out of the window, I suspected that I would not spend this night here alone. There was a car parked opposite me and now people were eagerly unpacking for beach camping. Why not? The stretch of beach was perfect for free camping in all its variations.

Failte, Welcome, Bienvenue,

My two bugbears got me out of bed after a short night. Yesterday, the local youth apparently still had a beach meeting so it was a bit noisy until midnight. Cars drove in and out with a lot of noise, fishing gear was unpacked, and the village girls were charmed. However, no further attention was paid to the two overnight guests. Around midnight the haunting disappeared.

In the morning, I took the dogs for a long walk, discovered that half the village was baptised MacNeil (source: cemetery, gravestones) and later took a nap. We managed to pass the time well until noon.

At this time, I started my way to the **"Highland Village"**, because I wanted to have a cheap parking place. The event was scheduled for two o'clock and there was enough time for an informative tour. The dogs were welcome guests and everywhere in the houses we were welcomed in Gaelic (Failte). The reason for this was that at the end of the 18th century, the Scots came to this country with much hope for a better life. But conditions were at least as harsh as in their homeland, if not worse. A great many emigrants came from the Outer and Inner Hebrides and names of origin such as Barra, Uist, Lewis or Skye were not unknown to me. After all, I had also travelled extensively to these austere islands not so long ago.

With a good airing, I put the two dogs in the camper, because there were too many people and too much excitement. The location of the open-air event was beautiful. There was a wide view of the strait and the two waterways. Thank God the sky was overcast, so the announced 27°C didn't matter too much. I didn't necessarily have to sacrifice a day for the concert itself. Some local artists performed, sang about Scotland and the sea and the music with guitar accompaniment was not varied. I was probably spoiled by the performance in Louisbourg. I had the feeling that for the audience the music was secondary: it was more of a social event. The main thing was to meet and have a chat or two. Next to me, a numerous family had established itself on the lawn, where someone was always talking. Finally, I moved because I had come for the music and wanted to make some recordings.

After two good hours, I left the venue. The amusement was scheduled to last until 6 pm and that was too long for me. Just at that time it started to drizzle in true Scottish fashion.

Afterwards we squatted in our parking bay at the "Grand Narrows", got our bellies full and slept in anticipation of the new events. Tomorrow we wanted to tackle a first section of the "Cabot Trail". I had estimated two to three days (300 kilometres) for this, depending on the weather and driving conditions

Iona NS – Heritage Village

 Private remarks

Oops! Not quite so fast! First, we have to get the Scots, the Irish and the Arcadians behind us! We were able to start at around nine o'clock, as my darlings had already asked me to go for a walk at half past six, wagging their tails! (If that's what it takes…). After all, there was just a break in the rain. That's right! Until now, there has always been a cool shower in the morning, so that the beginning day felt humid, nice and warm. Cape Breton Island also has that in common with Scotland.

We drove across the "Little Narrows" for the third time, passed the campsite in **Whycocomagh** again and soon found ourselves on the so-called **Ceilidh Trail**. Here in the small villages, the tradition of getting together again and again for musical gatherings (ceilidh) is still firmly held. There is fiddling and dancing everywhere. That's why this stretch of the #19 coastline has been given this unusual nickname. I find it "unusual" because you absolutely cannot deduce the pronunciation from the spelling (Ceilidh = KAY-lie).

As expected, it had become hot and humid again and my two companions were longing for a bath. Ok, then it'll be the turn of the *Glenora Distillery* in **Glenville**. It is Canada's only single malt distillery. I wasn't keen on a guided tour because those who have been to Scotland have been served plenty of them. Here, at least, Knuffi found a small stream to dive into.

Inverness does not have much in common with its sibling city of the same name. Two beautiful sandy beaches invited us to linger. I treated my two fellow travellers to a little refreshment before continuing north. My short-term memory is failing me completely. Now, I can't remember this beach at all, only the petrol station; there is no photo to help me either. All I remember is that it was another one of my spontaneous decisions. Apparently, my mental computer is overloaded.

In **Margaree Harbour** I let my intuition take over again and came to a beautiful little bay with a sandy beach and dunes. Here we first had a long lunch and included the place in our considerations as a night camp. Dripping wet, I put both dogs back in the camper. Their soaked fur would keep them cool for the next few days. We could continue on to **Chéticamp**. Chéticamp is an eternally long street village and today all hell had broken loose. There was a week-long Arcadian festival going on, with self-expression and a street parade in full swing – and us in the middle of the traffic jam!

Well, at Margaree Harbour we had entered the French regions of the former Arcadians, who are also firmly attached to their tradition. Suddenly, in the supermarket, there was nothing but French buzzing around my ears. I was looking for the carpet museum *Les Trois Pignons* because the crocheted carpets of the Arcadians were and are highly valued as a handicraft. This time-consuming craft is still maintained today. Since I was stuck in a traffic jam anyway, I patiently crept through the whole place. As usual, the end of the parade was at the north end of the village and the turning point, right in front of the museum I was looking for.

There were still quite a few parade participants on the road, listening to the musicians. Nevertheless, I found a corner for my box. The visit to the collection did not take too long, the tapestries on display were enormous. Some of the work involved must have been gigantic: I was deeply impressed. The only thing I found a bit confusing was the name "crocheted tapestries". I would rather call it a "looping" technique because you work on picking from the bottom and then pull the thread upwards through the fabric in a loop.

On the way here I had not found anything adequate to my chosen sleeping place. I tried the island of Chéticamp with its campsite and lighthouse. The campsite was terrifying, and the lighthouse was only open for day visitors. Besides, the lighthouse was in an open field with a herd of cows so I turned around and drove back twenty-five kilometres. Then I knew where I would stay.

The parking bay was still packed at five o'clock, but we were able to drop anchor just an hour later. A wonderful spot, which was absolutely safe (as a local resident assured me) with a wonderful view of the harbour and the hysterical cries of countless seagulls. We ended the day in the small bay with a picturesque sunset, a few fishing boats finding their way back and now only the red and green lights of the harbour entrance still flashing. With this end of the day, the Cabot Trail could easily wait 24 hours.

Addendum: Unfortunately, the collection of scarecrows mentioned in the guide no longer exists. Instead, I found a museum of masks, which was only closed today because of the parade. Let's see if we are luckier tomorrow.

 Private remarks

Chéticamp - Carpet Museum

 Private remarks

Cape Breton, NS

Cabot-Trail

500 km

 Private remarks

Cabot Trail Part 1/Local holiday

My two tots let me sleep today. It was already half past eight when I opened my eyes the next time. That would delay our departure considerably! Well, at ten o'clock we were ready to go anyway and thankfully said goodbye to the hospitable place. Perhaps we would come back on our return?

At the Mask Museum just before Chéticamp, I was successful this time. Here I also learned why the scarecrow collection of Joe no longer existed: his family did not want to continue the legacy after his death. The *Centre de la Mi-Carême* in **Grand Étang** saved a few of them and put them on display outside. The centre also had a studio attached to it where everyone could give free rein to their imagination.

Now the Cabot Trail!

Who John Cabot was should be known to everyone by now as he would appear again later that day. Although it was a public holiday, there were not too many visitors on the three-hundred-kilometre round trip. Many manage this route in one day but I wanted to give myself two or three days to do it. I was told that the Cabot Trail is one of the most beautiful roads in the world. Well, maybe in the rear ranks…

Right at the beginning there was a wet belly to freshen up and a red chair to explore. In any case, the approach was eventful, especially as the road spiralled relatively steeply upwards. Thankfully, there were many stopping bays where you could easily stop to enjoy the view. Bright blue skies would have been an advantage for the photographer, but I preferred the light cloud cover, because I had been sweating enough over the last few days. There were also an infinite number of turn-offs to larger or smaller round trips, between twenty minutes (for us) and several hours (for the trained). The starting point of the *Skyline Trail* of three hours was particularly crowded. Better not! We enjoyed our walk on the boardwalk through the high moor, between the carnivorous (insect) plants and small ponds.

However, it wasn't only the road along the coast that was to be marvelled at, there were also numerous curves, hairpin bends and views through the mountains. I wanted to get to **Cape North** at the tip of the peninsula today. I had scouted out a campsite there. In addition, many whale watching tours started from the cape. The weather cleared up and after a 17% gradient I had a wonderful view of **Pleasant Bay**.

Although only signposted as a secondary route, the road to the north was easily passable. I had already had other experiences just like at **Cabots Landing PP** where we came across a beautiful, kilometre-long sandy beach and a well-kept surrounding area. Unfortunately, the facility closed at 9 pm. Until then, I still had in mind the "Jumping Mouse Campground" in the **Bay of St. Lawrence**.

The desire to do so vanished abruptly when I saw the "ecological" facility. Ecology here apparently meant "messing around" and everyone doing as they pleased. There was neither water nor waste disposal, not to mention electricity. Only the nice elderly lady, apparently the owner or administrator, would have been happy to keep me as a guest. But under no circumstances would I pay to stay here, so I excused myself with an urgent need for electricity and quickly escaped.

Very well! What to do now? It was thirty kilometres back to the main line. I saw a camper van parked at a low altitude at the harbour, next to the ticket kiosk of a whale-watching company. Sometimes I need to be cheeky! I asked about tomorrow's departure times and agreed to join the tour. Very politely, I asked to be allowed to stay here overnight. No problem at all, I was told. I could still manage one night with my reserves…

So now we are standing above the small harbour of **Bay St. Lawrence** in beautiful evening sunshine and will now take a walk along the harbour before I get back into the inclined position. I'd rather pay thirty dollars for the boat tour than twenty-five dollars for the messy campsite with NOTHING.

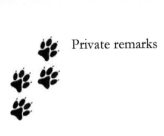 Private remarks

Cape Breton, NS – Cabot-Trail

Private remarks

Whale-Watching

Excellent location and good sleep! The sky was a bit cloudier than yesterday. "Well, I guess it will be the same as always!" I thought to myself but took the precaution of packing rain gear. As my camera battery was a bit low, I added my camcorder to the equipment as a precaution. I opened the window for the dogs and asked the nice gentleman at the kiosk of the Whalewatching Tours "OSHANA" to keep an eye on my open vehicle.

About twenty people met at the boat down at the harbour and we expectantly started at around half past ten. Then a downpour pelted down on the open boat that literally "washed" down on us. Confident of victory, I unpacked my rain gear. Oh no! I had caught the rain trousers, not the cape! So, like 90% of the participants, I hurried to the captain's small cabin. Tight now, but relatively dry

With a sonar system, the entrepreneur organised several smaller whales in the open sea, and we soon got to see a larger group of the species. Now I was indifferent to the rain. Although the rain was running down my collar from the cabin

roof I hardly noticed it because of my excitement. The animals sometimes came right up to the boat. Red light on my device! No more battery! Shit! Today was not my day! I unpacked my camcorder, which I wasn't quite familiar with yet. I hope it can stand the rain! It was dripping from everywhere and I was soaked to the skin. The jumper was soaked as well and stretched heavily. My hat was dripping considerably but at least it protected my eyes. Wonderfully comfortable! Nevertheless, I persevered in the open like so many other brave participants. Then a quick thought about the open windows in the camper crossed my mind – can't change anything now anyway! Then we'll just keep swimming!

The boat swayed up and down! Of course, this also influenced the pictures I took of the animals. You could get dizzy. The big mammals huffed and puffed like grandmother on the cellar stairs. Up and down! Up and down! With the sonar device you could follow their communication very well. Well, I guess I'll have to do a lot of editing. I just filmed away, checking again and again whether my device was still working. It still seemed to be coping with the rain after all.

After about an hour and a half of showering, the captain turned around and took us to a wild bay with sea lions and cormorants. Here again the same problem: as soon as I operated my zoom, I could no longer hold my hand steady, and the camera bobbed wildly up and down with the ship. How do professional filmmakers do it? Tripods are probably also useless. They also rock along!

After about two and a half hours the adventure was over, and the sky was dry again. How else? The camper had survived the rain, and I quickly jumped into dry clothes. A warm jumper was just right! Anyone can go whale watching when the weather is nice, I thought!

Due to the lousy conditions outside, I had little desire to pursue the Cabot Trail south in more detail. I did take the recommended diversions from **South Harbour** via **White Point**, but apart from a few bluffs with short views and a disastrous road, I got little out of it. In good weather, I could imagine this route was very interesting.

Then I started looking for a campsite. The National Park could only offer me a place without service for 26.- CAD in **Broad Cove**. Another offer of "nothing for 25.- CAD"! I still had time and drove on. The next National Park, **Camping Ingonish**, didn't even have a waste disposal station for the same price! So, on we went! I filled up in **Wreckhouse** as a precaution because there was no gas station for the next fifty kilometres! Camping? Not until **Englishtown** again, at the ferry!

The Cabot Trail now wound up and down the coast. The further south we went, the nicer the weather became, until the sun finally broke through and I started to sweat in my warm jumper. The road should also be a pleasure in the opposite direction on the seaside. Beautiful bays, imposing red cliffs… We found the place just before the ferry, a camping for 80% permanent guests and situated directly on the water so the prices were correspondingly high. We were charged over forty dollars with tax and had to pay extra for the shower. I bit the bullet and thought about the past four free nights.

The generator just couldn't run that long, but I needed a lot of electricity for the next few hours. I had writing to do, homework to catch up on, pictures to review, videos to check, all the batteries to refill… My evening would be full. There was a quick "fish and chips" (because the desire to cook had sunk to almost zero) and a relaxing beer. The dogs dived into the cool water. The shore was steep and rocky, studded with large pebbles and not very inviting for a walk with my wobbly joints. Consequently, I threw myself into work and managed to finish my travel reports up to today.

Music in the Barn

We had a lot of time today. I made the most of the expensive campsite for as long as I could, and we didn't leave until around lunchtime. For today I had planned a (hopefully) very special treat, which I had discovered in an advertisement.

We continued south along the Cabot Trail. Darn it! The red brake light wouldn't go out. Please, no problems! I thought... Maybe my car lacks fluid? Luckily, I had found out which container was responsible for the brake fluid during the oil change. I opened the bonnet at the first place I could stop at and removed the cap with a pair of pliers. Lo and behold! The brakes were indeed lacking lubrication. One section was completely dry! Well, I still had the bottle from the workshop and some spare from the previous model and I filled it up to the brim. It was getting exciting to see if I had found the solution! No, still the red light! I stepped on the brake a few times to get the lubrication process going. The light promptly went out. What a technical genius I am!

Why so much loss suddenly? That was a mystery to me. Was there perhaps a small leak somewhere? Were yesterday's braking manoeuvres too strenuous for the vehicle? After all, I had usually used the engine brake on steep downhill sections. In any case, I will keep an eye on the matter and buy a new bottle or visit a workshop if necessary.

After this little midday excitement, we drove on to **Baddeck**. I urgently needed a post office to send a priority letter express to Germany to revise my cancellation with 1&1 (phone company) as soon as possible. I could only do online banking with a German mobile phone number. The cancellation came into effect at the end of August. Delivery in five working days, cost 61.- CAD! Correct! Not a misprint! Canada Post's prices are extremely high. I had already paid CAD 18.- for a simple registered letter between Toronto and North Sydney a few weeks ago! Well, I hope it's worth it. Now I must keep up this nonsensical contract, even though I don't use my own phone or internet connection at home! I don't like to give my bank account details any which way.

The Cabot Trail now wound its way north again through a densely wooded area. We took a short break at **Lake O'Law** in the Provincial Park, and I stowed the groceries I had bought at COOP (Baddeck) on all the shelves and in the fridge. There had already been a certain nervous emptiness there for a few days as shopping is not always possible in the small villages.

We found *Egypt Road* to **Margaree Valley** straight away. There must have been a hayloft where Gaelic fiddle music was played every Wednesday. However, number 691 was not a barn, but an exquisitely converted rural hotel complex in the middle of the forest, with hotel rooms or small chalets from 200.- CAD upwards a night, on the extensive grounds (normaway.com). At first, I thought I was mistaken, but then I spotted the red barn building and in reception they confirmed today's event. And… I was allowed to stay overnight on the premises! Very hospitable…

I was just about to get out with my dogs when someone tapped me on my shoulder. I turned around. Standing there was the nice couple with grandparents and son from Luxembourg, whom I had met on the whale watching tour. Of course they had a bit more money in their purse and they had rented a chalet for two nights. I was not jealous of them: my chalet goes everywhere with me… But that's how small the world is!

The evening delivered what the advertisements promised! This is what I imagined Irish fiddle music to be like! The Highland Village of Iona could be discarded! There were young musicians throughout who mainly showed their talent individually. It was interesting to observe how differently everyone played the same instrument. The man at the piano was also excellent and played the keys with all his energy and speed. A quick glance at the fiddler was all it took to agree!

I got a good seat for my 15.- CAD, where I didn't disturb anyone when I shot my video clips standing up. One example of each participant was shown on the screen; anything else would have been too much. Besides, I didn't want to just see and hear the music just on the screen, I wanted to enjoy it. Of course, each of my travelogue participants gets a sample sent along as soon as I have edited and arranged it. But in order to do that I always need constant power, i.e. a campsite.

Afterwards, there were several square dances for the audience, but unfortunately, I could only watch passively because I didn't have a partner: I would have dragged him mercilessly onto the dance floor. After all, I used to be at home in this genre and I could be totally absorbed in this music. It took me a long time to fall asleep when I got home because my head was full of sounds and rhythms. In any case, this investment was better spent than on a campsite.

Nova Scotia
Mainland

Eastern Shore
Marine Drive
Halifax
520 km

Private remarks

Today we made our move! That meant we left **Cape Breton** and headed south. The **Ceilidh Tail** was also very nice to drive in this direction. The #19 led through nice villages, wooded hills and agricultural land. The coastal footpath also runs along it. I wanted to walk it a little with the dogs. However, there was hardly any shade and so all three of us were soon panting back towards the cooler caravan.

The **Canso Causeway** connects Cape Breton with the mainland of **Nova Scotia**. Originally, the Cape was an island. We drove the Marine-Drive #344 towards **Canso** (town). At the beginning it was boring, at times even ugly with all the industry on the coast. Later, however, the landscape became lovelier and the road better. Often it went directly along the coast with pretty views of the Strait of Canso.

As usual, however, there was hardly any opportunity to stop and relax. The possibility of a bathing beach *(Shoreham PP)* appeared after about fifty kilometres and later we came across a beautifully situated camping site **(Guysborough).** Unfortunately, for 20.- CAD, this campsite had neither showers nor electricity – but it was wonderfully located on a hill with a view of *Chedabucto Bay.* Since I wanted to save my money for the time being (see postage!), I trusted the town of Canso and found a car park at the harbour. Here I will now prepare a little for the next few days and shimmy my way along the coast from here. We've done a good 200 kilometres today and are a little tired after the winding road. The dogs were able to get into the water several times, so they have already been baptised on the East Shore.

Sherbrooke

My brake fluid test during the night had unfortunately come back positive. A large wet spot had stained the cardboard box I had left underneath the motorhome. I would probably have to visit a garage. But before that, I quickly sent an important e-mail to friends as I had found a good free hotspot next to a bakery.

At the COOP in town, I asked a local for a workshop. Just up the road! I went there and they were already waiting for me. The secret message seems to work incredibly fast in NS. Three gentlemen took care of my matter and stuck their heads under the bonnet, talking together. Apparently, they had nothing else to do. They found the cause of the leak but couldn't find a replacement part in the short time available. After all, today was Friday and they didn't work here on Saturday either.

I didn't want to stay in this dump until Monday, because it was out in the boonies. They would have a nice sandy beach for me, though, right nearby! Very friendly, but no, thank you very much! I stocked up on some fluid for the next emergency and would try to find a garage in Halifax. The problem wasn't too big at the moment and the brakes were working correctly. Besides, the loss since the day before yesterday was only slight, as I could see with a glance into the fluid chambers. On the other hand, I was finally able to get my horn working. Thank God, I hadn't needed it until today, but in case of emergency... Now I am not only visible, but also audible again! However, a new part was due, and I once again had to pay 75.- dollars for repairs.

Look at the fuel gauge! I thought I would have enough for the next towns along the Marine Drive but I was wrong! Between Canso and Sherbrooke there were hamlets, bays, creeks, trees and brooks, but no fuel despite the fact that the distance between the two towns was about a hundred kilometres. Eventually, I did get a little too nervous and was overjoyed when I found much needed fuel at a small gas station near **Sherbrooke**. My a… had indeed gone to pieces! In this heat! I would have been stranded in the middle of the forest, in the wilderness! I'll never behave again so recklessly! This has been the second time! Unfortunately, I hadn't read my guidebook carefully enough…

All right! Now I was ready for the next foolishness. Unfortunately, I had to skip some of the smaller sights for a given reason. I drove through the interior to Sherbrooke, always on the lookout for an overnight place to stay. Absolutely nothing! I'll probably have to go to one of the expensive campsites. In an emergency, I saw a not particularly inviting car park in the village. Unfortunately, camping was forbidden on the extensive grounds in front of the "Living Village".

Sherbrooke used to be a lively little town, which in the 19th century made its living from shipbuilding, timber and the nearby gold mines. At some point the economy went down the drain and the dwellings fell into disrepair. Several enthusiasts got together and restored the houses piece by piece, bringing them back to life with the original craftsmen. Today, people dressed in period costumes walk around among the eighty or so buildings, immersing the visitor in the atmosphere of the turn of the century. About 25 houses can be visited. Sherbrooke Village is thus a bourgeois counterpart to the military Louisbourg on Cape Breton.

My two four-legged friends were allowed to accompany me on the leash and sniff around all the houses. Of course, that always gave me something to talk about with the staff. The two-hour tour was varied and interesting. The gates closed at five o'clock and I quickly bought an unusual wooden spoon in the souvenir shop.

I asked the lady at the counter if she knew where I could stay for the night. Yes, she had often seen mobile homes parked opposite the small picnic park on the St. Mary's River. At the *Salmon Museum*, there was a large esplanade, and the picnic areas (with a camping ban) were just opposite. Despite everything we tried our luck.

We are standing next to the road at the museum now, but I think there will hardly be anything going on at night. Here, nobody really cares who stays where, how and when – if you find a spot. At most, salmon fishermen come here, as the low river is known for its fish stock. Honestly, in Mexico I would never risk this under any circumstances.

Marine Drive Part 2

Predictably, the night was quiet and trouble-free. We set off again under a white-blue sky on the Marine Drive heading west, which now bears the number #7 from Sherbrooke.

The whole drive was not sensational, rather calming, if it hadn't been for the winding road. There was nothing to complain about in terms of road quality this time. Wooded inland stretches alternated with sections directly along the Atlantic coast. Again and again, there were small rocky islands off the coast. One could well imagine that in earlier times smuggling had its stronghold here because the coast is absolutely unmanageable. Even today, a not insignificant number of locals are said to have financed their cottages through this source of income. Today it is no longer "only" alcohol or cigarettes; profit is made with much harder substances. This was told to me by an (almost) local on the whale watching tour.

We stopped at several small picnic parks to take a picture or two. Not all provincial parks in Newfoundland are the same in Nova Scotia. In this Canadian province, small rest areas near or a short distance from the main road usually go by this name and invite you to have a snack. They are equipped with outhouses, rarely with waste bins (i.e. take your trash with you) and have no hiking facilities. Only occasionally do they offer a simple camping option separate from the picnic area, sometimes with, sometimes without a shower. There are no hookups at all. If you are lucky, you can at least dispose of your waste and fill up with water.

Now I understand why an employee looked at me so strangely when I asked him for a season pass like in Newfoundland. Here, the use of the facilities is free of charge, but at the campsites they charge hefty prices of 26.- CAD upwards. In all these parks it is forbidden to stay overnight and at nine o'clock in the evening the barrier is closed. They probably also check any stock that has wandered away. In other words, the search for free overnight accommodation is extremely frustrating. As already briefly described, the shores are densely populated or there is impenetrable jungle. Boat landing places at small bridges or on rivers like in the Yukon, for example, do not exist at all; I always liked to park there.

If a settlement calls itself a "harbour", this does not mean that there are moorings for fishing boats. Occasionally, small churches or cemeteries offer a place to stop. Very often they are built on hills to reach as many believers as possible but these are unsuitable places to sleep in a camper van. There are many other similar examples though. The best are still small museums like yesterday's or today's, which offer an empty parking space after closing time – if there is no "overnight" ban posted.

We drove about a hundred and twenty kilometres this way today. One bay after another, one forest after another, one hamlet after another, one bend after the next. However we were able to make a longer stop at **Taylor Head PP**. The kilometre-long white fine sand beach invite you to laze around, and my two companions had a lively time in the water. Even Wurschtel now regularly manages to go into the water up to his belly, even with a slight swell, which had been unthinkable in the past. The maximum water temperature of the Atlantic is 15°C in summer!

At around two o'clock, the bay was still almost deserted, but after our lunch it filled up visibly. Since Wurschtel was constantly trying to save our lives, there was no chance of a midday nap, and slightly annoyed, I started the journey at half past two. Now real Atlantic weather awaited us: rain, thunderstorms, sun, steaming roads… all over again!

In the late afternoon I started looking for a suitable place to spend the night. If need be, I would have stayed at a campsite; even though forty dollars for the night seemed a bit expensive. Unfortunately, these are the average prices here. The only one on the route that would have come into question was fully occupied. After all, it was Saturday. I had already thought so. In faint hope, I took a diversion along the coast with beach signs to **Clam Harbour Beach**. Same dilemma! Thirty-six kilometres for nothing – my expectations kept spiralling down. I was apparently a bit spoiled from the last few pitches. Then chance came to my rescue, as it often does.

We passed a small "Heritage Village" near **Lake Charlotte** at the re-junction with #7, an old post office and general shop in one, with opening hours from 11am to 4pm. Great, at four o'clock they would all be gone, the sign "closed" on the door and the level car park free. Tomorrow we'll be long gone by eleven o'clock. I'll need to bite the bullet and stay at a commercial campsite, because after four free nights we're running low on water, even though the tanks are nowhere near their full capacity. Hopefully we'll find a place near Halifax so I can take a closer look at the city.

Dartmouth/Halifax opposite

We got hold of a campsite! The closest one there is to the centre of Halifax. It is a municipal facility of **Dartmouth** (that doesn't mean it is cheap!) and it is in a recreational area on a small lake. They charge just under CAD 40 a night at **Shubie Campground** with electricity and water; showers are available at extra charge. There is a bus connection to the ferry that connects the twin town with downtown **Halifax**. This way I can leave my two dogs alone for a while. For their comfort, I can keep my air conditioning on! Half a day of sightseeing is usually enough for me.

From my place I am immediately in a wonderful forest area for beautiful walks! You wouldn't believe it: paths are marked where the dogs are allowed to roam freely. There is also a nice "dog beach", so I won't complain about the price. There is even a small discount for ADAC members as, apparently, a lot of Germans come here. I think Condor has extra cheap flights to Halifax in their programme. Nearby I saw a rental station of "Canadadream" motorhomes, a company often frequented by Germans.

As our arrival time was still in the morning, we could have a look at the allocated sites, but we had to wait until 1pm to check in. Not far away, I found a Walmart: I would check it out and do a little shopping. A quick examination and it was clear to me that it also allowed free overnight stays. I wasn't sure how long I would be stuck here with my repairs: we'll find out tomorrow. In any case, I have booked the campsite for three nights. A little luxury is good for the heart!

I took the dogs for a long walk in the forest and around the lake until we were allowed to move into our pitch. Outside there is Atlantic April weather with threatening cumulus clouds: sometimes white, sometimes grey, sometimes black. Then another shower pelts down and the sun that follows turns the landscape into a sauna. To be on the safe side, I stocked up on some cheap T-shirts in the shopping centre. I

spent the afternoon comfortably at the PC and will continue to work on my videos this evening. Now we're going for a walk to find the bus stop for the #55. Then it will be enough for today...

Shubie-Camping / Drama in several acts

<u>Monday:</u>
Appointment tour:
* Brake fluid just around the corner (appointment tomorrow).
* "Petsmart" for dog groomer (7am appointment tomorrow), five kilometres away
* Heater "Fraser RV" 20 km away (appointment on Thursday at 8 am).
* Four loads of laundry done and a big walk with the dogs – and the day was over.

<u>Tuesday:</u>
* Morning wasted with a walk,
* workshop: 2x wrong parts delivered/new order and new appointment for tomorrow
* work on the PC
* both dogs for 130.- CAD – look respectable again.

<u>Wednesday:</u>
* long walk,
* 1 pm workshop: correct part delivered, but connecting part defective/ new order and new appointment for tomorrow –
* again intensive PC work in the afternoon

<u>Thursday:</u>
Drama 1:
"Fraser RV" at 8 am/heating problem checked/repair would take several days/probably line from power to heating eaten away by mouse/whole parts of WoMo have to be disassembled/good customer service: no charge for working time.

Drama 2:
seven different attempts to find a propane station/feel like bookbinder Wanninger (Bavarian sketch story) who is always sent on without success – get to know half of Dart-
283

mouth/highway system very confusing, would be lost without GPS/CAA as last port of call/find a dealer for me in Halifax – 25 km away/appointment for tomorrow morning

Drama 3:
the part for the brake fluid finally fits and I become 280.- CAD lighter.

I've had enough for today! I'm going for a long walk with the dogs and then I'll sit down at my desk! I'm curious to see what tomorrow will bring. The weather is changeable and humid at the moment. Despite all, I enjoy the comfort of the air conditioning in the camper.

Friday:
   Halifax doesn't like me! I started today at eight o'clock, under cloudbursts, to the propane dealer in Halifax. We drove through rush hour traffic over the MacKay Bridge and even the GPS had problems with the short exits. Once missed, you end up in normal traffic. However the dealer could still be found. Meanwhile the sweat was dripping over the hat into the neck and out again at the toes. There I bought a sinfully expensive adapter with which I would be able to fill my tank at every pump that fills normal bottles from now on: if it does really work…

   This morning I spent time at Walmart and bought countless CAD 5 T-shirts on sale, new carpets and blankets for the camper: today I don't feel like saving money. Then I worked on my mails for two hours at the free hotspot in front of the wholesale market and after that I drove twenty kilometres back to the campsite: the dogs have to go out! Although I put the third "waterproof" anorak on – the other two are already hanging out to dry – I was soaked again in ten minutes. The downpours finally stop at four o'clock, but now I don't feel like going into town either so I'll spend the rest of the afternoon on the PC.

A glimpse of Halifax
Halifax likes me after all!

After a short night due to problems falling asleep – I probably sat too long at the PC again – I was woken up by my friends at about half past seven. Duty was calling, the bladder and the digestion were pressing. With a heavy heart I crawled out of my corner and had to get myself going. At least yesterday's rain was gone, and the sun accompanied us on our first round. In good Bavarian: today a small part of Halifax would be on the programme. I didn't want to extend my stay again for financial reasons and tried to include as much as possible in my walking-sightseeing tour. I turned on the air-conditioning for the dogs as a precaution, as you never knew how quickly it could get uncomfortably warm here. After all, I pay a lot of money for this service!

I took the half past eleven bus to the bridge terminal (MacDonald Bridge). From there, a twenty-minute walk took me to the ferry to Halifax. I could have taken another bus, but this gave me a better view of the city skyline and its natural harbour – the second largest in the world. Sydney in Australia has the largest one I was told.

At a quarter to twelve I had reached the other shore. First, I wanted to tackle the strenuous part of my tour and I puffed up the hill to the clock tower and the citadel. Just beyond the harbour, it gets uncomfortably steep, like in San Francisco or St. John's, Newfoundland. The historic clock, which is also the landmark of Halifax, was just striking noon. Suddenly there was a horrible bang. I had completely forgotten that a cannon was fired from the citadel over the city at noon every day. It wasn't just me alone who winced. Halifax has that in common with Vancouver, although there are 6,000 kilometres between the Canadian cities.

285

I had forgotten my "Discovery Pass" in the camper so I didn't go inside the citadel, of which there is not much left to see anyway. Besides, the view of the harbour was limited by many modern high-rise buildings. A friendly guard didn't make a face when I photographed him at the castle gate; he was waiting for the changing of the guard. In the background you could already hear the bagpipes howling in return: "Edinburgh in Halifax".

I worked my way down again and roamed a few streets in the historic district. There wasn't much left of it, because in 1917 a huge explosion destroyed almost the whole northern part of the city. A munitions ship had blown up in a collision, killing more than 2,000 people who had gathered at the wharves as onlookers. More than 9,000 people were injured and the city took decades to recover from this disaster.

Some nice pubs in old buildings invited the traveller to rest and there was also an old cemetery to visit, where graves from the city's foundation around 1755 could still be found. Most of the gravestones were about a hundred years younger.

In front of the library, a thoughtful Winston Churchill greeted me among a crowd of pigeons and colourful iridescent birds. I did not know, however, what species the latter were. I simply liked them.

I walked along the "Waterfront", which stretches from the ferry terminal to Pier 21. There were some interesting ships to discover, from ocean-going yachts to commercial military amphibious vehicles that had been originally converted for tourist purposes.

In the Sea-Market, I was overcome by hunger and bought some fried noodles from a Chinese vendor. There were only a few chairs and tables, so like many like-minded people I sat down on some stairs and ate my "menu" out of Styrofoam bowls. Not exactly posh, but it filled the belly!

I discovered a Bavarian butcher with liverwurst, pressed sausage and beer ham. However, there was no point in shopping in the heat because I couldn't carry the sausage around with me for another two hours. Funnily enough, the sales staff understood neither Bavarian nor German.

With a heavy heart, I left and made my way to Pier 21, the jetty where the millions of immigrants and war brides (mostly from England) came into the country and with their labour helped make Canada what it is today. Often Halifax was not yet the destination of their hopes for a better life. That's why there was a special train station at Pier 21 that transported immigrants deeper into the country.

The museum was informative and interactive with many contemporary short films. How must those people have felt when they had burnt all their bridges behind them, for whatever reason, from whatever cultural background? Without friends and family in a foreign country with often a foreign language, an unknown future, sometimes with only a little money in their pockets and a small suitcase as personal belongings... I find the courage of each individual admirable. Canada has always been open to immigrants and that is how the tolerant mixture of peoples that makes up the state today came into being.

My feet hurt. I had to walk all the way back. A quick time check told me that it was necessary to take the ferry for my return. Unfortunately, I had to cancel the naval museum with the information about the Titanic. If it worked out, I would even still catch the bus to the campsite. It didn't work! The bus drove away under my nose. It was a matter of one minute at the most! I gesticulated and waved my arms after the #55, but no mercy! The next one left in an hour...

I asked a passer-by for the next taxi stop. The gentleman was very kind and called a vehicle by mobile phone. I didn't want to keep my doggies waiting any longer. Five hours in a camper van had been enough, so I sacrificed twenty dollars and was driven to the front door.

After four hours of walking myself, I now had to do an additional round with my two friends. Everyone can vividly imagine how much I enjoyed sitting at my notebook afterwards: with my legs up, typing my report. Then dinner was cancelled for me as the day would end relatively early for me today: lack of sleep, sightseeing, a long run to the bus, a run with the dogs, work on the PC,...

 Private remarks

Private remarks

Extreme anchor
in the harbour
of Halifax

Private remarks

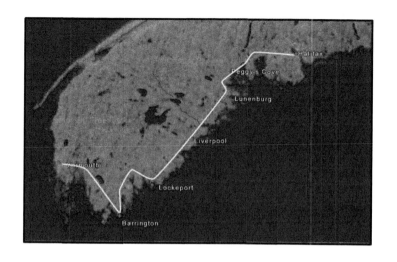

Lighthouse Trail

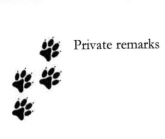 Private remarks

Lighthouse Route Part 1

Ten hours of sleep! I probably needed it badly. After all, yesterday the day had already ended for me at nine o'clock. We could take our time, because today there was only one item on the programme: the camper had to be cleaned!

Freshly polished, filled and emptied, showered and disposed of, we ventured once more across Halifax to get onto the Lighthouse Route on the south coast, west of the city. Finally, we reached the #333 road and after a pleasant drive we were in **Peggy's Cove** at lunchtime.

Normally, the small fishing village has about 60 inhabitants. But because it has the most photographed lighthouse in Nova Scotia, its little houses clinging picturesquely to rocks and the unique landscape around it, it was teeming with visitors. Like ants, they crawled around the lighthouse and up and down the rocks. Although parking spaces were scarce; we managed to get one anyway and set off as well. The car park attendant told me that before nine o'clock in the morning there was complete silence and after 5pm the whole spook disappeared again. I could compare this with the island of Capri in Italy, where I had experienced something similar. How can the "natives" stand it... every day?

We threw ourselves into the mass migration and diligently took photos. I didn't want to come home without Peggy's Cove loot. Somehow, I found myself thrown back to Newfoundland in terms of scenery. The only thing I could resist was climbing the huge rocks. The barren landscape and the large boulders are still relics from the Ice Age.

Lunchtime and a *siesta* in the well-ventilated camper. Only Wurschtel couldn't keep his mouth shut and had to grumble at everyone who passed by the door. Somehow, I still managed to shut off his barking in my brain and find a short sleep.

A second round to the cheerful-looking church, then we escaped the crowds and turned left. We would not make it to Chester but maybe there would be another opportunity on the way. We stopped briefly after another three kilometres. On the left of the road was the impressive memorial stone commemorating a *Swissair plane crash* in which all 200 occupants died in the sea. There was also an impressive view of Peggy's Cove coast from here.

The **Lighthouse Trail** led us along the coast with ever-changing views of fjord-like bays, dotted with countless sailing ships at rest. Probably every next house here had such a floating vessel. We drove about two thirds of the way around **Margaret's Bay**, with several nice little (ice-cold) sandy beaches and a few expensive campsites, all in the 30.- to 40.- CAD category. That was too expensive for me. To me Nova Scotia seemed to be almost 10.- CAD/night higher on average than Newfoundland in camping prices.

At around half past five we found our evening destination. In **Hubbards** I discovered a friendly harbour with enough pitches and a small green area. There were even decent toilets on site. Quiet and almost ideal for our needs! Here we settled down. On an informative tour, there were also no overnight bans to be found anywhere. The harbour doesn't seem to be frequented by "bad parents", because some respectable boats and even a private jetty with a seaplane could be spotted. We were just in time for that…

Peggy's Cove

Private remarks

Lighthouse Route Part 2
The way is once again the goal

We left our hospitable campsite in Hubbards at about half past eight. The GPS wanted to take us to **Chester** by the quickest route, but we cheated it and took the #329 along the coast. First, we had Margaret's Bay on our left, then **Mahone Bay** after the southern bend. Cosy little fishing villages came along, lots of forest and well-kept larger and smaller estates. On this curve we drove about 40 kilometres, sometimes with a view of the bay, sometimes with a view of the small hidden lakes in the interior of the small peninsula.

Chester was just right for a little morning walk, and we strolled a bit through the shady streets and along the cosy harbour. Since the first holiday hotel was built there around 1900, the small town with its ideal sailing conditions quickly became a refuge for stressed city dwellers. After all, Highway #103 is the shortest and most direct route from Halifax to here. This is how nice summer residences, a small playhouse and an active sailing harbour with several local artisans originated.

Our next destination was **Mahone Bay** with its beautiful churches. I wanted to stroll around a bit, but the larger car park was too far away from the centre, and when I spot-  ted something suitable, I couldn't find a place to turn my car around. Well, we'll just drive straight on to Lunenburg. We got there at a decent hour for lunch.

Lunenburg, of course, was once again a hive of activity, which meant that it was crowded with tourists. Searching for a parking space was fruitless even though I drove around the bay, towards the golf course, as one of my guides recommended, with a clear view of the colourful UNESCO World Heritage Site. There was indeed a stretch of beach where many larger and smaller artists with painting ambitions were cavorting at small picnic tables. We fit right in so we parked on the promenade. I found a spot that was flat and would fit my vehicle with no street invasion; there were no overnight bans in sight either. The walk to the centre took about fifteen minutes. Great! This is where we'll set up camp!

First we had the obligatory lunch soup and the usual *siesta*. Around two o'clock I hitched up my two "mice" (Wurschtel held short and Knuffi locked to the belt) and we set off for the city centre. Like everywhere in North America, the old buildings have been converted into souvenir shops, restaurants or guest houses. But this did not detract from the colourfulness of the overall picture. The only thing that disturbed the photographer was the constant tangle of cables in front of the houses. Can't they find another solution? At home, the mess would have been fixed long ago.

The biggest attraction was the **"Blue Nose II"**, a perfect replica of the famous regatta ship "Blue Nose I", which is depicted on the 10-cent coin. Like its predecessor, the ship was built at the same shipyard in Lunenburg and is currently being restored and so was therefore not open to the public. Next year, the schooner will set sail again with human cargo.

We trudged up and down the steep streets, criss-crossed and got to see many pretty properties and in total we managed a tour of almost two hours. Despite that, I was thinking about maybe going a little further as I still had enough time.

As often happens, fate took the decision away from me. I really must get into the habit of stopping when I lift my head up to read or visit something. However, I didn't do this at the *Hackney Carriages* down at the harbour, and as a result I once again tripped over a curb and fell flat. This time it was the left side that was hit. Two helpful gentlemen helped me up and the owner of the horse-drawn carriage offered to drive me and my two companions to my motorhome. I noticed once again how extraordinarily helpful and friendly Canadians are in normal or emergency situations. The old man almost thanked me for giving him the pleasure of driving me… Thank God nothing was broken, neither my glasses nor any bones. There will probably be some bruises on my left buttock and shoulder tomorrow. Of course, I had "Mobilat" and my tried and tested painkillers at hand. I cooled myself down with the frozen sausages, which I inadvertently defrosted for dinner tonight. Now we'll sleep with a view of Lunenburg harbour, and I will not be driven away from this spot. At worst, I can say I'm unfit to drive. But I can't imagine anyone objecting to my parking situation, even though there are residential houses on the opposite side of the road.

PS: To be polite, I asked a gentleman using his lawnmower if it would be any problem if I obscured his view with my big box tonight! "I'm the neighbour! No one lives in the house…!" Great! No guilty conscience on my side!

Private remarks

 Private remarks

Lighthouse Trail Part 3

Heeding yesterday's "subtle" hint from my psyche, we arranged the day quietly and comfortably. We woke up at around seven o'clock with picture-book weather. Not a single cloud in the sky; pleasant dry temperatures and a light breeze. Lunenburg lay clear, albeit in the morning shade ahead of us. Our "Ocean View Villa" had once again proved to be a good value. On the first morning round I spotted a bird of prey fortress on a mast that had escaped me yesterday. But it was perfect for a picture in these light conditions!

First item on the agenda after a relaxed breakfast: the small fishing village of **Blue Rocks**, only six kilometres east of Lunenburg. We landed in a different world, far away from any tourist hustle and bustle. A few paddlers took their first beginner's lesson and fishermen chatted about their everyday life. The houses stuck like shells to the rocks or floated on stilts above the water. Someone had decorated his Christmas tree with buoys. Several sailors in white were cavorting in the deep blue bay. There was not only one picture to fall in love with…

Second item on the agenda: shopping at the supermarket. Apart from some personal trifles (German bread), I bought a bag of carrots as a treat for the coachman's horses and a collection of sweets for the helpful gentleman from yesterday. I wanted to show my appreciation for his support, but I didn't want to give him any money. He was quite astonished when he saw me climbing out of the camper almost without any complaints and was happy about the unexpected recognition. With many good wishes, he then sent me on my way.

Just in case, fill up the tank! I had learned from my experiences. After all, there was room for another eighty litres in my drunkard. I was on the safe side again. We took the #332 south. The hustle and bustle died down and the road was once again the destination. It went along the water under a white-blue sky and the landscape and the ambience around it became more rural. I enjoyed the well-kept wooden houses, always decorated with lots of flowers. Somehow this decorative mentality reminded me a little of home in Bavaria. There, too, flower arrangements and gardening are very important.

What now? Wait twenty minutes for the cable ferry from LaHave? That was too long for me; even though I still had a ticket for it from before. As I had time, I took the bay out to **Bridgewater**. Bay is actually wrong, because it was the estuary of the *LaHave River*. But then, just before Bridgewater, I abruptly slammed on the brakes. There was a park signposted on the left and it was not marked on any of my maps. It was a beautiful, wooded area with good walks, picnic areas and access to the water. It was just right for our lunch break so we parked in the shade and set off. We tramped through the forest for a full hour and the dogs had plenty of time to pursue their sniffing needs. The car park was so uncrowded that even Wurschtel didn't find it necessary to grumble and so I completed another hour of *siesta* without interruption.

306

Afterwards, we drove back along the LaHave River on the #331 to the south – on the opposite side! A short stop at the *Fort Point Museum* was a must. There, the buildings of the former lighthouse were picturesquely situated on a promontory in the river. With a few exhibits, they reminded us of a French fortification from around 1600, when LaHave was briefly the capital of Arcadia. Several mementos of the first German settlers were also to be discovered.

The drive continued picturesquely. Each cottage on the hillside had built its own little private jetty on large stone blocks in the water, adorned with friendly Adirondack chairs. We didn't drive too long, though, because we were tempted by **Crescent Beach** with its eternally long white sandy beach. But first I wanted to visit the *marine museum* on one of the small islands. Usually, these facilities close at 5pm. So maybe this could be a place to spend the night.

Interestingly, the museum was housed in a disused church and crammed with all kinds of collectibles. No entrance fee was charged. You could get to this marine museum on two adventurous wooden bridges that connected the islands of LaHave. Unfortunately, I saw a barrier in front of the car park! Ok, there would be no chance to spend the night here! Oh well, we'll just turn around!

Back across the two wobbly bridges; I discovered a tiny car park at the end of Crescent Beach. Three cars and me! … and a passable access to the beach. But we didn't want to risk that with my few kilos on the wheels.

We are not quite level now, but our rear end no longer invades the street and a parking ban is nowhere to be discovered. The traffic should be reduced to zero in the evening hours. I still cherish the hope that the car in front of me will disappear, then I could arrange myself a little better. If that car moves to the small estates behind the sand road, that doesn't bother me either.

We strolled for over an hour "off leash" on the deserted beach and my two friends frolicked as much as they wanted in the water. I have a strong suspicion that we have found a suitable place for us for the next night.

 Private remarks

Lighthouse Trail, Part 4
Beach and Lighthouse Combo

We didn't get very far today; the day was just too beautiful for that. We didn't want to spend it only in the car, so we took a closer look at the lighthouses and beaches along the following stretch of coast. The water was warm enough to wade in, but it would have been too cold for me to swim. At the last beach we had to wade through a knee-deep ford, which was not quite the same height as my dogs. This time Wurschtel was also forced to swim. It wasn't quite to his liking, but he survived it twice. Knuffi wasn't exactly thrilled either, but she paddled eagerly to keep up with me.

1) Port Medway: with a small park around the lighthouse

2) Medway Head: the old and new lighthouse on the headland behind Port Medway, accessible on Gravel Road

3) Port Medway: the old parish hall, formerly a church

4) 2 Beaches of Beach Meadows: one dog-friendly, the other developed, but… with an overnight ban!

5) Liverpool lighthouse

6) Central Port Mouton: dream beach of Carter's Beach

As you can see, we were not the only ones on the beach that afternoon, but we would be the only ones as soon as night fell. Then this piece of earth will be ours alone!

A few curiosities on the side: it's not hard to guess who the first settlers were here…

 Private remarks

Lighthouse Trail, Part 4 and Carter's Beach

Private remarks

Lighthouse Route part 5
Final stop Shelburne

I woke up on a magical morning on the beach. The night had been somewhat painfully interrupted as my bruises from the fall had not yet healed completely. I remembered them every time I turned around. Never mind, it could have been worse.

Enchantingly calm and shimmering soft pink, the beach and the water lay before the rising sun. It was pleasantly cool, and a gentle breeze stirred the waves. Some ducks were performing diving tricks, a fishing boat chugged in the distance: pure romance... Only a few early risers were out and about, so we left the hospitable place at around half past eight. I wanted to have a look at the much-praised *Thomas Randall Provincial Park*. Going there as a non-camper is not at all worthwhile, as the day-use area was very small compared to the size of the park. Hiking trails were closed, and the so-called "Sandy Beach" was one big pile of stones. The beautiful beaches were only accessible to paying campers. The pitches have zero service and cost 26.- CAD. Actually, an outrage! The only advantage for me was that the waste disposal station was outside the area, so after four days I could renew my water and empty the tanks for free without having to stay at a campsite.

I drove back onto the highway #103 and turned back onto the Lighthouse Trail at exit #23, around the next bay. In retrospect, I could have saved these coastal kilometres if I had headed straight for Lockport. There was little view of the water as it was forest dominated.

At lunchtime, **Lockport** delighted us with a few old cottages, a small harbour and a beautiful, immaculate sandy beach. We walked along the beach after the walk in the Provincial Park had turned out to be a bit short due to the circumstances. It was aptly called "Canada's Ocean Playground" on the Nova

Scotia car signs: indeed, a sandy playground on the Atlantic, the entire coastline. There we had our usual long lunch break until there were too many bathers for us.

For the afternoon I had planned to go to **Shelburne**. This small harbour town is described in the highest terms in the guidebooks. It was founded by Loyalists around 1750 and grew into a "boom town" due to its lively shipyard activity, but later lost importance and today has about 2,000 inhabitants. However, the town still has its importance as a supply centre for the surrounding area. Its historical centre on the waterfront was rediscovered by filmmakers and plays a leading role in the historical film "The Scarlet Letter". Even a community hall was reconstructed and incorporated into the historic buildings.

This time, I left my companions as guards in the motorhome and set off on my own without any "stop and go" to take pictures. There were museums in some of the old wooden shacks, a shipyard with dories to visit and I also took a pleasant stroll along the marina.

We had a good parking space down by the water and so I started thinking about spending the night here. But first I wanted to have a look at the localities near the lighthouse, a few kilometres to the south. No, I didn't particularly like it there – too exposed; that's why I went back to the village, where I found a sign for a public free parking space. It was the large parking area in front of the yacht club! Not particularly suitable for starting the generator either and I urgently needed power for my technical equipment again, so this wouldn't do.

It was still relatively early in the day, so I decided to try my luck further along the Lighthouse Trail. Shortly after **Churchover**, there was a rattle in the box and my journey was "over" … The familiar sound made me think of the fan belt! But not after 7,000 kilometres! That can't be! This time (almost) in the middle of the wilderness! I now had a Canadian mobile phone, but far and wide no number from the CAA or any other road service.

Accordingly, I put my hazard lights on, threw my reflective vest on, set up a triangle or pylon and stopped the next best car. A friendly lady of my age immediately agreed to call the breakdown service, but until the bureaucracy got going, another helpful gentleman came along and gave her the address of a towing service in Shelburne. My saving angel went there and sent an emergency service. I think it took less than an hour before I was hitched up and once again allowed to drive back to the village at an angle without any effort of my own.

The friendliness and helpfulness of the Canadians is simply overwhelming again and again. "I'm glad if I could help you... ". The boss of the workshop himself had me in tow. He made a place for me to stay behind the building and even provided me with electricity. It was too late for a repair, so I had to wait until tomorrow.

Now I'm in Shelburne on a free pitch for the night, I can recharge all my devices and finish writing my travel report in peace. The only thing I miss is the view of the Atlantic (as a substitute, used car tyres) – you can't have everything! So, now I'm going to sleep, because tomorrow the mechanics will be at the gates at eight o'clock. I'd better stop jumping around in my pyjamas and get into bed.

Private remarks

Historical Shelburn

Private remarks

Lighthouse Trail, Part 6
Another lazy day

They didn't surprise me in my pyjamas after all! I had set my alarm for six o'clock and was freshly washed, combed and ready when the mechanics appeared. I had even had my breakfast. The damage and the culprit could be determined and found. As far as I could tell, some bolts had turned the wrong way and overloaded the V-belt, which was why it would have broken after such a short time. They would try to repair the damage cheaply, safely and in the fastest possible time. Your word in God's ears, I thought to myself. However, I would have to be a little patient. That won't be a problem, I can't drive without a fan belt anyway!

As the car was safely parked at the workshop, I first took the dogs for a walk and then went to the information centre to check my e-mails. The museums were open, but again, I wasn't interested enough in local history to shell out eight dollars. I found another nice motif with one of the well-known "dories" and wandered back to my beasts.

The mechanic surprised me with the good news that the matter could be cleared up faster than expected. So once again I paid 380.- CAD for the tow and the repair. Good thing I had my financial cushion for that. This time the towing was only a third of the last bill.

I got on Highway #103, the motorway. According to the lady at the information desk, the diversion of 75 kilometres on the Lighthouse Route was not advisable. Apart from the forest, there was nothing else, so my motorhome was allowed to really speed for a few kilometres. Our next destination was **Barrington**: it was only a tiny village, but it had three museums. I wasn't going to pay five dollars to climb up the lighthouse and the local history museum interested me less, but the "wool

321

mill" aroused my interest. It was a workshop for wool processing, completely geared for waterpower. Here they took care of everything, from washing the wool to automatic combing and spinning. I discovered a beautiful tapestry with appliqués and two pairs of knee socks with old knitting patterns. In my youth, I had produced several foot warmers with complicated patterns myself.

Afterwards, I was attracted by the beaches of **Cape Sable Island**, which juts far out into the Atlantic and forms the southernmost tip of Nova Scotia. We crossed over via a causeway at *Barrington Passage* and beautiful, fine sandy white beaches invited us to take a walk. For the dogs, the water was welcome; for me, ankle-high was enough because of the temperature. Wurschtel had the ideal camouflage colour "silver-grey" and was hardly distinguishable from the sandy surface.

We made our route clockwise, with me already taking a longer lunch break at the first beach. The short night had made itself felt and I allowed myself a long rest. This beach is just one example of the vastness of the coast. In the distance, the highest lighthouse in NS could be seen. It stands on a separate island and can only be reached by boat.

Time was running out and we had to decide where to sleep. Any stretch of beach with restrictions would have been possible. Why not park right by the dam, on a wide and flat area, with lighting and a boardwalk. That seemed very safe so we placed ourselves in a corner and I made dinner for everyone first.

I was a little annoyed by a racing boat that was cruising on the water with considerable roar and noise. Then suddenly everything was quiet. I looked out of the window and saw a crowd of people slowly but steadily growing and waiting on the shore. You wouldn't believe it, but the boat in question was being towed upside down to the jetty by the coastguard. Someone must have been too cocky and capsized. Now everyone watched the young gentleman busily bailing water and they helped him pull his racing vehicle ashore. I wouldn't like to know how much chat developed between the spectators. On a separate issue, tomorrow we're finally head-ing around the eastern bend of Nova Scotia, up towards Yarmouth. There the Lighthouse Trail will come to an end, and we will find a campsite again!

Lighthouse Trail, last section

This morning I looked as old as I was! The campsite was secure, under lights, but there must have been a disco or a crazy beach party somewhere. Until half past three in the morning, one crate after another squealed and hissed past me. Car doors slammed incessantly, and loud clucking accompanied the running engines: it was unnerving. I probably would have slept more peacefully in the reserve on the coast with the bird conservationists. Now you know that before I did. Anyway, at around eight o'clock I got up with rings under my eyes and took the day slowly. I did some shopping at Sobeys and got back on the Lighthouse Route #3 to **Pubnico**. Here I encountered purely ethnic Arcadian territory again. Everywhere you could see the Canadian flag and the Arcadian flag flying. This mentality reminded me a little of Bavaria. We are also a separate tribe, although we were not expelled or deported like the Arcadians. We honour our white and blue colour and uphold our traditions. This population group in Nova Scotia also holds its flag high, somehow in defiance of the Scots.

I visited the museum village "Arcadian Village" on the peninsula in the south. Each of these small villages was somehow called "Pubnico" once with a "low" in front, then an "east, a "west", an "upper" or a "little", sometimes even combined... The small complex was embedded in a salty marshland with a wide view of the bay. Except for two buildings, I was able to let my two four-legged friends run with me. I therefore completed both buildings with original furnishings and hardworking women first, then grabbed my friends and explored the grounds with them.

One of the ladies was cooking soup and making jam, the other was baking bread for a communal meal tomorrow. A blacksmith was making a strong nail in front of our eyes and telling all kinds of stories. I also learned that the Arcadians are the only French people who still count the same way in their language as we do and have not adopted the complicated addition system of the Napoleonic way of counting, which still annoys me today, as I always have to start concentrating from "sixty" onwards. Those who know French as a foreign language can sing a song about it and use a calculator...

After the visit to the village, we had our traditional lunch soup and an unusually long *siesta*. Maybe I was still tired from the previous night? I didn't want to go on like this. After two hours I was back among the living, but with little energy. Accordingly, I crossed the WALMART overnight stay off my list and drove to the nearest campsite. It was about 15 kilometres from **Yarmouth**, the second largest town in Nova Scotia, with only about 7,500 inhabitants. After six free nights, I was allowed to treat myself to some luxury again. For 40.- CAD a night, I could pass through the *"Campers Haven"* and get a place with all connections. Otherwise, there was really nothing cheaper along the entire route. I would have been satisfied with water alone! Instead, I enjoyed an unlimited hot shower right after arrival and felt like a human being again…

Private remarks

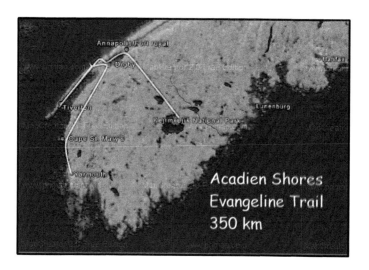

Acadien Shores
Evangeline Trail
350 km

327

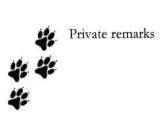 Private remarks

Acadien Shores
Evangeline Trail

Cleaning the camper is not really the most pleasant work on a Sunday. But since almost all days are a Sunday for us, I could get over it. It was simply necessary to remove the sand dunes inside and here at the campsite I had enough electricity available. But that also meant we couldn't get on the road before noon, and half a day of glorious weather would inevitably go to waste.

We made the best of it and drove via **Yarmouth** (7 kilometres) to **Cape Forchu** lighthouse, about ten kilometres south of town on a promontory. It's so picturesque that you can even find it on the official Nova Scotia tourist brochure. Yarmouth is still economically important despite its small population, but it doesn't have much to offer apart from two museums and the ferry port to the USA. So I decided not to visit the town.

Since there was also a nice circular walk at the lighthouse, we didn't notice how quickly the time passed. Only my hunger pangs made me realise that it was already almost two o'clock when we climbed back into the car.

I planned to drive to the next Provincial Park and take a break there. Somehow, however, we drifted off the path and ended up in an inland park instead of the coast. **Ellenwood Lake PP** was in the middle of the forest, blessed with a campsite and a beautiful swimming lake that was only frequented by very few people. We stayed here for a while, and once again I combined lunch with dinner. Soup alone was not enough for me today, so I added bacon to the pan, German bread and long stored fried eggs. Mustard gherkins rounded off my gourmet meal; the rest was given to the dogs.

From now on I listened to my GPS again and let it guide me to #1, the **Evangeline Trail**. I followed the instructions to the letter but I had to cope with several cross connections in the form of gravel roads. However, they were well paved and sufficiently wide that no problems arose. Finally, I had the coast in front of me again.

This stretch of coast (Yarmouth to Digby, Annapolis Royal to Wolfville) is named after the heroic figure who was responsible for the expulsion of French settlers (Arcadians) by the British. The poetry creation that commemorated the deed is the epic verse by the American *Henry W. Longfellow*, published in 1847, which depicts in epic breadth Evangeline's lifelong search across the continent for her expelled lover Gabriel. Old, broken and ill, she finds him again in Louisiana shortly before his – and her – death. Many of the coastal villages are French in character and honour their Acadian past.

We found the first wide sandy beach at **Port Maitland**, firmly in the hands of the Provincial Park and so hopeless for us as a night's lodging. I turned around and fate (road #1) brought me to **Beaver River**. Just past the town I found a signpost to a public beach, however the car park was so tiny that it was only enough for six cars and I was too fat for that. I therefore stopped in the middle of a field of fragrant hedge roses and waited for the "crowd" to disperse soon. But when I saw the beach goers approaching with driftwood for a campfire, I realised my hopeless situation and moved on. In any case, the three of us had a long and wonderful walk on a kilometre-long beach, completely off-leash. As a result, we kept on looking. The turnoff at **Salmon River** turned out to be a loser. The long beach at **Mavilette** was also in the hands of the "provincials", but there was no sign of a ban at the car parks behind the dunes. Although we would keep that in mind, I was still attracted by the little lighthouse at **Cape St. Mary's**.

That's where we are standing now and we're not going anywhere else. A peaceful place, high above the sea, the rocks and the small fishing harbour. We have had another wonderful walk and are out of sight of the houses and the road below us.

Despite all the idyll we are not alone today, for a very special cyclist has pitched his tent a short distance away. His pedal is adorned with the flags of Canada, Nova Scotia, Acadia, the provincial flag of Newfoundland and the Republic of Newfoundland. He himself is from Ontario. He has now pitched his tiny tent and will soon retire to his little kingdom. We had a great chat, the dogs made fast friends with him, and he tried out his rusty knowledge of German, as he was once married for a short time in Frankfurt. Slowly the lights of the coast appear, after a beautiful sunset. We hit the right note again!

331

Evangeline Trail Part 2

Woke up once again to bright sunshine under the lighthouse... He had worked diligently all night, keeping the sleepers at his feet safe with the flashing light. My neighbour had also just crawled out of his mini tent and so I could let the dogs run free. We arranged to meet later in my camper for breakfast. I enjoyed hosting the illustrious fellow. He had so many stories to tell and was very interested in history, from which of course I also benefited, as well as being friendly and unobtrusive, which I particularly appreciated.

For this reason, breakfast naturally dragged on, and it took some time before I had everything ready to leave. Once again, there was no hurry, as I wanted to take the dogs for a long walk on the beautiful long *beach of Mavilette* before continuing my journey north. Unfortunately, we parted ways here, as his next destination was Yarmouth in the south. There was a fond farewell, a quick *adieu* horn and he was out of my sight. The wide long sandy beach, now immaculately untouched after the tide, comforted me a little after the loss of his company. Repeatedly experience has taught me: you always meet people on

these trips where the chemistry is right from the start. You just must get involved and perhaps make the first move. The rest is usually done by my dogs.

We continued north on #1 and made a short stop at *Meteghan Provincial Park*, appropriately named Smuggler's Cove. This had to do with the fact that the cliff here has several caves where smuggled rum used to be stored in the days of Prohibition. At low tide, it was safe to enter the rocks and get to the stored goods. This cave was twenty metres long and five metres high. There was plenty of room! Again, of course, we took advantage of the friendly surroundings for a longer walk.

The symbol of the Evangeline Trail is a stylised church. The reason for this is the large number of enormous churches in the many small Acadian communities, which were so out of proportion with each other. For example, in **Church Point** (meaningful name!) you find the tallest wooden church in North America. I had to search for a long time before I found a vantage point to capture the entire building in height and width. The camper van next to it looks rather puny.

Gilberts Cove with its picturesque lighthouse was our next stop: here we had our lunch break. There was a small café attached, but it closed at 4pm. The car park here would have been perfect as a place to spend the night, but it was too early for us, even though the sea and several short walks were tempting.

Our destination for the day would be **Digby**, the capital of the scallop. Here I would surely find a place to stay. I found one on the boardwalk and the waterfront. However, it did not promise to be very quiet. At the information office, I asked about the museum schooner and its equipment for "harvesting" the scallop, but it had closed three years ago: a book revision was due.

Where could one buy this prized delicacy scallop? I didn't want to go to a restaurant but the fish market at the harbour was still open so let's go there! I bought a package of these highly praised mussels, the (American) pound for 14.- CAD, not quite 500 grams, content approx. 12 pieces. But then I had enough for two meals. I also took a bag of fresh halibut for only 5.- CAD. I was able to eat that twice, too. There was space in the freezer again since I had removed all the accumulated ice the day before yesterday, so storage was no problem!

At the information centre, I was advised to drive the seven kilometres to the lighthouse: it would be worth it. "Lighthouse"? My ears perked up again. Indeed, the headland jutted far out into the water and the lighthouse stood on an exposed spot. It's hard to believe that in the past ships were warned of fog with rifle shots and simple campfires, or later lamps with whale oil. For us, the flashing light has become a matter of course. However, I read that about one and a half kilometres west of here, many a ship and its crew had met a tragic end: 42 wrecks were counted by 1950. Campfires and rifle shootings were apparently not very effective. Everyone can probably tell where we will spend the night today. I had half my mussels for dinner with a fantastic view of the sea. I had already made my planned salmon disappear at noon. For dessert, nature served me a dreamlike sunset.

It is now getting noticeably cooler in the evening. Autumn is creeping up very slowly but surely. I don't need my dogs in order to sleep yet, but the duvet is the order of the day again. The camper is slightly chilled in the morning and the days have become shorter. The odd tree is already starting to colour up. It is still a little early, but considering the long and dry summer... After all, we had almost two months of beautiful weather with only short interruptions, which is also proven by the pictures.

Digby Nack and Long Island

A day is only interesting when you wake up and have no idea where you are going, where and how it will end. Such a day had begun again today. The only thing planned was the general direction. We wanted to go down the long "finger" southwards from Digby. The night at the lighthouse had been quiet and trouble-free. All three occupants seemed to have slept well. We were therefore able to set off at half past eight in bright sunshine.

First stop: "Sobeys" to get some bread and selected sausages and cheeses. I know, everything has its price! But I was tired of the same-tasting sausage from Walmart! I'd rather spend a few dollars more!

Second stop: "Tim Hortons", to finally check my e-mails again! No one had thought of us! But wait! Not true! At the second address I found two letters from occasional writers! Otherwise, I had to keep my writing short, because I was using all the battery! That was annoying at times and so I only sent "Nova Scotia 3" on its way.

Third stop: The small *Provincial Park "Lake Midway"* on the long peninsula **Digby Neck**. The route from Digby was not particularly varied because it went almost constantly through wooded areas. You rarely saw anything of St. Mary's Bay on the left and even less of Fundy Bay on the right. Since the dogs needed some exercise, we took a little break at this freshwater lake and there I discovered a working water tap, not too far from the entrance, so I was able to refill my tank: the next free nights were also secured. The more expensive alternative would have been called *"Whale Grove Campground"*.

Fourth stop: we found **Sandy Cove** by chance, which was only advertised as Bay Street. An immaculate round shape with deep blue water, but the sandy beach was marred by sea-weed, very soft and therefore tiring to walk on. You could also see a few crumbling fishermen's huts and a broken wharf. We didn't particularly like it here, so we turned back after a short and tiring walk: the beach looked more inviting in the picture than it really was. Then turning the camper around was also a challenge.

Fifth stop: *Ferry to Long Island...* I was fighting with myself over whether I shouldn't turn around. I had to wait almost 45 minutes for the next crossing. If the two islands were as monotonous as the route here, the time spent would not pay off. I did get in the approach queue, but in such a way that I could still get out.

My book had praised the quality of the lobster and scallop rolls at the little café on the jetty and I was hungry anyway, so I devoured a soft roll of each kind. They were well filled, tasty and seasoned with a little too much mayonnaise, but worth the price (hot dogs are cheaper, that's for sure!). Now I only have 25.- CAD cash in my pocket! That's not the world!

While waiting for the rolls and studying the brochures, time passed, and I had just enough time to eat my lunch before the ferry left. The decision was made and I crossed over. The whole thing didn't cost me anything because I still had the combined ticket from the very first ferry port near Iona, although I had no idea at the time where all these state ferries worked. Now here it paid off.

Tiverton was the name of the port of call. Just around the corner there was a whale watching company of a special kind. I had already done such a tour at Cape Breton in pouring rain and with a normal boat. The special thing about this company was that the "Ocean Exploration" company stationed there employed Tom Goodwin as a guide. He is a biologist known in this country who has already worked with Jaques Cousteau and Greenpeace. He himself steers the Zodiacs and is of course open to all interested questions. I afforded myself the luxury in this bright weather today and paid a whopping 75.- CAD! Praise the credit card!

I got to talk to a few young people in front of the house and learned that they were all serving as volunteers at Tom's and expanding their knowledge on the side. One young man had just finished his A-levels in Frankfurt and wanted to do something completely different. A young woman from Croatia had run out of money while travelling and she had decided to start working with the scientist. Unfortunately, I didn't find out what had inspired the Chinese man.

I still had a good hour before the meeting point and so I set off for the lighthouse. Now I was really starting to sweat! What a narrow road! It was almost too narrow for a normal car! But I couldn't turn around either because the path was lined with bushes and trees. For better or worse, I had to drive to the bitter end and hope for somewhere to turn around. Why had no one warned me? At the end of the road, I met a Japanese man who didn't seem to have a good grip on his rented car. I first guided him into a small detour so that I could pass, then he was able to disappear and in his small gap I was finally allowed to turn around! Quickly I took a photo of the old tower and then I proceeded to get out of the mousetrap! Fortunately, no oncoming traffic intervened during the retreat.

Either they would have taken off, backed up or I would have run them over recklessly…

At 3 p.m. we finally got all dressed up and looked like the men from Mars. There were only fifteen of us on this tour, one third of them German speaking! At breakneck speed, we drove along Long Island for about 45 minutes out into the Bay of Fundy under glistening sunlight. For those sitting at the front of the boat, it was more like a ride on the ox, because your feet hardly found any grip, the air cushion on the edge of the boat bounced with every wave and the impact on the water each time was hard. The phenomenon was explained with the receding tide and the contrary blowing of the wind. As the senior member of the group, I had wisely been relegated to a fixed seat in the middle of the boat. There, my vertebrae were still violently compressed, but at least I had a foothold.

Then the first humpback whales came into sight. Three specimens rested snorting on the surface of the sea. Their fountains shone rainbow-coloured over the water. At first, I tried to take a few pictures or capture them on video. Then I got tired of all the magic and put all the equipment away. I really didn't feel like looking at the animals only through the viewfinder of the camera, only to be annoyed later that I hadn't caught this or that moment right. I don't have to prove anything to anyone! One's own eye is much more flexible when observing.

In this sunny open-air theatre, I much preferred to enjoy the elegant diving of their tail fins, the cheerful waving of their long lateral fins or the aerial jumps and somersaults out of the water. What power must be inherent in an animal weighing so many tonnes to break free from its lightness in the water and perform such leaps in the heaviness of gravity. I was fascinated by their agility. We were also able to follow a mother with a "baby" for quite some time, but that "baby" already beat the size of our boat by far. In this way, more than two hours in the *Bay of Fundy* flew by and we started our way home at around five o'clock. Again and again, I had to smile at the various contortions of the other passengers when they were on their crazy photo safari. Ok, ok, you must show your offspring at home what you have seen…

The day was over but tomorrow had already taken shape. We would spend the night here at the harbour and watch the ships coming towards us at high tide. People have cleverly adapted to the tidal phenomenon by constructing floating docks that lower or raise with the help of beams at low and high tide to compensate for the difference in height.

PS: It is now 10.30 pm and I am standing at the harbour quay now almost within sight of the boats.

Long Island to Annapolis Royal

When I heard a rhythmic hooting around half past two in the morning, I knew immediately what it meant. That's right, when I lifted the blinds a little, there was a dense fog outside and a Newfoundland feeling came over me. How lucky we had been yesterday! I turned over once more with pleasure and shooed Wurschtel away from my warm sleeping place for the umpteenth time! What a stubborn dog he could be…

In the morning, however, the sun was already peeking through the haze and soon the fog had disappeared from the bay. The boats from the previous day had sunk back to their lowest level.

For today, I had planned a walk to *Balancing Rock*. The small hiking trail was barely four kilometres from my sleeping place. I calculated 45 minutes for the many steps and the path, as it was always slower with the dogs than when walking alone. The path was very nicely laid out between the woods, sometimes comfortably even, sometimes with a plank path. The 200 steps

down to the rock and the viewing platform were still acceptable, but I was already thinking about the way back. I let the dogs run off the leash which gave me my hands free, because with the short leash they always stopped each other.

According to the description, I was confronted with 200 million years of Earth history. The entire coastline was a pile of upright basalt rocks, just this one floating freely in space. The scenery reminded me of the Scottish island of Staffa. It too had rock walls of a

340

similar shape. When will the whole thing lose its balance? I hardly think we will live to see it…

Sporty as we were, we then puffed our way back up the many steps. The most frequent command for the dogs was: "And… wait!" – which they did diligently on every landing. How happy I was to see the flat path again after the exertion! Thank goodness there was a small bench to rest on and a typical red Canadian maple in the colours of autumn!

How should we continue the day now? If I pressed the gas a little, I would get across on the ferry at eleven. No sooner said than done and shortly after eleven we were back on the main route to Digby. I had read that there would be a big motorbike meeting in town from today until the weekend. I had no business being in the hustle and bustle of hundreds of bikers. We would therefore drive around the city. Before that, however, I took a relaxing break at **Midway Lake** and its park. We had a quiet spot, the dogs in their shade and water, I with my chair and my books. After all, I needed to be informed about the route ahead. It was a tranquil couple of hours and around three o'clock we set off for **Annapolis Royal**. The diversions via **Bear River** didn't pay off much, although it was described as worthwhile. Instead, the roads were about the quality of yesterday's sea voyage… and cost time.

"Annapolis Royal"…   I'll tell you more about that tomorrow when I've done my tour. For tonight I found a place to sleep in the centre of the small town, in a public car park, where nobody can scare me away. I took the dogs on an orientation tour of the historic district, had dinner (fresh haddock with vegetables and rice) and now I'm finishing my writing and studying the localities a bit more. The weather seems to be changing, clouds have moved in over the bay. Good night!

Annapolis Royal

Today, this small town has only about 440 inhabitants and is located in Canada's oldest European settlement area. Everywhere you go you come across the eventful history of the French and English immigrants. Almost every house (150 in number) has a historical background and dates back at least two hundred years. Today they have been converted into bistros, tourist quarters, restaurants and souvenir shops and others serve as museums. In the middle of the centre you find *Fort Anne*, which dates from the time of the wars between England and France in the 17th and 18th centuries. The town became the British capital of Nova Scotia until Halifax took over in 1749. So much for the history in brief… I'll just do a little tour of the town for my readers. Later, there are two other delicacies planned. I left the dogs at home this time to have a clear run for pictures.

Another item on the agenda for this afternoon was **Port Royal**, located about ten kilometres outside Annapolis Royal. The weather was ideal for this, although it had rained this morning and I therefore crawled back onto the couch before my walk; there was no need for the usual *siesta*. The first French settlers established a trading post there in 1605. The site was rebuilt in 1939 according to original drawings by Samuel de Champlain. One absolutely felt transported to the Wild West during the tour, exactly like the facilities from the old films. The crew slept in four-bed rooms, the lower folk in the attic. The boss had his own suite with a bed on the first floor. I found the wooden construction of the roofs particularly fascinating.

Actually, I had planned to visit **Victoria Beach** at the very end of the bay. After all, this "beach" was probably directly opposite the Lighthouse that had granted me hospitality for one night in Digby. Unfortunately, the beach was just a pile of stones, and the path was ultimately impassable with my box. I didn't want to end up in such a predicament as in Tiverton again. I spontaneously decided to drive to the **Kejimkujik** (unpronounceable) **National Park** today. If they could offer me a place with electricity, I would be very grateful as all my reserves were slowly running low and lower. We would easily do the fifty kilometres with our eyes shut! And by doing so, I would finally manage to get all my activities in order again. If the weather cooperates, we will spend the day here with walks, going to Annapolis Royal again to sleep. Then we'll be ready for the next four or five days.

Private remarks

Private remarks

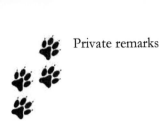 Private remarks

Kedschi-mmh-kuh-dschik

No, we didn't make a detour to China! This is how one of my guides pronounces the name of the Canadian **National Park Kejimkujik**. Now everyone can practise until they get to Nova Scotia and will be able to pronounce the name correctly!

Anyway, we started getting ready to check out by eleven; but showers, internet and dumping were on the agenda before we left. This morning I got a bit bogged down on the map to co-ordinate my further plans, so breakfast was had in a hurry. Never mind, they still let us out through the gates at noon.

The branching hiking trails are widely scattered throughout the park, and you always have to drive quite a few kilometres to get to the next starting point. Only about a fifth of its total extent has been opened to vehicles. The highlight of the park, however, is canoeing. The huge lake with its well-signposted canoe trails and wilderness areas for camping is a Dorado for water sports enthusiasts. That's why the campground with its more than 300 pitches is well frequented, although I was still lucky enough to get a nice big one with electricity yesterday (Thursday). The prospect of a free pitch over the weekend was zero because the coming Monday was a high holy holiday (La-bour Day) and thus a long weekend was announced.

This holiday also marks the end of summer. Work and school start again, and it gets noticeably quieter everywhere. So quiet, in fact, that sometimes some parks and campsites close as early as mid-September because the season is over for them. It can happen that on an autumn day in 30°C you stand in front of closed gates and discover the sign: "Closed due to danger of frost!" Of course, this poses one or two problems for my return journey. Time will tell… but it's not that far!

Today, at any rate, we enjoyed the sunny autumn afternoon and set out on two short hikes. The first one led us along the lake with its many islands and branches, the second one took us to small waterfalls and on a round tour through the high forest. Together with the late lunch break and the two circular walks, we easily filled the time until 5pm. I wanted to start back at this time, as "Port Royal" only closed its doors at half past five and the day before yesterday I had already rated the car park as very suitable for a stay. It would be quieter here than in the centre of Annapolis with its current biker festival.

We quickly bought some groceries for the next few days, as everything would probably be closed on Monday, and hid almost invisibly behind a large tree at the car park. The traffic along the road should die down soon, because there are only very small settlements on this peninsula.

 Private remarks

Valley of Annapolis to Truro
(Bay of Fundy – Minas Basin)
270 km

National Park Kejimkujik

 Private remarks

Annapolis Valley and Minas Basin

As expected, we had a peaceful and restful night in the shelter of Port Royal (... like other travellers in the past!) and were able to start again at 9am in an enterprising mood. I really had a good nose with the choice of my sleeping place, because today there was a weekly market in Annapolis, and I would either have been driven away early or wedged in until lunchtime.

We first filled up with petrol and later drove to the car park of the funeral home, because there was still room for me. There were no funerals today! My dogs guarded the camper and I went on a photo safari in the sunshine! The whole affair was called "Farmer's Market", but craftsmen and bakeries were in the majority.

German bakery with fresh pretzels! ... and they even spoke my mother tongue! ... not like in Halifax at the Bavarian butcher! I had enough bread at home, but I could afford two pretzels. Let's see if they really taste like home! I was so excited that I didn't even ask for the price, so I had to swallow hard! The baker wanted six dollars for the two pieces! That's about 4.20 Euros! Inflation could go on for a long time to reach this price level. But now they were packed! They will be eaten bite by bite with all devotion...

I was stuck for a long time at a vendor with beautiful leather dog leashes and fought a bitter battle with myself. My two four-legged friends were dear to me, but the prices would have put an enormous strain on my monthly budget. Common sense prevailed, and the lady was a bit disappointed after I left without her having achieved anything. In one corner there was the smell of potato pancakes and quite a few people were sitting on benches in front of the stall eating them. But I was still so full of breakfast that I wasn't particularly drawn there.

I had already stocked up on fresh blueberries from a local vendor at the petrol station, and it looked considerably cheaper than at the market. Yes, blueberry season has been going on in Canada for a good two weeks now and you can find various delicacies prepared with blueberries everywhere. I didn't really want to buy anything, I just wanted to wander around a bit and soon I went back to the camper with my two expensive pretzels to quickly buy some cheap chicken legs at "Foodland".

Knuffi has had her diarrhoea again for days and is always more than picky about what she eats. No tinned food, cheers! Dry food only when I'm starving! The cheap sausages from the supermarket? No, thanks! Cheese maybe after a little consideration! Doesn't my mistress have anything chicken-like in the fridge? She does… and will spoil this old lady with noodles and boiled fowl!

I imagined the much praised and climatically protected **Annapolis Valley** with its apple tree cultures to be like South Tyrol. But there was no question of that. There was hardly any espalier fruit to be seen and the so-called fruit tree orchards belonged to various private houses and were not to be understood as cultivated.

This weekend there was something different on the Evangeline Trail. It was the weekend of motorcyclists and bargain hunters. Every second household held its private flea market under blue skies, called a "garage sale" or "yard sale". Maybe someone will buy some of my junk for a few cents? Some households exhibit alone, others together with friends and turn it into a social event right away. This kind of shopping is especially popular with Americans, and I know from experience that my friend Dee can't pass up a yard sale. After all, she has a lot of grandchildren to give presents to. Whether these things later go unnoticed is anyone's guess.

The **Annapolis Valley** is about 160 kilometres long and a maximum of 24 kilometres wide. I hoped to get a small overview from a viewpoint park, the **Valleyview PP** near **Bridgetown**; but the view was only into the green and was unsuitable for photography. We stopped there in the shade for my lunch break with the first buttered pretzel and the first portion of blueberries and cream.

As we had only covered forty kilometres for the time being, the winding route through the valley was enough for me and I soon settled down on highway #101, which runs parallel to the Evangeline Trail. I wanted to get back to the **Bay of Fundy** with its stunning tides. I turned off at exit #11 and oriented myself towards **Blomidon PP**. This is highly praised in my guidebooks in terms of its location. Because of the long weekend, I didn't think there was a chance of finding a campsite there anyway but it costs nothing to ask...

The park is 183 metres above the sea and Minas Basin with the highest tides in the world. Now it was high tide time and there was nothing to see of the red rocks and the washouts in the sea. Tomorrow morning the situation would be different.

They had a place for me and my two rascals! There was no electricity here at altitude, but the view and the size of the site made up for that. If someone advertises our generous space, they should look at the following photo for comparison. Be-

355

tween me and the neighbour to my right, or left, there is no further parking space. Unbelievable, isn't it? I'm happy to pay my 26.- CAD for that. The pitches in the forest are also immensely spacious and everyone is provided layered protection by trees and hedges. It is one of the most beautiful campsites I have visited here in Nova Scotia.

The weather seems to be changing and so I have only booked for one night for now. If we are lucky for another day, I will add another night. Then the long weekend will have passed, and the hustle and bustle will be over.

Tide in Minas Basin

As you can see from the following pictures, we did not extend our stay. The weather was double-edged and so I preferred to devote myself to low and high tide in Minas Basin. I arranged my departure time so that I would be down on the beach at low tide (at around eleven o'clock). I could take my time, after I had slept more than badly that night but I had only myself to blame for that. For one thing, I had been too lazy last night to really level the car and for another, the branches of the neighbouring trees hit the body of my camper van so hard in the prevailing wind that it constantly screeched like chalk on a blackboard! A horror sound for me!

It was then impressive to see the vastness of the receding water. Where yesterday there were waves crashing against the rocks, there was now brown mud and clay-like ground. Where the water had first receded, the ground was firm and dry; but further out, the ground resembled a rusty-brown sheet of ice on which one was in constant danger of slipping. I preferred not to risk that now, as you could still see the bruises from the fall in Lunenburg on my thigh. I therefore only ventured halfway out into the vastness of the sea. But that didn't stop Knuffi from getting a brown nose and me from getting my feet wet like in my childhood days.

This was the first prank! The second was called **"Scot's Bay"**. For this I had to go back almost to Canning and take the #358 several kilometres northwards. There was a small provincial park in the village that made the pebbly bay accessible. When I arrived, the water was still very far out, but it rolled over more and more powerfully while I was talking to a Polish immigrant in my mother tongue. The point of contact was, as so often, the dogs (he had a black pug with him) and then we chatted for over half an hour about Canada, the work situation in Nova Scotia, the USA and God and the world. It was so nice, as if we had known each other forever.

I couldn't and didn't want to get to the top of **Cape Split**. For one thing, there was still a hiking trail of seven(!) easy kilometres to conquer at the end of the road; and for another, the car park was so full of excursionists that there was certainly nothing left of the romantic wilderness described. I turned around without getting out and drove via **Wolfville** to **Grand Pre**, the "national shrine" of the Acadians.

A slender fieldstone church commemorates the Acadians, who were forcibly expelled between 1755 and 1763. They had settled here since 1680 and reclaimed usable land from the sea by building seawalls. Of course, a statue of Evangeline, a bust of her storyteller Harry W. Longfellow and a memorial to the expulsion were not to be missed in the small open-air museum. In the little church, the story of her deportation had been illustrated in several paintings.

We drove out to the beach, hoping for a parking space! No chance: overnight ban! An eternally long search in Wolfville… Every parking space was banned or only accessible with a pass. Not even on the university campus were there unrestricted parking spaces. As nice as the town appeared, we couldn't be bothered with it today. We drove several kilometres back to the Walmart in **New Minas** and here we are now standing undisturbed. It might get a bit noisy around us today, after all it is the eve of Labour Day, and the young people are celebrating. Well, then we'll sleep a little longer tomorrow morning... Anyway, I had the opportunity to check my mails and write some important letters. The first battery on my tiny device still does the job.

 Private remarks

359

September 1st, Labour Day
Glooscap Trail

The night in the car park was more peaceful than expected. At eleven o'clock the young people had had enough of their "Remmidemmi" and from then on it was quiet. So, we slept into the holiday until eight. There was no hurry because it had rained lightly. How far would we get today? What would the day bring? On the plan we had the continuance of the Evangeline Trail around Minas Basin and its extension.

The route is called the **Glooscap Trail** and has a stylised Indian as its symbol. In Mi'kmaq beliefs, Glooscap is the most powerful god figure with a creative and teaching function. According to legend, he created Minas Basin with a stroke of his paddle while hunting beaver. He led people to knowledge, but also punished those who harmed the community. He taught the people the existential basics like fishing, hunting and farming.

Our first port of call was the remains of *Fort Edwards* in **Windsor** where the green ramparts and the oldest log cabin in Nova Scotia are still standing. What did I discover on the plaque with the description? A cross link to Scotland (the Isle of Skye). The saviour of Bonnie Prince Charlie, Flora Macdonald lived here with her husband for some time after the ungrateful prince failed to contact her. She later moved back to her homeland, where she is also buried. I can still remember visiting her grave memorial two years ago in the pouring rain.

Fort Edward has the sad history of being one of the main assembly points during the deportation of the Acadians in 1755. The old wooden building itself dates back to 1750, so it has surpassed the old tavern in Annapolis by a few years in age. If we had driven a few kilometres further yesterday, we could easily have spent the night next to the fort.

Windsor is small but has two beautiful historic houses to visit. In former times, the small town was prosperous and famous for its shipbuilding, and they sold high quality sailboats all over the world. Almost nothing remains from the past, as is the case almost everywhere in Nova Scotia.

A short excursion: once a blessed province with trade and agriculture, today only about one million inhabitants live around the coast. You can tell from looking at these little houses by the roadside that these inhabitants are not spoiled with wealth (especially in the north). In fact, many of them lack the financial means to keep them alive at all. Understandably, the young people go to Alberta to work in the oil fields because there is a lack of work here. The older people are left behind, living on a meagre basic pension, and paying no taxes to the state. Subsequently, the provinces also lack money for social services and various government services.

My search for lighthouses continued north, around the bay of the *Avon River*. It was silted up now because the tide was out. It's interesting how far the water recedes here. I was able to capture a shot of such a wrung-out river later.

After a good 40 kilometres, I arrived at *Walton Lighthouse*. Once again, a picturesque spot – without water! During our lunch break, water came rushing into the bay. I read on a sign that the speed of the incoming water masses can be around 20km/h, depending on the nature of the ground and the natural obstacles.

It was not very far to the *Burntcoat Head Lighthouse*. The descent of the route was very badly signposted and only after a

U-turn did I find the right way. This lighthouse was even more romantically situated than the previous one, but the hope of spending another night here also failed, as before: "No Overnight!" Despite the fact that it was already a little late, we made our rounds and observed the rapid change in the water level. I preferred not to take the dogs onto the slippery rocks, which of course caused Wurschtel to protest most vehemently. All those present were amused by his behaviour but I was rather embarrassed.

Having found nowhere far and wide where we could lay our heads for free tonight, my last hope was the little *Lawrence Museum* in **Maitland** with its car park. I had the right nose, no prohibition sign! Much more interesting: right next door was the "River Runners" company, for which I have booked tomorrow. I'll tell you what it's all about on Tuesday, if for whatever reason I'm still able to do so in the evening. Good night for today! I'm dog-tired and I can't wait to lie down.

Tidal Bore

On the *Shubenacadie River* near Maitland, you can not only watch the Tidal Bore, but also ride it. You board the boats at low tide and ride upstream with the tide. Where there are sandbanks at low tide, the enormous suction effect of the river narrowing creates rapids and whirlpools, which rafting companies take advantage of. You ride up the river with the tide, so to speak, in the opposite direction. The sailors ride right through the front of the waves, finding the appropriate rapids along the way to get the adrenaline pumping. The "River Runners" at Maitland were such an undertaking.
(www.tidalborerafting.com)

During high tide, water is forced into a river course and a wave or several waves are created that run against the direction

362

of flow of the river and whose water level deflections are above the still water level.

The extreme form, the flood surge or bore, is observed in only a few places worldwide. It is restricted to areas where the tidal range is particularly large. Certain tides and estuarine forms can favour its formation. Boren can either occur as a single breaking wave or be followed by several smaller waves. Larger ones can be dangerous for shipping, but also pose a challenge for surfers.

Since I would only be here once in my life and this natural spectacle is not often witnessed on earth, I joined in this afternoon for 75.- CAD! The flood would start around 4pm and we had to show up one hour before.

Equipped with the oldest trousers and T-shirts, as well as aged shoes, we were put into yellow protective jackets and wrapped with red life jackets. The zodiacs were much smaller than those used for whale-watching, so there were only seven of us on board, plus a charming female boatman.

Unfortunately, there are no photos of our own of this venture, as a waterproof camera would have been necessary. The pictures in this report come from the advertising brochure and from the employees of the company. However, if I am lucky, I will soon receive an email with pictures taken by the boatman from the other boat. They will then be forwarded.

As the senior member of the group, I asked for a place further back in the boat. There I wouldn't get the full shower from the waves, but it was still enough to totally soak me: the brown water drenched through even the smallest opening of the protective jacket. It was a fantastic experience to ride the waves and I didn't regret the investment. But after two hours, the up and down and all around was completely enough for me and I was wet down to my underwear. At around six o'clock it also started to get chilly and in the wet clothes you started to freeze. The service on site, however, was great. There were hot showers to rinse off the brown residue and hot drinks to warm you up.

You could really see that the boatmen were enjoying the trip immensely this time. We were alone on the river with three boats and an empty safety boat. Thanks to the past Labour Day and the end of the holidays, the number of people interested in taking part in the trip had suddenly dwindled. Where there were usually thirty boats, there were just the four of us in action. Of course, we could lunge, slow down in a sharp bend and then throw ourselves unhindered into the waves. Screaming and yelling was the result.

Now I've experienced that adventure too, just as I parasailed on a beach in Mexico back in the day. I enjoyed it each time and I know what it feels like. Although I won't become a fan of any of these sports, one must accept every offer at our age.

For tonight, I'm sitting on yesterday's museum hill again. In the morning I went to a WALMART in Truro, 40 kilometres away, to buy new credentials for my Canadian mobile phone. It was one of the rare WALMART Markets with an overnight ban emblazoned on it. Moreover, the internet annoyed me so much that I wasted more than an hour (and precious battery) on technology without getting any results, and turned back without having achieved anything, so to speak.

Yes, by the way, you don't have to show up at the Interpretive Centre for the Tidal Bore. You must pay a five-dollar fee to get onto the bridge that slides into the river. As it was low tide, this money would go down the drain! However, it was exhilarating to watch some youngsters having their own personal sledding party on the loamy ridge. They may not have looked bad afterwards!

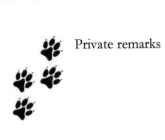 Private remarks

Truro

The weather didn't have much to offer this morning and so we left our convenient campsite at around 9am. We didn't take the short route to Truro this time but drove the slightly larger loop on #215. I had two destinations in mind: firstly, the big elephant (excuse me, the mammoth) which was supposed to indicate dinosaur finds; and secondly the Indian Glooscap, after whom the road had been named.

I missed the first target and found no primeval animal far and wide! Either I didn't have my eyes open properly or the signposting was really bad. The Indian and the Heritage Centre of the Mi'kmaq could be seen from far away at exit #13 of the motorway. I wanted to look for a drum as a souvenir, as I imagined it would look quite decorative next to my other figurines in the living room but the selection was too small for me and the price a bit too high. I just picked up a map of Truro at the information desk because I wanted to have a look at the tree sculptures.

We were able to stop in front of a supermarket in the centre and had Queen's Street and Princes' Street with several desired spots right in front of us. Not so long ago, the city fathers had the glorious idea of having artists sculpt dead trees as historical monuments.

In the oppressive heat, all three of us wandered down the two streets with our tongues hanging out. To be honest, the sculptures were not really to my taste. I found it particularly disturbing that they had been covered with a sandstone-coloured coating and thus lost all tree character. Only the root foundation was recognizable.

In this sultry weather, *Victoria Park* was the best place for us, I thought, and I found my way there relatively quickly. Excellent! A large car park without an overnight ban! Worth considering if the Walmart doesn't want us. During our lunch break it started to pour. This finally cleared the atmosphere, and we could enjoy a breath of fresh air here.

This morning I had changed the bed linen and the soiled clothes from yesterday were also waiting to be treated. On our tour, I had discovered a laundromat. I played poker: if there was a free parking space nearby, I would start the big wash. If not, we would drive to the next campsite. Finally the dirty laundry had won the poker game. We had a free parking space at our disposal! I therefore devoted the next three hours to five loads of laundry: I had "only" been collecting for almost four weeks…

Shortly after five o'clock everything was fresh in the cupboard again, this time even washed in hot water! Now we had plenty of time to look for the vantage point on the Tidal Bore. The incoming tidal wave in the opposite direction of the river should be particularly easy to observe here. We immediately found the small road near the motorway. The viewpoint was next to an abandoned motel, a bit off the #2 to Maitland. And… with a large, unobstructed car park.

I asked a few locals how safe it was here, and they eased my concerns. I could stay here overnight without any problems. Then why go back to the park, I said to myself. We sat and waited. The show would start at half past seven. First, more and more people came and then the tidal wave rolled in, right on time. It wasn't very high, but it was very fast, considering the way it crawled up the river (or more accurately, galloped). The water birds had fun and let themselves drift with it. I had my fun too because I managed to capture the spectacle of nature on film. The weather had its fun because the clouds had cleared and there was pure sunshine. The sun had its fun because it could offer us a fabulous sunset… fun for everyone!

Now all three of us are sitting or lying around tired in our corners. It's already getting dark shortly after eight o'clock, so the evenings are getting longer again within our own four walls. If we don't oversleep tomorrow, I can witness the spectacle once more. According to the local tide calendar, the wave comes again at 8.06 am, after the tide has gone out during the night.

The battery on my laptop is just enough to proofread. Tomorrow I urgently need to recharge it in a campsite – after four nights off!

Not without my lighthouse …

Our sleeping place turned out to be trouble-free and with breakfast we were prepared for the morning tidal wave. At this time of day, there were nowhere near as many spectators as last night. There was a dense morning fog over the river, but unfortunately the sun did not manage to dissipate it in time. Still, I think the Tidal Bore fog-picture is meaningful to the overall mood after all.

It was time to stock up on food, dog food and petrol before we set off on new explorations. The next seventy kilometres on the #2 were not particularly exciting, but wonderful to drive in glorious sunshine. Here a bit of forest, there a small peaceful village and every now and then a view of the *Bay of Fundy*, which did not shine sea-blue but clay-brown towards us – a nice contrast to the bright blue sky, the green of the trees and the colours of the Indian summer.

We stopped for lunch at **Five Islands PP**. According to Indian legend, when Glooscap threw a handful of earth at a beaver, he created the five islands off the coast. The park has a miserable access road at the moment, but the picnic benches are close to the water and at low tide you can walk extensively and far on the seabed. In addition, there are some hiking trails with magnificent views for sporty lovers. We ourselves only climbed a few metres and already had a wonderful overview.

After a short lunch break with half a kilo of strawberries from the farmers' market and the accompanying portion of (calorie-reduced!) whipped cream, we ventured out to the sea-bed once more. This time it was also muddy and wet, but not as slippery as in the first attempt in Blomidon. It was amazing and fascinating to see how far the sea had receded. Quite a few stone seekers were out trying their luck in semi-precious stones.

My next destination was a suitable campsite for tonight. After four days, I needed electricity again for my various batteries and urgently had to get online to finally charge my mobile phone; I also had to do some paperwork.

There was not much choice: the PP had no electricity and Wi-Fi, the "Diamond Shores" no Wi-Fi since yesterday – so we were left with the expensive "Five Islands RV Resort". We have full hook-up, that is, water, electricity and sewage connection, good internet and right on the water too. But we had to pay 41.- CAD for it. I really need a day without action again. I'll let the weather decide tomorrow whether we want and will afford the luxury of an extra day. Oh yes, lighthouse! I almost forgot, the Five Islands Lighthouse! Here you go! Maybe a few more atmospheric pictures of the nightfall...?

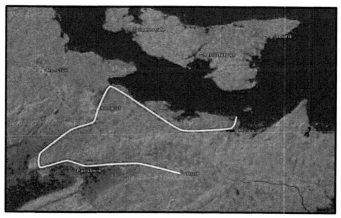

Nova Scotia - Finale

 Private remarks

Short – and even shorter

After our daily stages had almost never exceeded 70 kilometres lately, we broke the record today. We covered just 25 kilometres on the odometer. But not without reason: once again I had slept miserably during the night, or rather not at all until around 2am. Out of sheer desperation, I talked to an employee of the telephone company via the "chat line" to get some problems out of the way or to have them explained to me: it was really entertaining. I wonder if they always use "night owls" who have an open ear even at impossible hours for cases like mine. Around half past three I got some rest and of course woke up in the morning with double bags under my eyes.

Being tired, I didn't feel the need to move around too much on the road. However, paying for the expensive campsite again went against the grain for me. I took care of all the necessary emails and used the hoover for a short time after breakfast. My room was in dire need of it.

Finally, it was time for a shower. It was bad enough that I had to pay so much for the showers – more than ever before! – and none of them worked! Maybe I was angry… There I was in my Eva costume, wanting to wash my hair and not a drop came out! I returned to the camper van without having achieved anything, dressed only in a makeshift outfit. After all, I had to check out at eleven o'clock.

But instead of offering me another solution, the lady at the reception only apologized and pointed out that I only had five minutes until the hour in another shower! As if she could not have delayed the check-out time under these circumstances. I would like to stress that this was the first money-grubbing campsite I had encountered on the entire trip. They even had higher prices for card payment, which was a first too. Therefore, hands off the "Five Islands Resort"!

Out of sheer anger, I overlooked the turnoff to yesterday's lighthouse and was on the direct route to **Parrsboro**. I wanted to settle down at the Lighthouse for the rest of the day and relax. Well, not then! Parrsboro also has its lighthouse – but only accessible at low tide! Almost directly in the centre of the small community there was a large open space by the river. I took advantage of it, fired up my hot water system and took a wonderful and long shower in the middle of town! I had saved some water... If only people sometimes knew what goes on in a camper van! Well, the blow-dry had to be cancelled, because the necessary power was too high even for the generator. But with the wonderful weather, my hair dried very quickly.

Now I was feeling better again, at least mentally. Physically, I still felt like a giant marshmallow – soggy, soft and chewy. I guess the best thing was a walk along the harbour with the Wuffis at "half" low tide. Nevertheless, you could already see the desolation of the little ships as they vegetated on the ropes without water. I got into conversation with a couple of nice amateur fishermen – father and son – who, to my credit, re-membered their German. Both had been stationed in the army in Germany. At the end, I had a piece of paper in my hands with a name and an email address: "Just for an update ..."!

A short nap on the beach, a short lunch as well. In the mean-time, we could almost walk to the lighthouse on dry feet. But we drove to the *Ottawa House* on another beach, after the "newcomers" had recommended it. A wonderful double bay opened in front of us, with a small island off the coast (Par-tridge Island). The two beaches and the hinterland of the is-land are a paradise for stone collectors. Again and again, there are interesting finds of minerals and semi-precious stones. I also stocked up on them as souvenirs, but not laboriously sto-len from the beach; I bought them for a cheap price in a small "rock and mineral shop and museum" on the way there. It was funny that they calculated my treasures by weight, using an ancient scale that must have served earlier gold miners reliably. One pound for 4.03 CAD incl. tax… Maybe they would need a little polishing and grinding?

I also wanted to see the inside of the stately *Ottawa House*. The ground floor serves as a meeting room for literary and musical events. A thoroughly winning atmosphere, I thought to myself. On the upper floor, all kinds of memorabilia from the former owners have been collected. There is almost no reminder that when it was built in 1775, there was once an important shipyard on the beach in front of the house. The Ottawa House stood at a busy junction of two important connecting roads and was also accessible by rail: some pictures prove this. Later, it was converted into a hotel with 21 rooms, until one of the Canadian Premiers chose it as holiday home.

The next item on the programme was the geological museum with its information centre. Two friendly ladies let me into the museum without admission because it would close in 45 minutes anyway, but I had enough time to learn about the prehistoric finds and the fossils. Not far from here, at *Wasson Bluff*, fossilised dinosaur footprints have been found and a whole lot of fossils. Normally you are allowed to look over the shoulders of the scientists at work in the museum but today they had already gone home. Well, if the museum were to close, no one would ask who occupies the RV space. Tomorrow I will be the first visitor!

Weather change

Now I finally had it, the fog over Fundy Bay! Until then, I almost didn't believe the reports about this part of the country. Never mind, we've had so many wonderful days and the gloomy mood won't last forever. We were up early and on the road before the museum opened. Finally, we were "rounding the bend" of Nova Scotia. Oh, it's wonderful when you're fully rested again. First, we were looking for three lighthouses in our corner: we found all three of them, one even with a scary story on site.

The lighthouse stood right at the water, also protecting a shipyard and telling the story of the ghost ship "Mary Celeste".

On November 7th 1872, this ship set sail from New York, destined for Genoa, with a cargo of 1,100 bottles of pure alcohol. On board were the captain's wife, his two-year-old daughter and seven crew members. Twenty-seven days later, on December 4th, the Mary Celeste was discovered adrift in the North Atlantic, near Spencer's Island. Irritated by the motionlessness and the uncontrolled course of the ship, the captain of the second ship boarded the schooner: they discovered nothing there but abandonment. The Mary Celeste was not damaged; there were no signs of piracy. The doors and windows were unlocked, the quarters of the captain and his crew seemed untouched. Coats hung on their hooks, tobacco lay handy for smoking on the tables and items laid scattered around. The captain, his family and crew had disappeared without a trace. Two sailors brought the ship to Gibraltar without finding a solution to the mystery. There were several hearings and investigations and all sorts of assumptions were made, but the captain, his wife and the crew remained missing. For ten more years, the Mary Celeste sailed the North Atlantic, but it was always haunted by misfortune.

The ship's owners had their problems hiring seamen for the ghost ship. Then in 1885, the ship ran aground in Haiti. It is a pity that the plaque from which I took this story said nothing about the whereabouts of the alcohol. Was it still on board or had it also disappeared? How many more drunkenness offences were there in the area? Were the many bottles also untouched?

The third lighthouse was the jewel box among the three. It stood on a rocky promontory in the middle of the sea, washed by mighty waves and flanked by steep, erosion-damaged cliffs. At **Cape d'Or Lighthouse**, three different ocean currents meet and gnaw at the rock with all their power, aided by the powerful energy of the tides. The lighthouse keeper has a few rooms available for rent, not all with en-suite bathrooms of course. A wonderfully romantic place, in fine weather just as it is today with wind, fog and drizzle. We set off, circled the area, and puffed our way up again.

Now we were scraping the big bend to the north. Sixty kilometres of country road with only forest and almost no human habitation. Several times I found myself letting my thoughts wander and daydreaming through the monotony. Not entirely without danger! The volume of traffic was so low that I could count my encounters on the fingers of both hands. Somehow it really did me good to see small houses again and the structure of villages.

It's interesting that 40 kilometres south of **Amherst** you find the *Joggins Fossil Cliffs*. Thousands of fossils from the Carboniferous period (about 350 to 280 million years ago) have already been discovered in these sea cliffs, which were declared a UNESCO World Heritage Site in 2008. Most of them are plant finds, but an entire forest of upright fossilised tree stumps has made the site famous. They contained the fossilised remains of "Hylonomus", the earliest reptile ever found.

The energy-efficient and environmentally oriented centre offers several guided tours, from half an hour (included in the entrance fee) to several hours. For me, the thirty minutes was enough in the bad weather. Besides, I'm not a geologist and have enormous problems distinguishing rocks from boulders or recognising fossils in them. If I have it pointed out to me, it tends to work out though! I was not afraid to bring up this problem and lo and behold, I was not the only one among the fourteen participants! It's just that no one dared to admit what a greenhorn they were... The museum itself was also excellently prepared and cleverly arranged. It was well worth seeing, even if you don't know much about the subject. After all, the cliffs walk you back three hundred million years in the history of the Earth. Unimaginable dimensions... we were travelling at "half" low tide and the water receded much further in the course of time. The famous tree stumps were still under water at the moment, and you had to hike quite a distance to the spot. Something for enthusiasts!

Thinker's Lodge

The day started as it ended yesterday: rainy... But at least it was dry when we set off at about 9am. I quickly took care of the drinking water supplies and put myself on the safe side with the petrol. As an aside, I asked the cashier if there was any way I could refill my propane in the area. It had now been a good month since the last (dripping wet) fill-up in Halifax and

I had very often done free camping. Yes, just around the corner, at the laundry… I thought I had misheard. Laundry? What have they got to do with propane?

Slightly sceptical, I followed the directions. If it failed, the world wouldn't end. I was sure I had several litres left in the tank. Indeed! Behind the laundry there was a large propane tank with matching equipment. And the owner was already about to leave for the day – mind you: today was Sunday! I had thus completed the first problem-free propane procurement in months! Unbelievable! I was there with 23 litres, about half the capacity. Now I would easily make it to the border crossing into the USA.

I set off on the **Sunrise Trail** – yes, towards the sunrise. The route lived up to its name: the sun was going up higher and higher. The road ran beautifully through the wide marshland that the Acadians had made fertile with their dykes. In between, the sea shone deep blue and the red colour of the rocks and the beaches contributed to a harmony of colours. Within a few kilometres there were three provincial parks to explore. The first, **Tidnish Dock PP**, provided me with domestic water and was situated on a rather rocky bay with annoying mosquitoes. The name comes from the fact that here, at low tide, you can still see a railway station that was once intended for an ambitious project. At the time, the tide was still too high.

The second park **(Amherst Shore PP)** had closed its day area and only opened the campground. This was on the other side of the road and several metres away from the bay, so we turned around without stopping.

In the third park **(Northport Beach PP)** we had our long lunch break. We wouldn't get to Pictou today anyway, so it didn't matter how and where we spent our Sunday. The weather was perfect. The tide had gone out, gradually revealing the beach and its red sandbanks. We went for a long walk, of course before I enjoyed my lunch outside, watched closely by my four-legged friends to see if any of the chicken leg would fall. Unfortunately, mistress wouldn't let that happen under any circumstances, because Wurschtel had diarrhoea again and made a mess of several carpets in the camper during the journey. He had tried to tell me, but unfortunately, I hadn't understood… Accordingly I got the receipt and had to pay the bill!

Where did the time go? It was half past three again. We would only make it as far as **Pugwash** before we had to find a place to stay for the night. I'm not very politically engaged; I've never heard of this place and its significant charisma. Well, I read a little about it in my guidebooks and wanted to see the place with its salt mines and the *Thinker's Lodge*. If the place might be known to anyone, it would be by the term *Pugwash Conference on Science and World Affairs*. The first of these was held at Pugwash after Albert Einstein suggested a meeting in 1955 to discuss the dangers of a nuclear war.

Cyrus Eaton, a wealthy US industrialist, offered to sponsor the meeting – on the condition that it took place in his hometown in Nova Scotia. So it came to pass that in 1957 thirteen nuclear scientists from Cold War countries (including three from the USSR) met in what later became Thinker's Lodge, a large but otherwise rather inconspicuous residence on the Pugwash coast. Some participants were billeted in the neighbourhood, some were given rooms in the house, and some were allowed to stay in comfortable sleeping car compartments of the railway company.

All in all, it seemed more like a casual "class reunion" than an Earth-shattering gathering. The relaxed atmosphere did much to promote a willingness to talk. A big contribution was also made by Cyrus' wheelchair-user wife, who was responsible for the comfort of the guests and unobtrusively organised everything from dinner to afternoon coffee.

How do I know these little background details? Once again, I had the luck of the clueless. We arrived at the house and walked around the place. There wasn't much to see. Let's see if the door is open. It is! Dogs into the camper, Monika into the house!

"Sorry, we are already closed due to the end of the season! But you are welcome to have a look around!" Thankful, I made my rounds and found some interesting documents. A friendly woman approached me and invited me to a cup of tea. Why should I refuse? It's just another long night! I had no idea then that it could be a really long one.

"Oh no! I'll show you the house first, if you want…"! You bet I do! Private tour! I learned a lot of details about this conference, the reproduction of which would go beyond the scope of this article. For anyone interested, the internet should be a treasure trove. It was fascinating to learn what an open mind Cyrus Eaton was and what energy was in his will for peace. I became more and more fascinated by this personality who even received the Lenin Peace Prize from the Russian President – the Russian equivalent of the Nobel Peace Prize. Josef Rotblat, one of the mentors of the movement, also received this prize in 1955. For the first time in my life, I discovered the existence of this award.

On the veranda where the most powerful people in the world moved, I was now allowed to enjoy tea with three other ladies, with a magnificent view of the Northumberland Strait. The dogs were welcome and could roam freely in the house and garden. The house was being cleaned, as the premises had been rented out to a wedding party over the weekend. Scientific conferences on peace and environmental policy are also held here from time to time. Unfortunately, the original buildings were partly destroyed in a fire in 1996, but the surrounding neighbours were able to save a lot of furniture and valuable objects. Now, apart from the house for the staff, the two houses have all been newly renovated, including the former lobster factory, which was later used as a dining hall.

We had an amusing conversation on the veranda about my travels, about working in this museum and the spirit inherent in this site. For me, these encounters were not pure coincidence. There was more to the whole afternoon for me – but I cannot define what.

Evening was approaching and as we were about to leave, one of the ladies offered me the option of either staying with her on the property or in the courtyard driveway of Thinker's Lodge. It should be clear which I chose!

As a farewell, I was handed a banana cake. It had been for the company and had been left over. I waited a while until everyone present had left the property and then sat down in the entrance arch. As a precaution, I found a letter stuck in the windscreen granting me overnight accommodation on the property if someone complained.

Now the MoWuKnuffels are sleeping and moving, from 7th to 8th September 2014, in an area where the most powerful people in the world met not so long ago and personalities like Yuri Gagarin stayed. After all, it is my very own still living age (year of birth 1951) and not distant grey past.

The participants' efforts to avert a worldwide catastrophe through a turnaround in political thinking did indeed find a continuation in follow-up conferences and further negotiations. The focus is still on weapons of mass destruction, but the range of topics has broadened – abolition of international borders, environmental policy, economic prosperity…

 Private remarks

Plugwash, NS – Thinker's Lodge

Private remarks

The next morning

Somehow, I felt like saying goodbye! A cloudless sky woke us up. We couldn't wait to see the friendly lady from yesterday and so we set off at about nine o'clock. Today we went a little criss-cross through the countryside. We made our first stop after a short while at the **Gulf Shore PP**, as Wurschtel was starting to get annoying, and I didn't want to clean up again, so we did another morning round there in a stormy breeze and only eleven degrees air temperature. The reddish beach was still very narrow and the waves quite violent. After the walk for Wurschtel happened without any visible success, we climbed back into our camper, freezing. Don't you dare! Something could still happen…

Tatamagouche was our next stop. I was interested in the museum of a giantess who toured the world with a famous circus. Unfortunately, the museum was only open on Saturdays and Sundays – end of season! Well, let's have a look at the railway hotel. In this small town, the abandoned railway station and its trains have been given a new purpose and turned into an "Inn". The restaurant is in the dining car, and the individual carriages each have two sleeping flats. The waiting hall became a cosy breakfast room, the ticket hall a souvenir shop: the whole affair had a fabulous character.

From now on, the road led us a few kilometres inland to **Balmoral**. There was a small *Provincial Park, Balmoral Grist Mill*, with a former flour mill as a museum. It is very picturesquely situated on a stream and was operated by waterpower for a long time. It was only towards the end of its active life that it was connected to the electrical grid. Although it is still operational with its old equipment, it is only set in motion for demonstration purposes.

While one lady explained the entire technology, the grinding process and the complicated construction, another employee took care of my two dogs, because they were not allowed inside the old walls. The woman was grateful for this task, because it made it easier for her to wait for possible other museum visitors and Wurschtel was distracted from his diarrhoea.

Pictou didn't offer much in the way of a harbour, so we drove straight to **Caribou**, where the ferry to PEI (short for Prince Edward Island) was leaving. The next departure was scheduled for a quarter to three. We had plenty of time for a long lunch break in the queue until the boat left. The crossing time was 75 minutes. You only pay on the return journey. If you take the Confederation Bridge, you save a few dollars, because the ferry is more expensive than the bridge toll.

One last look at the harbour from the ship and we happily closed the next chapter of our round trip in bright sunshine. We'll see you again in the next travel report!

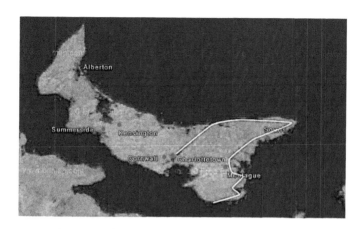

PEI or P.E.I. or Prince-Edward-Island
East Costal Drive

 Private remarks

Prince Edward Island

The welcoming committee was ready and waiting when our ferry docked at *Wood Island harbour* on PEI at 4pm. A large flock of cormorants had gathered for our arrival! After unloading, we first headed for the *Wood Islands lighthouse*. Proud and far-sighted, it sits enthroned on a small meadow plateau with plenty of room to run around. We made good use of this, of course, after my two mice had been incarcerated in the camper van for almost two hours.

Well, then! Where do we start? On the boat I had studied the guidebooks a bit and found out that there are not too many places of interest around here. The main attractions in this province are the beautiful beaches, agriculture and cattle breeding. Culture and history have taken second place.

So let's drive counter clockwise along the coast. There are several provincial parks with camping facilities and developed sandy beaches. We followed the route with the starfish, called *East Coastal Drive*. It was getting close to the time when we would have to start preparing for our night's lodging. We tried a few detours from the main route, but they led nowhere. Then we were successful: *Cape Bear lighthouse* welcomed us with the sign: "Sorry, we're closed!" This was very convenient for us as hardly anyone would show up at this time of day. The road to the bay was a little narrow, but we were alone in the open. Once again a lighthouse gave us nightly accommodation, directly on a small cliff. As the full moon rose and the waves of the incoming tide glittered silver in a starry sky, the evening mood became perfect. When I looked through my window from my bed, I saw directly into the water, without an obstacle. It was as if I were floating on the shimmering waves.

391

The young man and the sea

After a restful and quiet night, we continued north under clear skies. Let's see how far we get today. In retrospect, I'm not sure whether it was worth all the winding around the individual bays, or whether it wouldn't have made more sense to head straight for the individual destinations. As a first-time visitor to the island, one was always concerned about missing something.

My first stop today was the port of **Gaspereaux**. Why that one in particular? No idea! My gut sent me there. It was a friendly little fishing port for local fishing. I asked a young man about the fish caught and he told me that it was mostly herring and mackerel. Tonight he had finally been lucky again and would take home a good catch. For eight nights in a row he had returned to the harbour without any results. However, he could not tell me what circumstances caused such failures. It must be frustrating to spend eight consecutive nights without earning a penny. Here, too, the regulation of fishing quotas forces every fisherman to take on a second job to make a living. The economic situation is just as miserable as in Newfoundland or Nova Scotia. But here at least agriculture still flourished.

Panmure Island was our next destination. Once again, a proud lighthouse adorned the end of this peninsula with a narrow but kilometre-long red sand beach. Narrow perhaps because it was still high tide.

Buffaloes on PEI? There was indeed a park with bison not far from our last stop. We had to see them, of course. *Buffalo PP* was not very well signposted, but when we had almost missed the animals, I spotted the entrance. I turned around and took my camera. These huge animals came quite close to the fence and I left my two "warning signals" in the car: they would be allowed to let off steam later.

I took the direct route to **Montague** and **Lower Montague**. I wanted to find out what was behind the beaver (National Historic Site) on my map. Both guides were silent about it. We came across a dirt road to a place where three rivers came together. It was one of the first settlements of a French merchant on PEI – interesting perhaps for school children and their local history knowledge. The log cabin with a kitchen has been reconstructed and a few information boards have been put up at the excavations. Cosy for walking and squirrel hunting, so not particularly exciting…

I was more interested in the strange buoys in the river and the even stranger ship. When asked, I was told that these were mussel beds and that the ship was harvesting mussels with its special construction. It was a nice quiet setting and just right for our lunch break. I didn't want to rush, so I took a nap for an hour after lunch, as usual. We would arrive somewhere this evening!

We continued driving a long arc around **Cardigan Bay**, without much contact with the Atlantic. The whole stretch of coast was shielded from the coast by cornfields and other agricultural fields. As I said here I saw fewer run-down houses than in Nova Scotia. Each property was surrounded by a large plot of carefully manicured and trimmed lawn. Stables were always well away from the dwelling units, and one saw a well-stocked machinery park set up around them. We 're finally here! A harbour for the night wouldn't be bad, I thought! I

393

didn't like the first one at **Cardigan Point**. The second attempt was **Annandale Harbour**.

What was that cluster of people doing at the gallows? That's when I saw it: they were about to hang a huge tuna! But by the time I had slowed down, grabbed my camera, switched my lights off and jumped out, they had already laid the fish on the ground!

Nevertheless, it was very interesting to see how this huge specimen was handled. They even used a chainsaw to decapitate it. Wasn't it Hemingway with his "old man and the sea" who had lost the fight against a tuna? (No! – against a marlin) This young man here had won it. He showed me the not-so-massive fishing rod and the relatively small barb to which the fish had succumbed.

Three men were busy cleaning it, gutting it and packing it. Then the huge animal was put on ice as quickly as possible and loaded into a container for removal. Some joker offered us the heart of the animal and even bit into the raw meat. Along with some of the other spectators, I refused the possibility of having such a "yummy" breakfast. Yuck!

With the spectacle, it naturally turned into early evening and I asked the lucky guy if it was possible to spend the night here in the small harbour. Absolutely no problem! The Lord probably gives it to his own in his sleep… we can save the camping fees once again. However, I urgently need to dispose of the waste tomorrow and treat myself to a little luxury. After five days of free accommodation, that's probably appropriate. The harbour master stopped by briefly and officially allowed me my pitch. Nice people, here too…

Private remarks

Take a break!

When I woke up this morning, I had the urgent need to put the control stick aside for a little longer. So, without further ado, I decided to take a full day of rest. The sky was pleasantly clear and we continued our journey directly from Annandale to **Red Point PP**, with a stopover for emails at "Tim Horton" in **Souris.**

Staying one night at a Provincial Park was too short for me. I would be stressed again with all the preparations for the next day. No, we wanted to treat ourselves to a full beach day and just laze around. You wouldn't believe how exhausting it is to have to take care of everything yourself on a trip like this. If you are tired of driving, you must cook, the dogs whine for exercise and food, the inside of the camper looks like under Hempel's bed (as we say in German), the windows are more blind than transparent, the dust overlays the colour of the dashboard… Do I still have enough fuel, propane or water? What does my further route look like? What do the travel guides say? Don't I urgently need to go online again? … And then I sit at the laptop for up to two/three hours in the evening to write the travel reports and edit the pictures … Some people call that a holiday! So, now I hope that each of my letters gets the right appreciation!

Red Point PP is right by the sea with a small firm sandy beach that doubles in width at low tide. The season is over, and it is easy to get a place. Tonight, there'll be ten of us guests with a capacity of a hundred. It is a little elevated on the cliffs with steps to the beach. There are many sunny meadow pitches, and they charge a moderate price: 30.- CAD/night with electricity and water, including hot shower and free waste disposal. Some other money-grubbing campsites should take a lesson from this. We arrived here late in the morning and could therefore enjoy the full afternoon in the sun and on the

397

beach. The water is so warm that I can easily wade in it; swimming would probably be too cold for me.

Now it is sunset and countless seagulls are looking for food on the lawn. It looks like Hitchcock's "The Birds", only here they are white and don't attack the camper vans. Any event and they are suddenly up and away...

Day of rest?

Maybe tonight is just the right time to tell you a little bit about PEI, not too much, so no one gets bored!

PEI is the smallest province in Canada, only 200 km long and a maximum of 60 km wide. Thanks to its bay-rich coastline, the island has 800 km of beaches. However, one can find a variety of other stretches in the literature. Since the water here warms up to 20°C in summer, the island is a popular holiday destination among Canadians. Now that everyone has "flown" back, as school started last week and the daily work routine as well, the campsites are almost empty and usually close around September 20th or early October at the latest.

There are two connections to the mainland: one is the ferry from Caribou, which we used; and the other is the 13 km *Confederation Bridge*, which we will use on the return trip. Of course, the transfer costs money, but you only pay when you leave the island. Our option is the slightly cheaper one, because, as mentioned above, the boat is more expensive.

With about 140,000 inhabitants on 5,648 km², this province has the highest population density in Canada. Hard to believe when you drive through the more northerly areas. The majority of the population has British ancestors, only 11% speak French. About 60% of the people live in the countryside and subsist on farming and livestock. The potatoes from the red sandstone soil and the freshly caught lobster from the Atlantic are appreciated all over Canada… That must be enough! If you want further information, you can "Google" it.

Rest day with a question mark: we were able to sleep in and have breakfast in peace but that was all. Carpets were washed (Wurschtel's disaster), the windows cleaned, the fridge defrosted and cleaned, the furniture dusted, the camper vacuumed, the statistics updated, the contribution to the new car insurance for next year paid by phone and all batteries charged…

I didn't make it to the shower, because after the *siesta* and the walk by the sea, the dogs and I were hungry and the temperature outside was no longer pleasant. The morning had started with sunshine, but soon the sky got overcast and now the wind was blowing mightily here on the plateau. Thank goodness it stayed dry so I could do my so beloved housework.

We have another little gnawing guest in our home. However, the critter is highly intelligent and cunning. I set up three mousetraps, first stocked with cheese, then chocolate. Never once did I hear it snap or click, but each trap was empty when I went to check.

I have to find a solution for this tomorrow, otherwise I fear for my cables. The defective heater is probably also due to a small rodent. Since the animal is hiding somewhere behind the cooker and in the sink cupboard, my two dogs have no chance of locating it. They sometimes sniff a bit at the cupboard, but they don't really care about our flatmate. Much more interesting are the relatives in the wild…

Tomorrow we have a few more things to do in Souris and then it's on to East Coastal Drive. Good night for today… See you on the next "day of rest"!

A little refreshed going northward

Ludwig Uhland (German Poet 1787-1862): „Singe, wem Gesang gegeben!" (Not all who own a lyre are lyre-players...) – But not in the "Singing Sands". There is a stretch of beach just north of the campsite that calls itself that. We wanted to hear the sand "sing"! The dunes of **Basin Head** are known as "shifting sand dunes" not only because of their high mobility, but also because the sand here has a high silica content, so it supposedly squeaks under the soles of your shoes. The islanders call this phenomenon "singing sand."

Well, it didn't work for us. I heard absolutely nothing, no matter how hard I strained my eavesdroppers. Perhaps the loud swell and the strong blowing wind were to blame, their sounds masking the delicate plant "sand". I don't know! Maybe the sand was tired after high season and didn't feel like it any more... There was an ecological tour of the National Park on the way, but two hours was too much for me. At least it had been enough for the first morning run of my four-legged friends, because it was uncomfortably cold, cloudy and windy.

A bit chilled, we continued to the easternmost point of PEI, adorned with a (yes, that's right!) lighthouse and the hint of the end of the world! At East Point, the wind was already blowing around our ears again. Interestingly, I found the first major wind farm on my trip nearby. As much as the Canadians take care of their environment, e.g., with waste separation, I discovered very little alternative energy, although the islanders really have enough wind to take advantage of it!

The next section of road was a good 50 kilometres long and didn't have much to offer. The population became more scattered, the blueberry fields more frequent and agriculture more intensive. Of the sea, which licks the Gulf of the St. Lawrence

Current, I saw relatively little. However, I observed how the strong wind drove the clouds towards the water and the sun got its chance.

It was nice and warm in **Greenwich** at lunchtime. No, not in Great Britain! Greenwich, situated in front of a part of the PEI National Park, which adorns the northern coast in three sections. A drop of bitterness: I wasn't allowed on the beach with the dogs until October 15th. I couldn't wait that long... so instead, we walked the hiking trails far from the beach on the **St. Peter's Bay** side in a two-hour walk. It was just too wonderful outside to spend the time in the camper.

I struggled with myself. Should I spend tonight on that spot or drive the sixty kilometres to the capital **Charlottetown**? We had the well-maintained #2 as an option. Charlottetown had a WALMART for our night stay and quite a few wholesale markets for shopping. My fridge was almost empty so I opted for the latter option. However, it was already half past five when we left. We would most likely be heading into darkness. Not exactly my passion...

Shopping done, WALMART found, overnight ban discovered, dog-tired and disappointed... What to do when you don't know your way around a big city at night? I had no energy left for the campsites; they were too far outside the city. Besides, my information was not updated enough to trust it in the dark.

I decided to head back in the opposite direction. Some village would surely have a church with a car park! Heavens! Just as I turned the corner of *St Peter's Road*, I saw a chemist's shop with a large square and a fast-food takeaway in front of it. This was it! Here I could safely settle down without being disturbed. (Then the morning after I discovered that, I had ended up near a small church in a residential area). I quickly stowed all the groceries, fed the dogs, and hurriedly made myself some sandwiches. I didn't feel like cooking now at ten o'clock... As a precaution, I stretched out in bed in my tracksuit, ready to jump, because I still distrusted the unknown area. However, nobody seemed to be interested in RVs and it soon became quiet around us. I think my second foot was not yet in bed when I fell asleep and that's why I postponed the report until Saturday. Despite a long *siesta*, I was so worn out that I completed my first sleep cycle in a state of exhaustion.

 Private remarks

"Singing Sands" and shifting sand dune

Most Eastern Point of PEI

 Private remarks

Charlottetown

As expected, the night was trouble-free. I had slept like a dead woman. At some point both dogs had come to bed, but I had hardly noticed. The morning rhythm gradually roused our spirits and warmed us up. Seven degrees outside and twelve degrees in the camper were not exactly luxurious. But with washing up, preparing hot water and making tea, warmth returned to the camper and even Wurschtel stopped shivering. My God, the little guy is so sensitive to the cold! Every blanket is gratefully accepted from 15°C down!

We drove towards the city centre to the information office. There I got a good tip for a free car park nearby, a city map and internet access. I had to do some office stuff and get rid of some emails. That took more than an hour, so I released my four-legged friends in the late morning for a city walk.

Again, we were out for two full hours and saw pretty much everything historic that was outdoors. The city centre is not large and can be easily covered on foot in this amount of time. There are a few pretty and respectable mansions, many brick buildings, well-kept green spaces and a big park. However, we didn't see any cruise ships at anchor like the ones advertised in the brochures.

Two hours of sightseeing with two dogs on the leash are endurance training in high format... Tired, we reached our rolling home again. Even the dogs seemed exhausted: the many smells and the countless corners of the house all had to be marked and sniffed. Then they had to obey mistress's orders when taking photos... Almost too exhausting for a single dog's life!

All three of us treated ourselves to a hearty snack and a long nap. Afterwards we had to walk again, because I wanted to drive to the other side of the bay, where the actual fort used to stand, even before Charlottetown was founded. There are no more remains to see, but the site has well-maintained walkways, and you have an unobstructed view of the "skyline" (with only two high-rise buildings – hotels!) of Charlottetown. Although the distance as the crow flies is only a maximum of four kilometres, the road around the bay is thirty kilometres.

No sooner said than done! We walked for another good hour over terrain that has been hard fought over and seen much grief. Today, everything is peaceful and friendly.

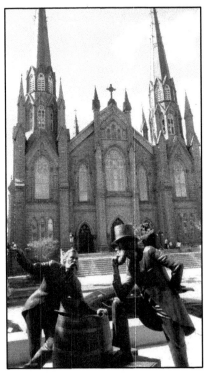

We sleep in Charlottetown by the harbour, in an abandoned free car park. I feel safe, even though I am standing here alone. Life is moving all around. It's eleven o'clock again and I haven't added any pictures yet. They will have to wait for tomorrow! I don't feel like it any more...

Charlottetown PEI - Downtown

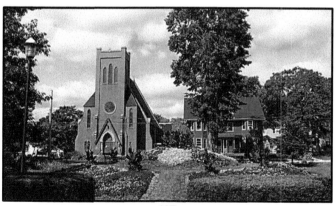

 Private remarks

PEI Nationalpark II

I had decided to stay in the inexpensive parking in Charlotte-town and to start several round trips from here, which I would otherwise not be able to fit in my plans on my entire loop. As Charlottetown is very centrally located, all my destinations could be reached in an hour or less.

For this reason, nothing pushed us to set off early and so we leisurely made our way along the #15 to **Brackley**, where the middle part of the national park was lo-cated. Here, mighty dunes, a fair amount of wind and changeable weather awaited me. Once again, my four-legged friends were not allowed to go to the beach. I didn't feel like it either, because if you're used to company, any solo trip gets boring. I quickly took some pictures and we headed towards **Dalvay** in the east, where there were a few hiking trails in the hinterland that we could explore.

On our way there was another – right! – a pretty lighthouse at a small harbour. This miniport was teeming with offers for deep-sea fishing, but most of them were "closed, due to the season being over!". Before that, however, a PP with camping saved us from being overwhelmed – they were kind enough to let me dispose of my waste free of charge. I was also able to fill up with service water again without hin-drance. That gave me room for other three or four days.

First, I wanted to do trail 1, to the bubbling spring. It was good to walk but the weather was crazy. Sometimes it drizzled, then it was dry again and later it rained uncomfortably. After one and a half hours we arrived back at the camper. After the midday rest, I really didn't feel like walking the same length of the "farmland loop". No, thanks! We therefore drove the #2 back to our harbour place.

Today I wanted to cultivate my culture a bit and visit a small theatre with the local literary idol Anne Shirley, called Anne of Green Gables. More about that tomorrow, because I won't get home before half past ten and I certainly won't be writing a travelogue then.

.

Anne of Green Gables total

Yesterday evening was a complete success and this morning even more so! During the night I had heard an inexplicable humming that came from the harbour and thought that the oil tanker would surely be in action. But no oil tanker! On my doorstep there was a handsome cruise ship waiting to disgorge its people at this time of day. Now I finally had my "pot" like the ones in the Charlottetown advertising posters! After the disposal round, the dogs were back in the camper, and I was ready to go to check out the ship. One of the security guards

even let me get close to the floating colossus. He would put a maximum of 450 passengers ashore, and the taxi drivers and several buses were already greedily waiting…

Here in Europe, the literary redhead *Anne Shirley* is hardly known. In Japan, the stories of the vital *Anne of Green Gables* are standard literature in secondary schools. In Anne Frank's novel, the book only appears briefly as a name; she was reading it in her hiding place. The creator of the lively and spirited Anne of Green Gables was *Lucy Maud Montgomery* of Cavendish in PEI, 40 km northwest of the capital. The girl is fictional and somewhat similar to our "Troublemaker" (*Trotzkopf*) and is also often compared to "Pippi Longstocking", but after reading the book at home, I would opt for the first one.

About 700,000 tourists visit the various Anne of Green Gables-related museums in and around Cavendish every year. Anne is, from a business point of view, the most important

411

tourism factor in the province of PEI. The book still sells half a million copies a year in North America alone. Every year, up to 10,000 Japanese come to Cavendish, supposedly the most popular foreign destination after New York, Paris and London.

Of course, I also visited as the 700,001st visitor to the iconic place that influenced the author's inspiration. She took her cousin's house with the "green gables" as a model and set the plots there. The whole area is now looked after by the National Trust and the building is furnished with contemporary furniture as described in the novel. It is only too understandable that I found more Japanese than Europeans on site. In all, I counted five full coaches after we showed up.

We walked the paths, so we had more than an hour and a half of movement. There would be a lot more to tell, but I don't want to bore anyone who doesn't know the story. We got home in time for me to get some food in my belly before I turned my mice into guard dogs.

As I had seen the musical "Anne and Gilbert" the night before in that very small theatre (125 seats), I treated myself to "Anne of Green Gables – the Musical" in the main theatre of the city this evening and had a lot of fun. Yesterday it was easier for me to follow the humorous dialogues because the

orchestra was only piano, cello and violin. Tonight, a full orchestra was involved; the music fluctuated between loud and classical. But the stage possibilities were of course much more varied in the small theatre. Each performance had something of its own, and I was satisfied that I was spending my money here instead of at a campsite.

Last day in Charlottetown

We didn't want to take much more advantage of the hospitable car park and this morning we set off for our last excursion. Before breakfast, however, I had to get out taking pictures, because two cruise ships from Europe arrived in the morning sun. A taxi driver told me that in the next half hour about 3,000 holidaymakers and about 1,000 crew members would flood the island. He had not been there yesterday because the ship "only" had 450 passengers and was not worth it for him and his fleet. Today, however, he could earn his bacon. I had already suspected something like this because my car park was visibly filling up with coaches. During my walk, I had already counted 25 vehicles. It was time to change direction.

I had chosen **Point Prim** in the southeast, again with a lighthouse, of course. The 11 km long headland juts far out into the Northumberland Strait and is home to PEI's oldest round tower. We had a fun sunny ride, with a little mudflat walk in the red sand. Afterwards, we all looked like red pigs, including wet lines where the sand had got caught. My two mice, however, had the most fun playing with and catching empty scallops.

While the sun still held out, I took the direct route to the headland. It was not far away. Here we took our midday rest until a swarm of buses appeared. I wonder if they were from one of the ships. Nearby there was a well-kept provincial park with an adjacent golf course. Should we treat ourselves to luxury again? Did I want to play golf? Not really! Therefore, stinginess prevailed, and we drove back to our regular accommodation. I could charge all my devices and get rid of some emails at the VIC (Visitor Centre). We would still be ok for the next two days.

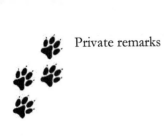 Private remarks

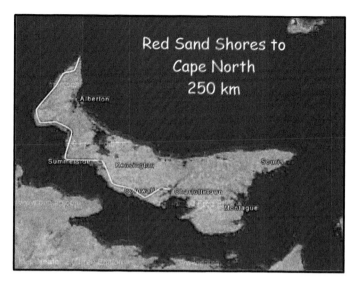

Red Sand Shores to
Cape North
250 km

 Private remarks

Red Sand Shores
Von Charlottetown to Summerside

Once again, a huge cruise ship surprised us in the morning in the harbour. It had arrived around eight o'clock and, as usual, buses and taxis were lined up waiting for passengers. I had the feeling that today would be even busier than yesterday. Let's get out of here before they trap us in the car park.

We had slept wonderfully and long that night too. I was in bed by nine o'clock last night, after three days of catching up on the laptop. After that workload, I was exhausted and felt most comfortable lying down. I was unresponsive for ten full hours and was happy to wake up to sunshine. We were so lucky with the weather!

Although I was not well disposed towards the local WALMART because of its overnight ban, I still had to pay it a visit as I needed a more effective mousetrap. It was still rumbling under my sink from time to time and the sly mouse ate away one piece of chocolate after another without falling into the trap. Now more sophisticated tools had to be used.

Smiling, the salesman explained to me that the most effective way to hide the treat was under flowers. The mouse would have to dig there first and thus surely fall into the trap. Ok! I will also deliver the flowers for the funeral. (8.15 pm – it just clicked! My electrical wires are safe again and the little mouse is in happy mouse heaven! Sorry...)

We had a first short stop on the opposite bay, at the no longer existing *Fort Amherst*. There we had the best view of the ship and the Charlottetown skyline. Besides, the historic site was on our way anyway: the road #19 – **"Red Sands Shore"**. Here, not only the coast was red, no. The houses, the earth, the churches, the water and the trees were too. See for yourself

417

at the beginning of this chapter! The drive itself was a pleasure with this sunshine and glassy water. The houses looked beautiful and even if the estate was small, there were green spaces all around that we could only dream of; every lawn was neatly mown and tended. The islanders also seemed to have a thing for discreet floral decorations.

At **Canoe Cove**, a diversion led us to a beautiful viewpoint park with a path to the water and a wide view of the bay: this is where we took our lunch break. The idea was good, because as it turned out later, the planned **PP "Argyle Shore"** was already closed due to the end of the season and the entrance was locked with a chain. Too bad! But we had had our run.

Victoria seemed very small to me, with a nice harbour and a restaurant jetty into the water. Otherwise, I didn't see too much of the village in the marshland. Among other things, it is supposed to house a relatively well-known theatre for this area.

I was drawn to the 13 km toll *Confederation Bridge*, which would take us back to the mainland in New Brunswick in one of the next days. Then more about this mighty structure! There had to be a global view of the bridge somewhere! I tried a private, sprawling complex, saw several houses or cottages not under a million euros and voluntarily turned around as quickly as possible before a law enforcement officer made me flee. If I had waited a little, this viewpoint would have appeared two kilometres further. Sometimes I'm just too impatient and afraid of missing something…

The same thing happened at **Chelton Beach PP**: closed for the season! I'll probably have the same problem at all the other places that don't have a campsite attached, which are open longer. Accordingly, my secret water sources have also dried up! After some confusion, I finally found the *Seacow Head lighthouse* in **Fernwood**: a beautiful spot! If there hadn't been a private residence nearby, I would have reserved this spot again for the night. Unfortunately, I saw no one far and wide whom I could have asked if I was intruding.

Another 23 km to **Summerside**. I urgently needed to refuel because the pointer had already moved alarmingly to the left. Even if you only drive short distances and detours, the kilometres still add up and by the time you look around, you have four hundred more on the odometer.

Right near the petrol station there was a large nursery. A lot of strange creatures were cavorting on their meadow in front of the facilities. Every year, this company organises a scarecrow competition and several of them were already on display, each more magnificent than the last. Let's see if I'm still here at the end of September to marvel at more curiosities.

Tonight we sleep at a WALMART once again, which is a lot more hospitable than the one in Charlottetown. Tomorrow we will have a look at the town and then continue to the North Pole, pardon the North Cape! Wurschtel keeps peeking out from under the partition curtain, asking me if I'm finally going to bed so he can come with me. No, my friend, first we must add the pictures so that we don't get behind schedule like the last few days.

 Private remarks

Summerside – „Scarecrow Festival"

 Private remarks

North Cape Costal Drive I

When I checked the internet this morning to get the weather conditions for the next few days, I was horrified. It wasn't'so much the daytime temperatures for the next two days that scared me, but rather the night-time temperatures. They were supposed to drop to 6°/7°C. I had to rethink my plans, because in this cold I needed heating and that was only available via electricity (see chapter Halifax!). Two provincial parks were still open on my route, so if I planned well I would be on the safe side.

I decided to take the aforementioned coastal drive clockwise and leave Summerside on the left for the time being. We took the #11 heading west. From Union Corner it always ran close to the coast with wide views of the water, which had turned red again as the level was low now. The tide was beginning to rise. Once again, we entered a purely Arcadian area with a French-speaking population and the typical blue-white-red flags and patterns on the houses. Significantly, the whole area between Summerside and the *Strait Coast* is also called *"Evangeline County"*. The generally Protestant believers were now replaced by Catholics.

The town of **Miscouche**, small as it is today, was of great historical importance. It was here that the Arcadian Convention was signed in 1884, taking as its national flag the French tricolour, with a single gold star symbolising Mary, the Mother of God.

The style of the churches, too, already showed the regional influence. Whereas the village Protestant or Presbyterian churches were simple, small, bright and white, the Catholic churches were powerful and dominant. One example was St. John's in Miscouche, another the "Virgin of Mount Carmel" in Mont Carmel.

Not far from Mont Carmel you find the small village **of Cape Egmont**. It is adorned with a special feature that has already found its way into "Ripley's - Believe it or not": the absolutely unique *"Bottle House"*. The three small houses are the work of *Edouard Arsenault*, who in the 1970s processed 25,000 glass bottles of all colours, shapes and sizes and constructed three amazing buildings from them – a chapel with an altar, a house with six gables and a pub. You could call him an early recycler if the word even existed back then. He gathered his building materials from all over the neighbourhood, the surrounding pubs, rubble heaps and helpful friends, painstakingly cleaning the bottles of dirt and labels until he could use them as he wished.

After a long photo session, we drove on to the old **Cape Egmont lighthouse**. If my guidebook hadn't warned me, I would have missed the gravel road just after the turnoff to the harbour. The lighthouse is located on a washed-out coast with several caves and bizarre weathering. The place would have been appropriate to stand free again, but 1pm was still decidedly too early to retire. The little siesta fell through because two tourist cars arrived at exactly the time when I did not expect another soul to show up. My watchful four-legged friends had to sound the alarm and the nap was over! So we drove on.

There was something to be said for arriving early at **Cedar Dunes PP**. We were able to walk along the beach and look at the black and white striped *lighthouse of Westpoint* with its small hotel attached. It is supposedly the only place in Canada where you can stay overnight in a lighthouse. There is only one guest room in the actual tower, but eight more in adjacent buildings.

I met very nice neighbours from British Columbia at the campsite. They have found a so-called "kitchen party" nearby and want to take me tonight. Then I won't have to drive back with my big box. Before that, we'll have dinner together in my castle, because it's started to rain outside and their small – but nice – pickup truck is somewhat limited in space for three people. The wavelength is right again, I think – with a poodle dog, of course!

I'll tell you more about the evening tomorrow. I think we will stay here for the two cold nights, because the park is small, well laid out and the beach is wide enough for a walk. Besides, at a price of 31.- CAD, I enjoy a senior citizen's discount here. One day more or less doesn't matter. The second PP I chose is open until 27 September. So that will fit my later schedule too.

 Private remarks

 Private remarks

Cold day again

With another cold night in prospect – the weather was lousy today (6°C outside) – I've extended it by another day. The sun is shining now (for how much longer?) but the wind is bitterly cold. In fact, gloves and headgear were called for again in the morning. Today we will do all the paperwork, turn the camper upside down and, depending on the wind strength and temperature, go for a long walk along the sea. The water is very choppy due to the gusts, which makes the beach particularly attractive.

Our trio had a lot of fun together last night. After a hearty dinner in my castle, we drove a few kilometres to the next village, **Burton**. The so-called *"kitchen party"* turned out to be a normal ceilidh evening in the village hall. When we arrived, the hall was already well filled, mostly by locals.

I got a good spot to take pictures in the back rows, so I could also catch up on the performances musically. My God! I would like to have a quarter of the temperament of the fiddler and mother of three children. It is unimaginable to me how one can tap-dance to the music like that while sitting down and at the same time let the violin bow jump over the strings at such a pace. Mother and son had come together for this evening, with an elderly lady at the piano. Her virtuosity was also overwhelming.

Then, in keeping with tradition, there were little treats during the interval, from cakes to sandwiches to cookies, with tea or coffee. As I was still stuffed from the evening, I preferred to watch the buffet guests. Tea and coffee are taboo for me currently anyway.

There are three customs at these evening events. Firstly, the guest who has travelled the furthest is welcomed; and secondly, you get a small gift for the "door price". This is a ticket number corresponding to the entrance ticket and thirdly a 50/50 box. You buy one or more tickets and the number drawn gets half of the amount collected. The other half goes into the community box. You can imagine who was the guest who travelled the furthest – together with my new acquaintances from British Columbia. I outdid them not so much by kilometres but rather by time zones. From here, there is a time difference of five hours to Germany, and "only" four to Vancouver. So now I have a riddle for everyone:

What do the first four letters in the picture mean? I discovered them above a door in the community centre...

At the North Cape of PEI

Today I finally had to do the unpleasant housework before we could start. After all, I didn't know when I'd get around to it again, so with a blustery wind and sun, all the carpets out and the hoover on. The dogs disappeared under the tree. After an hour and a half, the camper was superficially clean again. It was done, and so was I! After all, I had already washed loads of dishes before breakfast, because last night we sat together again for a merry round of goulash, pasta, salad and ice cream. Of course, it was getting late, and I didn't feel like doing the plates anymore. Since I had stayed at home, I also swung the wooden spoon, as we say in German.

Despite all the activities, we were ready to leave at eleven o'clock, had a nice chat with the ranger and steamed off in a northerly direction, almost always on the #14 along the coast.

The wind came from the north, and we had to steer against it. In **Skinners Pond** we tried our luck at the harbour with a walk. First the force of the wind ripped the door out of my hand, and then I could hardly get it closed. I had stood awkwardly, but after a quarter turn the entrance was in the lee and we could climb out.

As long as we ran with the wind (the lines flew horizontally and in serpentines), it was still relatively easy, but on the return I had to clench my lips to avoid getting the red sand between my teeth: that was less fun. A quarter of an hour upwind, a quarter of an hour downwind! That was quite enough and the dogs were also happy to get back into the quiet area of the camper.

The route took us further to the **North Cape**. There it was just as uncomfortable as on the beach. In addition, the whole cape had been decorated with a wind farm, which took away a lot of the original charm of the place. The exhibition about the wind farm in the visitor centre had to be paid for; only the washrooms were free. I didn't need any souvenirs from the shop or information from the exhibition (we have several wind farms in Germany), so I took my dogs for a short walk to the cairns, which are built at special places all over the world. The tide had already been out for two hours, so there was not a trace of Canada's longest rocky reef to be seen. On the other hand, there were warnings on all sides about the danger of the cliffs.

In view of this, we didn't stay outside for too long and ate the leftovers from last night's dinner together. After all, the hour hand was already pointing to three! Another hour of *siesta* and we turned south. We passed some nice little harbours, tried our luck in **Alberton** (a pleasant little town with a silver fox breeding past) and in the harbour of **Northport**. None of the places really appealed to me, so why not drive the fifty kilometres back to **Summerside**? We would still arrive in daylight, be welcomed with open arms at the Walmart and have a good starting point for the next two days. I also wanted to check out the town centre and visit the scarecrow exhibition. Maybe something had happened in the meantime.

We trundled around and at half past six we found our BC acquaintances on the spot. It had also been too windy for them on their tour and, like me, they had sought shelter between the houses.

Nevertheless, the camper still rocks violently from time to time at the mercy of the gusts. Tomorrow it will be windy again, according to the weather forecast, but the temperatures will rise again. For the next few days it will be possible to live without a campsite again.

 Private remarks

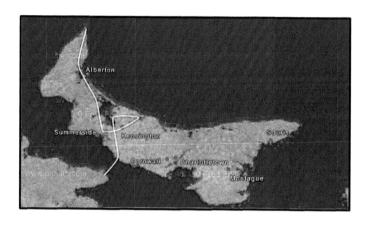

PEI – Farewell tour with music

 Private remarks

Farewell tour with music

Thank goodness I have my pictures to help me remember when I rewrite the trip report. Otherwise, I would have forgotten that I did a little tour of Summerside before my trip. Today (Sunday) there was nothing going on at the harbour. The VIC was still closed, so I set off on my own with my two four-legged friends in search of the murals of the town's history. I didn't find all of them without a map, but some were impossible to miss. In one, the story of a big town fire was told (sensibly on the fire brigade wall), then there were illustrations of the local railway (at the former station building – now a library) and a view of the bygone market street. We were walking  around for over an hour until I had had enough of the wind and cold and returned to the camper.

Another quick visit to the scarecrows. Today was the day of the award ceremony. There was not much more news but I found the new bingo group quite funny.

There was nothing standing in the way of **Lennox Island**, a route I had had to skip. So far – we said our final goodbyes to British Columbia (they continued to Charlottetown) and started north in a little stormy weather. This time we turned north in Miscouche onto **Lady Slipper Drive** – a pretty name for a highway!

The course of the Coastal Drive here was more like a zigzag route and led in a big loop around **Malpeque Bay**. There I spotted the sign "Ceilidh, Sunday, 7pm" twice. But where? Maria had talked about that too. Was it to take place in the pretty church or in the community centre of **Bayside/Grand River**? That could be found out for sure.

But for now, it was Lennox Island's turn, a seat of the "First Nation" and supposedly equipped with a well-stocked craft shop. I was still partly on the lookout for an unusual drum.

What I didn't take home was a drum, but a special knife made, interestingly, of flint, not steel, with the story of an Indian artist in it. Once again, I could not say "no" to the remarkable object and at a price of ninety dollars the piece was still within my means. The owner would have had other, larger pieces in stock, but I didn't necessarily want a bear jaw with teeth as a handle. All the blades were similarly made of sharply ground flint – including mine! – and for this reason they (like the earlier arrowheads) are not shatterproof. That's why the Indians switched to steel when they made the acquaintance with the white man.

Today, arrowheads still serve as protective amulets for the natives. They transmit positive energies and point the way in life. A long thin spearhead, broken into two parts, was given to the warriors on their last journey. The lady from the shop told me a lot about the "Native" and his knowledge of traditional spirituality. He lives hidden in the forest, no one is allowed to visit him without his permission. His knowledge and art are so all-embracing that even museums seek his advice. I guess I was on the right track again, just like years ago with the cutler in Arizona who turned out to be a master blacksmith.

I hope this excursion was not too boring! I, for one, am fascinated by such objects with a background. But I didn't just leave money in the till there for myself, I also found some appealing birthday presents for dear relatives, which did me a great service at home.

We still had some time before the musical evening. We filled it with a long walk on the Confederation Trail, sheltered from the wind. This is an abandoned railway line that stretch-  es 400 km through all of PEI and is reserved for cyclists and hikers only. We had caught a section near **Portage**, which went straight through sparse birch forests and wetlands. Here it was finally time to "cast off!" and sniff until we dropped. My two four-legged friends visibly enjoyed their freedom and I also enjoyed my free hands and had plenty of time to contemplate the onset of autumn.

From Maria and Arnie, I got the tip for a workshop with basketry. Baskets are hard to take home, but quilted items were soft and cuddly, so there were three pairs of potholders to take back and a table runner for my home – if we ever end up there again! This is also where I got the exact address for the ceilidh evening. It was indeed the detached church as I had suspected. St. Patrick's was beautifully situated on a small hill and, like our Leonhard chapels, could be seen all around. Across the road you find the parish hall. I asked one of the organisers if I could stop at the church overnight. "If I were you, I'd stand right in the driveway!" I wouldn't have dared on my own, but with the local blessing I was now off the road.

The evening was a little different from the previous one. The hall was almost full of locals and a "son" of the community was present with his band. At the beginning there were shanties and country, but later my favourite music took its turn. Again, the fiddler was a virtuoso and the lady at the piano weighty but very vital. At the end, all five of them brought a lot of verve to the stage, when they mainly improvised. A nice conclusion to my PEI experience. There is a lot of work to be done on film editing soon. I should still write the first New Brunswick day, but that day will also be anchored in the sup-plementary budget. I am dog-tired. Good night!

 Private remarks

New Brunswick's
coasts in autumn

Indian Summer

End of
September to
End of October

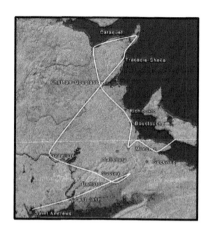

Private remarks

End PEI.... See you tomorrow in New Brunswick (NB)!

Unfortunately, I have to write about the last three days in a somewhat abbreviated form, as I'm behind schedule and otherwise my memories won't keep up. But the most important things stuck, and the pictures help me remember.

On Monday we left PEI via the 13-kilometre *Confederation Bridge* with a fee of 45.- CAD. Bright sunshine accompanied us again, but also a strong wind whose hurricane-like gusts hit the camper again and again in its broadside.

Since I couldn't take pictures from the bridge, I've put in a corresponding picture from Google Earth! It really looked like this! This bridge has connected New Brunswick and PEI since 1997. Before that, there was a ferry in summer and a dangerous sledge transport over the ice with natural horsepower in winter.

I knew little about NB up to this point, as I had not found time to read. I decided to drive to the next larger town and make plans there first. Sufficient material was provided for me at the tourist information office at the end of the bridge.

After a leisurely lunch break below the bridge at **Cape Tormentine**, I drove along the coast towards **Shediac**. I was looking for a campsite to get some shelter from the cold at night.

However, I was unlucky because most of the campgrounds were already closed, and the few open ones looked like chicken coops with overcrowding. No, better to freeze and look for a quiet place. I discovered a marina (*Pointe-du-Chêne*) shortly before Shediac with many closed pubs and shops. Here I could settle down safely in the shelter of a building to at least be safe from the fierce wind.

We remained untouched until shortly before midnight, then someone woke me up with a knock! It was the security guard of the harbour. He informed me that I was no longer allowed to stand here. This was the first time something like that had happened on my long journey. I pretended to be ignorant, told him that I was from Germany, that I couldn't drive at night, that I hadn't seen any prohibition signs... Then he relented and allowed me to stay the night if I didn't steal a boat. I could promise him this with a clear conscience. But sleep was now a thing of the past for several hours, because the wind moved some tinkling measuring instruments and with my eyes closed, I was on an alpine pasture with cowbells in the mountains. Of course, I crawled out of bed in the morning feeling correspondingly exhausted.

In Shediac I tried to find the huge lobster. The VIC was also nearby. There I took the precaution of getting a map of Moncton. I could also fill up my water, as there were garden hoses everywhere. **Moncton** didn't have too much to offer on Tuesday. Both WALMARTs had free parking at night and good

Wi-Fi reception, so I knew my sleeping place was secured for today. I did some correspondence and around noon I set off for *Magnetic Hill,* one of the sights of the city. The gradient plays tricks on anything with wheels. If you put your car in neutral at the bottom of the hill and release the brakes, the vehicle seems to roll backwards uphill. It's not just cars that defy gravity here. A stream running alongside the road also seems to flow up the hill.

You pay a five-dollar fee to explore this phenomenon. Since there were no crowds and I was alone in the field, I let my camper roll backwards up the hill several times. A strange feeling! The explanation is an optical illusion and can be explained physically.

Even in the photo it looks like the road is going uphill. After my fifth attempt, I looked for a parking space and strolled through the site with the dogs. Attached to the spectacle was a water park (closed) and a zoo to keep the tourists entertained. Even a covered

bridge (more about that later!) had been moved here for reasons of attractiveness. I took a quick look at the camper van and couldn't believe my eyes. I knew that pickup with a canoe… right, our paths crossed again at Magnetic Hill. We ar

443

ranged to sleep on one of the two WALMARTs later, but not before I took a photo of the car rolling uphill.

On Wednesday, we wanted to see the tidal wave together here in Moncton. You readers might remember the rafting trip on the other side of Fundy Bay (town of Truro) and the gentle wave of the Atlantic. Today I felt that the wave came in heavier and faster. Was it perhaps due to the location or the tidal phenomenon in general? You can see this very well on the video.

My new acquaintances were drawn to the south curve of NB, me to the east coast, towards the north. Would our paths cross again? A reunion in BC was planned for April next year at the latest – after my return from Mexico and everyone went their separate ways with confidence. I wanted to get as far as **Kouchibouguac National Park** today and take a breather there, because the weather prospects were brilliant.

A drove hundred kilometres of direct route, about 160 kilometres along the coast. This time it was a "Coastal Drive" with lots of views of the sea and the offshore salt marshes. The population was of Arcadian origin and their flags demonstrated their ancestry, or even just power poles painted blue-white-red. With the right eye, one could always glimpse PEI. The two coasts are not far apart. At around five o'clock I was glad when I arrived at the national park after a lot of winding: there were enough free places with electricity. Here I wanted to relax a little with my crew, enjoy the Indian summer, do some work that had been left behind and do a lot of walking. We all desperately needed some more nature and peace. I am still not sure about the further course of my route. Let's see what the next thoughts bring. Maybe the flash of inspiration will strike in time… In any case, the weather is expected to be perfect until Sunday, and we'll stay here until then! In addition, I have the best Wi-Fi possibilities at my location, so that I can use the internet again as much as I want.

Holiday in Kouchibouguac National Park

We let our souls dangle for four days! Nothing but walking, sitting in the sun, reading, hunting squirrels and watching bald eagles. The Canadian wild geese gather at the river to fill their bellies before continuing their journey; their chattering can be heard all day, but there is only a small photographic overview of the national park with the unpronounceable name from the Mi'kmaq language: "River of the Long Tides".

The river of the same name that flows into the park is wide, interspersed with sandbanks and surrounded by marshy meadows. Off the coast there is a sandy spit with a kilometre-long protected dune belt and sandy beach. The quiet and peaceful landscape – low forest, many small ponds, marshes, small rivers, and also formerly cultivated land that is now being reclaimed by nature – is a paradise for numerous water birds. So far, 225 different bird species have been recorded in the area.

The park has a 60 km network of cycle paths and attractive canoe routes. Of course, walkers and hikers are also catered for, from 20-minute circular walks to a 12 km hiking trail with wilderness overnight stays. The area is so large that you have to drive over 10 km from its entrance to the campsite. Now the campers are not busy and although at the weekend the site fills up a bit you have plenty of space around you.

(Pictures: Red orgy in the swamp are – a swamp area opened by boardwalks! Can't be beaten for colour intensity!)

Private remarks

Kouchibouguac NP - Indian Summer

 Private remarks

Inferno of fire colours

The decision yesterday was right when we believed the weather forecast. This morning everything was indeed overcast and it smelled like rain. I was therefore a bit more motivated to get my interior in order and once again throw everything out and clean it up, guilelessly and uncomprehendingly followed by two pairs of dog eyes.

At lunchtime, everything was done and we said goodbye in the direction of **Miramichi,** about 50 km to the north. There I wanted to make a stop at a laundry. While sorting, I came up with six full loads. After all, I hadn't done anything in this respect for four weeks. It was about time, before I ran out of my last pair of pants!

Even though the sun wasn't shining, it was still a brilliant ride. In the last three days, the Indian Summer had unfolded in its full splendour. This season is golden in Alaska; in the Yukon more dominated by the colourful tundra. Here you drive through a tree-high sea of flames. All shades of fire are represented, from soft orange to an almost purple leaf colour. The further north I went, the more the low ground vegetation played a part in the symphony of colours with light intermediate tones. One could have stopped a hundred times during these fifty kilometres to capture the play of colours in the camera. The basic motif would have been the same again and again, but still amazingly different and varied. That's why ideas like purgatory (only more pleasant) or the trial by fire from The Magic Flute came to mind.

I hope I can deliver some sunny pictures tomorrow. The weather is supposed to become friendlier again, but also cooler. Now it is raining in **Bathurst** at the WALMART and the night temperatures are supposed to drop to 5°C. Our route has taken us several kilometres north again. As there are no moun-

449

tains here to keep out the incoming cool polar air, there are often surprising drops in temperature: for example yesterday it was 27°C and today the daily high was 12°C. Last night I slept almost without a blanket and tonight I'll need my two dogs. I'll probably have to get them in bed as hot water bottles!

Again and again, I have to marvel at how small the world is. In the launderette I was busily doing my seven things when a younger man asked me with a familiar voice: "Now I'd like to know where you come from… !" It turned out that he was almost from my old home, from *Kochel am See*. He bought a cabin and a plot of land in the wilderness here twenty years ago as a young "drop-out" and now regularly enjoys his freedom, fishes for salmon and goes hunting. We had so much to talk about that I almost forgot my work. It turned out that we agreed on many things about our host country.

The wait for the dryers went by in no time at all and after three hours I was 25.- CAD poorer in loonies and quarters and a load of clean laundry richer. I stowed everything away and then headed off straight towards **Bathurst** before it got dark.

The town has a hospitable WALMART. We'll set up here and decide tomorrow which direction to take: either the Appalachian Range Route and down to Fredericton, or the coastal tip and back to Miramichi and from there to the River Route. We'll see what my gut feeling tells me then, provided it hasn't frozen overnight… If necessary, we'll just thaw ourselves out with the oven!

180 km Arcadia full

Now comes the season I hate so much! In the morning it is still dark when I do the first walk with the dogs and the day is getting shorter and shorter, the evening longer and longer. Earlier and earlier, I have to find a place to cling to, so that the darkness doesn't get in the way of my driving.

450

Tonight, I was more than grateful for Wurschtel's cuddliness. Jesus Christ! It was so cool! I went to bed in a jumper and tracksuit bottoms. Before that, I had to keep the oven on to keep myself warm. What else could I do without a functioning gas heating system. But I have to say the place warmed up quickly with this method, but cooled down again just as quickly. By then we were already in a warm bed.

This morning, the whole game backwards: jumping out of bed, oven, back into bed and out for morning exercises in bearable temperatures (at least indoors). Gloves and a headband were the order of the day. First aid: warm water for washing, warm water for rinsing, hot breakfast tea – that also awakens frozen spirits.

A good friend recently remarked that she always had to smile when she read about our miserable temperatures, as she knows how averse I am to the cold. Honestly! I can only bear it because I am fully conscious in Canada (!) and will surely move to warmer zones in winter… Only advantage: the mosquitoes are gone! The best solution was found while driving. The car really heated up, we were all sitting comfortably and "freezing" was a foreign word at that time. For this reason, I decided on the Arcadian Peninsula – 180 km from Bathurst to Miramichi (direct route 80 km). Maybe up to the islands? Take a breather halfway until tomorrow? There was a campsite still open in **Shippagan**.

I deleted the route over the Appalachians from my programme when I looked at the road via "Google Earth Street View", as well as the cross connection to it… Might be a bit outdated, but with the budget situation of the province of NB… We got going at around nine, took the bypass around Bathurst and then clockwise along the coast on #11. Many Arcadians who had been expelled from Nova Scotia in 1755 fled to this region. The peripheral location helped them to preserve their traditions and culture better here than elsewhere – the many Arcadian flags still show it today. In addition you see bins painted in Arcadian colours; telephone poles with Arcadian bases; an entire house in Arcadian colours; the lighthouse near the information office bristling with blue-white-red; a Living Museum with 40 buildings on the former Arcadian way of life; an Arcadian Museum, large and emblazoned Arcadian door plates with French names, etc. You could see them all… you truly could not miss them all.

We made our first circular stop at **Grande-Anse** beach with an original (closed) pub. Heavens! The wind blew through our bones! Quickly back into the protective camper. Where was yesterday's positive weather report? **Caraquet** (founded in 1757) is today the centre of francophone culture. No English! French please! But the slang is so breathtaking that you think you never heard this language at school! What were we doing on the offshore islands? Nothing really! Everything was closed for the season anyway. If we could do the whole round now, we would have a safe place to sleep tonight at the WALMART of Miramichi.

Shortly after **Tracadie-Sheila** I discovered a signpost to the beach. However, there were still another four kilometres to go. Here we took our lunch break and watched several fishermen standing up to their bellies in the moving sea. Brrr! One of them proudly took his evening meal out of the tide… two large fish? They were too far away to ask what kind of fish they were.

If I gave up my afternoon nap now, we would even get a little further south. Yesterday, while studying the weather reports for the various cities, I discovered that **Fredericton** was at least five degrees warmer on average than the local towns. So let's get on the highway #8!

But first I wanted to refill my propane. It wasn't urgent yet, but using the oven as a heater? Like a possessed woman, I searched for the petrol station described to me: three times over the big bridge in a traffic jam and back again, five times down University Avenue! "Very easy to find …!" according to another petrol station yesterday. In desperation I entered the search name into the GPS! Sure enough, it had "Irving" on #11 in the radar! Very easy to find!

Now I had both necks full again, with gas and with petrol! We had a good hour left to drive before dusk fell. 70 km to Doaktown, 11 km further to an open campsite! That fitted … In case of doubt, maybe the VIC had already closed, and we could stay in the car park overnight.

What I got was much, much better: in Blackville I saw a municipal recreational park on the river with lots of green, available parking spaces and not a soul. But there was a house with cars back there! It doesn't cost anything to ask! A men's club, probably various fishing friends: "Of course you can stay here overnight! No problem!   You just mustn't sing too loudly …" Heavenly! So once again we had found the ultimate place for our trio. And it was still warm at 6 pm! I could go for a walk with my two mice without an anorak. Now, at 8pm, it's still 13°C outside and 19°C in the camper without heating! We have survived for the time being … I will now fit in the pictures and then my day's work is done! See you again in the provincial capital Fredericton. Good night!

453

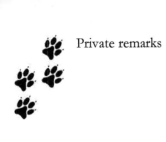 Private remarks

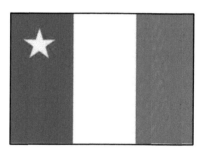

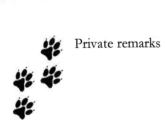 Private remarks

Provincial capital Fredericton

One hundred and twenty kilometres of paved road laid ahead of us today. Unfortunately, the sun had not appeared. Nevertheless, the drive through the colourful mixed forest was an experience. On our journey through NB to Newfoundland, I had already thought that autumn must have a special touch here. But the splendour of such different colours exceeded all my expectations. Added to this were the lovingly autumnal decorations in the individual houses and the hint of Hallow-een. I therefore did not get bored with these kilometres, alt-hough the route had been treated in a somewhat step motherly way in my guidebooks.

At a sign for a "Covered Bridge" we swung off the dual car-riageway and were blocked by a barrier shortly afterwards. We took the legs under our arm – as we say in my language – and set off for the small covered bridge into the valley to the Mir-amichi River, the salmon river par excellence.

There are still 62 of these bridges in NB and they are particu-larly common in the south. The roofing here is due to climatic reasons: a normal wooden bridge lasts 10-15 years under the given conditions, whereas a covered bridge lasts 70-80 years. Even expensive steel bridges rot quickly in the salty sea air if they are not constantly maintained. The covered bridges that still exist have been rehabilitated in the meantime, mostly with concrete foundations and steel girders, so that they can withstand today's traffic loads.

Once again, we ran into a couple who had bought property in Nova Scotia twenty years ago. At that time, real estate must have been available for a penny. Nowhere else can you find so many German properties on the Canadian coast as in Nova Scotia and New Brunswick. The economic situation at the time probably prompted many residents to sell their possessions.

Today the situation is not much different, as one can see with open eyes. "For sale" and again "For sale" is written on the houses. It should be noted, however, that Canadians have a different relationship to property from the one we have in Germany. While we build for generations and children's children, real estate ownership here is only a speculative object, to acquire a larger property from the proceeds of sale.

The average Canadian rarely lives in the same property for more than seven to eight years. At least that's how my friends have explained it to me. But when I look at the little houses here, I doubt this basic idea. I rather think that economic hardship is behind it. You just have to look at the daily price level; it is often surprising that the average family can survive. Most of the time, both parents have several jobs at the same time and those who have grandparents or uncles and aunts to look after the children are lucky.

But now from this little excursion back to Fredericton. First, we tested the WALMART for overnight accommodation. Bingo! We could drive into the city centre and have a look at the small old town. As I didn't know of any other parking possibilities, I stopped behind the town hall for a two-dollar parking fee, very cramped and risky. At the information office they referred me to a free RV park very close by. I waived my parking obolus and hurriedly got off the stool before any more cars would catch up with me.

A leisurely lunch break followed by a two-hour tour of the city centre. It's all well and good that Fredericton has so many pleasant green spaces with trees. But do hundreds of squirrels also have to cavort in the elms? It was just a tug and a jerk with my two four-legged friends. They wanted to catch every grey wretch but they turned up their long noses at them and happily hopped from meadow to tree and from tree to meadow. And I was allowed to see how I constantly kept my two beasts in check: if I have sore muscles in both arms tomorrow, I'll know why. The passers-by had a great time with us, but I didn't have as much fun. Heavens! I was exhausted after this tour. In the end I had both on such short leashes that they could hardly move from my side. I had no other choice!

Fredericton is located on the *Saint John River* and it is the third largest city in NB with a population of around 50,000. It owes its history to the thousands of Loyalists who left the USA at the time of the American War of Independence and found their "promised land" here. If you want to know more about its chequered history, including its allegiance to English royalty, you can look up hundreds of pages on the internet. I don't want to dwell on it here. There are wiser heads for that.

We walked (or rather rushed) along the waterfront to the drained lighthouse, rounded the cathedral, walked halfway across the railway bridge (now a pedestrian walkway), enjoyed some of the old wooden houses and, exhausted, reached our destination at the old garrison buildings, which now housed a museum, an art academy and several craft shops. According to my guidebook, the entire sightseeing tour could have been completed in about forty-five minutes but it took us almost two hours, thanks to the nimble grey ding-dong men... I had had enough and escaped for half an hour alone to the whole-sale market. It was wonderful to be able to walk three to four steps normally again without a sudden jerk and pull, despite the customers. As a reward, I bought a few long-sleeved shirts – after all, it was already autumn!

A trailer stopped near me and let its generator hum at extreme volume. I had already spent a long night suffering with this and couldn't sleep. Today I took heart and knocked the owner's door at around half past eight. It was like the joke about the rattling bicycle: "I can't hear a thing, it's rattling so loud!" In this case, the wizened little man was hard of hearing and I had to use more sign language to make him understand what was annoying me. I even offered to park further away should he have to run the thing any longer. But the driver was a real gentleman, took off and retreated to another corner. I didn't care what he thought about fussy German tourists. So my night's rest should be reasonably assured. Let's see...

Provincial capital Fredericton

 Private remarks

Fundy National Park

It lifts your spirits immensely when you wake up to sunshine again. The temperatures were still "in the basement", but by now we knew how to deal with that. Due to the favourable weather conditions, I decided to head for the Fundy coast immediately and leave Moncton again for later. It was only forty kilometres more, a pittance for a whole day. The drive went for a long time along the St. Johns River, which branches out into an infinite number of tributaries and sandbanks. Of course, autumn shone brightly in the sunlight and the colour play of water, vegetation and sky could not be surpassed.

At some point, the route took us onto Highway #10, which led us right through the middle of the province. Fifty kilometres of sparsely populated areas. Where do the children go to school here? What prospects do they have apart from becoming lumberjacks and hunters? Where are the jobs? What happens if someone needs urgent medical attention? By the time an emergency doctor arrives, the body has probably helped itself or given up. How does one spend the often long winter here at minus 25°C? Doesn't the intense loneliness make you depressed? What about neighbours, leisure activities… ? A lot of these questions or similar ones went through my mind and I realised the other side of the coin.

Shortly after the turn-off onto #10, I came across a very appealing information facility. They had housed the VIC in a nice reconstructed covered bridge, a clear indication that there were many of these small bridges in the area. The advice was extremely friendly and informative. Nowhere in my literature had I heard of Sussex. I should make a stop in the capital of murals. Why not? The sun was shining, which was excellent for photography, and we had time because our destination was called Fundy National Park. The clerk wanted to push another campsite on me, but I still managed with the national parks for the time being.

On the way, I made two small detours to marked wooden bridges. I had to try out whether I could get through with my box. A metre gauge just before the entrance signalled to me: "No danger"! Since there was no traffic in front or behind, I could risk taking a photo of my vehicle as it entered and exited.

Sussex is a typical North American small town, with a long main street dominated by low-rise shops, retail establishments and the usual fast-food joints. But its special feature is the murals (wall paintings): some very appealing, on the history of the small town and life past and present. We spent a good hour wandering through the streets and kept discovering new motifs. There was really a lot to see, from the ice hockey club to the former shopping street and cheerful farm life. This time at least we were spared the squirrel plague.

Sussex had a WALMART, but it was still far too early for a stop and so we drove on to the Fundy National Park, to the headquarters, just before the village of **Alma**. The campground there was still open for quite some time. As we were late, or rather the rangers got off work very early, we checked in with self-registration and found a place with full hook-up for just under 29.- CAD. I couldn't find the ones with only water and electricity in the twilight, so we settled for the night on the only available comfort pitch. Tomorrow we will see!

465

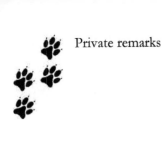 Private remarks

Flower Pots

I was feeling a bit exhausted again from the last few days of driving, but we still had to make our trip to the "flowerpots" today because of the favourable weather forecast. Rain was predicted for tomorrow; so we got out of bed and saddled up at around ten o'clock. The tides were ideal for our walk on the seabed. Low at 2.30pm, with three hours priming and three hours lagging.

However, we didn't take the direct route to **Hopewell Rocks** but took the #915 running along the coast, a little worse developed than the main road. I wanted to try the diversions to **Cape Enrage**. There, high above the sea, you find the oldest lighthouse in New Brunswick. At low tide you can supposedly still find fossils on the beach below, which are forbidden to collect and take.

Once you leave the *Caledonia Highlands* behind, a huge salt marsh stretches along the coast, home to numerous bird species and now sporting a beautiful yellow-brown colour in autumn. **Cape Enrage** is primed for the tourist rush. An adventure company offers a zip line over a small section of coastline in summer and several climbing tours. You must pay five dollars for the park fee and can then climb up various wooden walkways and stairs to several viewpoints. Of course, the obligatory souvenir shop is not to be missed. We only stayed in this area for a short time, because it was not possible for me to get down to the beach with my two companions, as the stairs and handrails were made of wire mesh and therefore unsuitable for dogs' paws.

Our actual destination for today was the **Hopewell Rocks** in the Provincial Park of the same name. This place was all set up for mass tourism, as you could see from the size of the car park. So what? Hopewell Cape is unique, even more so now that the sun was coming through in full. Thank God it was the off-season and the crowds were very small. The **Hopewell Rocks** are peculiar rock formations whose shape resembles flowerpots (with a lot of imagination). Shrubs and trees grow on top of the rocks. This is somewhat reminiscent of flowerpots, especially at high tide. At low tide you can walk between the peculiar formations (on the seabed so to speak); at high tide only the upper parts of the pots stick out of the water. Then you go around them by kayak with a guide, because of the currents.

I arrived just in time for a guided tour, but wisely left the dogs in the car. By luck I had caught the head of the guiding staff and we were only three listeners: two young girls and me. It was obvious that the smart gentleman was concentrating more on the other two ladies and just let me run along as an "old bag" (and a foreign speaker too). But that didn't bother me, because I had already read a lot about this natural attraction and so he didn't tell me much that was new for me. However his video recordings, which were mostly made by chance and showed very special events, such as a rock fall or the very rare northern lights over the rocks, were very informative. He also had to scramble through some rock holes with the two ladies, which I did my best to avoid.

I was perhaps glad that my four-legged friends were well looked after in the camper, because in places it was still very juicy brown on the seabed. We would have looked like pigs. It was enough that I returned to the car with muddy trouser legs and clay shoes. Only when you look at the isolated people in the pictures do you realise the gigantic size of the rocks. One day, the force of the tides will wash them out in the narrowest places. Then there goes the attraction "Flowerpots"! I think Canada will have to think of something new …

As I mentioned at the beginning, I was in the mood for a rest day. I couldn't imagine that with this wonderful evening atmosphere, rain was in the offing for tomorrow. But if it is, I can use this day to relax and catch up on my homework. It's also nice not to wake up to temperatures below 10°C for three days. So back to the National Park and a spot in the evening sun! See you!

Hopewell Rocks - Fundy NP

Private remarks

Molly's Kitchenparty

Despite yesterday's starry night, it rained heavily this morning: I hadn't believed the weather forecast. That came just in time for me to recover. I changed my place once more and now had a good internet signal again. I could finally finish the work I had left behind and send it on its way. There was also a lot of organisational work to do. In every corner a dog was sleeping and I took my time to work. With several short walks, the day passed peacefully, and the steering wheel was not touched for 24 hours.

In the evening I treated myself to "Molly's Kitchen Party" in the little wooden house at the bottom of the hill in Alma. I could easily walk there, equipped with a headlamp and a torch. The path was relatively well lit, however, so there were no tripping hazards lurking at night.

This kitchen party was a lot of fun! Everything was organised on a small scale. Two adult actors (probably mother and son) acted in a delicious two-man theatre and performed a couple of sketches with abandon, welcoming the audience to participate. In between, the youngsters had their turn. Of course, not all the harmonies were in tune with their age, but I admired the courage of the little musicians to play in front of such a large audience. There was even a tap interlude to applaud. As pleasantly dim and intimate as the lighting was, it was poor for my video clips. I could delete them all as soon as I got home. Thank God I had taken some photos this time. In the second part, the audience was involved in the musical performances, with rattles, spoons, washboard and canister. The little audience members especially enjoyed this activity and tapped and rattled along to the rhythm with concentration and appropriate seriousness.

Finally, the chairs were moved aside and a dance floor emerged. Whether anybody wanted to or not, they had to shake a leg. It was especially funny when a tall and a short person paired together. The many comical situations were rewarded by the audience with vigorous clapping.

As with every "Kitchen Party", there were a few treats to eat afterwards and this time hot cider to drink (non-alcoholic of course with so many children present). All the fun was available for 5.- CAD.

After an hour, the magic was over, and I puffed slowly like a steam engine up 120 steps to the campsite: going down had taken less than on my way home. Another short round with the pooches, typed today's text and then off into the trap. Tomorrow we continue to Saint John.

Saint John or: much ado about nothing

What nasty autumn weather! We started from the campsite at around noon and drove 130 kilometres straight to **Saint John** on the motorway. Grey in grey, windy and foggy with falling autumn leaves. A few more days like this and the glorious Indian summer will make this golden blanket degenerate into a muddy brown one on the ground. Well, we're heading further south soon, so nature will stay beautiful for a little longer.

I wanted to settle down at the campsite in Saint John for a few days and do some sightseeing from there. But that was no good! Although it was advertised for October 13th, it was already closed. Bummer! So once again we were left with the WALMART. Several other campers had the same problem so we all met again in front of the supermarket. At the end of the day, I counted seven guests.

Monday brought the promised sunshine so we set off for the information centre at the rapids. I needed the exact time of low and high tide. The "Reversing Falls" are the landmark of the Loyalist city; the powerful tides of the Bay of Fundy causing the St. John River to flow backwards here (as it does in Truro or Moncton) at times. The already wide river must squeeze through  a narrow gorge from a height of about 12m above sea level just before its mouth. The difference in height causes the water to cascade down several steps of the rocky subsoil when the flow is normal – i.e. at low tide. As the water rises, the height of the falls gradually decreases until the cascades disappear altogether. During a short phase, the river comes to a standstill. Then the water flows upstream through the gorge until the tide's highest point. This sounds quite exciting, but it takes ages and is only interesting in the time-lapse shot in the VIC.

We just arrived at the peak and would now have had to wait forever until the cascades were finally visible. That was too

boring for me, so I grabbed my two four-legged friends and marched through a nearby park, which was decorated with wooden figures of important personalities of the city. Of course, there was also a Mr. "Irving", an owner of countless woodworking businesses from days gone by. Whether this was to the blessing of Saint John or not remains to be seen. In any case, his paper mills and factories disfigure the cityscape and the surroundings of the falls enormously. The economic investments, however, have contributed to the fact that Saint John is now the second largest city in the province with about 70,000 inhabitants.

From a distance, I saw that a cruise ship was anchored in the harbour. I was drawn to the centre and the harbour at lunchtime. Without realising it, I parked for free in a paid area behind the sports arena. What does a stranger know?

Today I condemned my two four-legged friends to stable duty. I had absolutely no desire to watch Saint John at "stop and go" speed. Besides, they were not allowed to visit the market hall, and I didn't want to miss out on this gem. After all, it was one of the very few buildings that survived a major fire in 1877. Afterwards, the houses were rebuilt in brown bricks and designed very differently. This was the real charm of the small town centre. To compensate a little for the different levels, a long glass skywalk was built to connect the individual shopping centres. During my tour, therefore, I didn't feel the steep streets so much. King Street, for example, is considered Canada's steepest inner-city main street. I was on the go for almost two and a half hours and discovered many pretty doors or interesting shops. It was also amazing to see the size of the cruise ship compared to the harbour facilities and the reception building.

At *Loyalist Plaza*, I struck up a conversation with a nice person who was offering clay figurines and pendants for sale.

"Everything made of clay from Fundy Bay! I dug it out myself and baked the figurines! ..." Just out of a happy mood, he gave me a maple pin for my hat. Of course I bought a second one from him, for my second hat. He was more than proud when I asked him for a photo. (I just sent it to him by email!).

Slowly my legs were starting to ache. I also had to remember that my mice still needed exercise. Subsequently I took the skywalk again to get quickly past the library, the museum and the pretty entrance hall to my caravan. I wanted to spend the night at the WALMART car park again. However, I had planned to walk around the small lake in *Rockwood Park*. The walk was not that small and took over an hour. Both my friends had really earned this run, but please don't ask me what my poor legs said afterwards! Mind you, all without a midday *siesta*! But now quickly to bed! Tomorrow is supposed to be another beautiful day! "Carpe diem" – who remembers that?

Private remarks

477

Private remarks

Lots of nice people

Yesterday I was already happy about the friendly market trader, today I ran into an elderly couple who just handed me four cans of sardines from **Black Harbour**. In this fishing village that was on my route, there was a fish factory more than a hundred years ago. Today, the community celebrates itself as the "Home of the World's largest Sardine Industry". I was allowed to call a sample of it my own free of charge. Both were from the area and just like us, they were out for a little walk to the *waterfalls of Lepreau*. It was another beautiful day today and we had driven a long stretch on the #1 westbound. At the *River Beach PP* we found a barrier, so we thankfully gave up. As we were able to drive fast on the newly built highway, I also bypassed **St. George**, the granite town. Maybe we'll make a little trip there soon.

A campsite was still open in **Saint Andrews**. It was right on the tip of the cape, and I feared a high price because of its location. It was open until October 15th and that would fit perfectly into my plans. I checked in for 9 nights and was surprised to see the bill: with electricity and water only 18.- CAD as the post-season price: I liked that.

The site is spacious, right by the sea, and it#s about a 20-minute walk to the town centre, which is nothing more than a long main street along the water. This spot was founded in 1784 by wealthy British Loyalists who had previously made their home in Main. After crossing the border, they shipped property – and in some cases even their homes – and rebuilt here. Saint Andrews was spared by town fires and therefore has well-preserved examples of colonial architecture. Many wooden houses painted in all colours characterise the image of the old town.

Tomorrow the weather forecast calls for thunder and lightning, but on Thursday the sun will come out again We'll go on a few short excursions one day or the other or we'll let our wings hang down, depending on our mood. We've earned it after travelling almost exactly 15,500 kilometres since we set off from Toronto.

Many readers may wonder why we are taking such a long break here – the longest ever after Halifax on our journey. There are several reasons for this:

(a) The later I enter the US now, the longer I can delay my departure next spring. This can be of great importance climatically.

b) We must empty our fridge before crossing the border, because the Americans are (let's say politely) meticulous with agricultural products, vegetables, fruit and meat. It's best not to have anything on board. But my freezer is still at least half full. The dogs' treats and normal dry food are also taboo. That makes both dogs' hearts happy, of course!

c) We really need some rest, because I notice that a certain impatience with my animals is spreading through me. This is usually the surest sign to slow down a bit.

Curiosity satisfied now…? Then, good night!

"Carpe diem" concludes the first phase of my last travel project. The next 3,000 kilometres along the east coast of the USA down to Florida are purely private: I will be visiting friends I met on my many North American journeys. I will report back in detail from the Southern States (probably at the beginning of December) – if nothing comes up… until then, all the best! Monika with her two friends on four paws.

"La Cucaracha"/Central Mexico, Colonial Cities, Yucatán Peninsula in a private motorhome –
BoD-Verlag Norderstedt, ISBN: 9783754317884 Autorin Monika v. Borthwick erzählt von dieser folgenden spannenden Zeit.

Inhaltsverzeichnis
Einleitung

Neufundland

Nova Scotia NS

 Private remarks

Prince- Edward-Island oder P.E.I. oder PEI

New Brunswick – Küstenbereiche

Moncton – Kouchibouguac National Park

Acadian Shore – Fredericton

St. John – St. Andrew – USA

 Private remarks

Further travel reports of the adventurous trio with Monika von Borthwick

Highways und Gravel Roads - Volume I
* With the MoWuKnuffels in a
motorhome across the
North American continent.
 * From New York to Alaska

Highways und Gravel Roads Volume II
* A continuing story
* From the Arctic Circle (Alaska) to
the Tropic of Cancer
(Baja California)

Viva Los Topes!
* An eventful journey in a
motorhome with two dogs through
Central Mexico and the Southwest
                 of the USA
                 * Canyon State Utah

Winterwings
*Overwintering like the storks in Por-
tugal

 Private remarks

Rubber Tramps

Driving the TransCanada Highway in a motorhome from Vancouver to Ottawa

Chorizo & Co

Overwintering in Spain -

in a differen way

La Cucaracha

Mexican colonial cities and the Yucatan Peninsula with a camper van

 Private remarks

All books are also available as e-books in the relevant online shops.

Further information about the books, how to buy them in bookshops or directly from the author can be found at

www.monika vonborthwick.com
or info@mvborthwick.de

Here you will also find detailed information about the author's social commitment.

 Private remarks

Thank you

Normally at this point we should be reading a thank you to the helpers of the author such as lecturer, publisher, counseling, helpful wives, critical comments, …

Since the present book was created in absolute self-direction (images, layout, writing, language...), my thanks go to the following:

* My two dogs Wurschtel and Knuffi, who have faithfully gone through everything, helped me to never feel alone and to give me security as a guard and reliable alarm system.
* All the friendly and helpful people I met on my journey mentioned in the book and interested in our company.
* My reliable friend Patricia, who has translated this story into English with great love, competence and patience.
* My English friend Jennifer from GB finding the last spelling mistakes.
* My open-minded email readers and good friends who gave me the idea to publish my notes as a book.
* The indulgent readers of the book, who overlooked one or the other error devil benevolently. If you discover one, you are welcome to keep it!
* Last, but not least, the helpful hands at home, which took care of the vacant apartment during my absence, monitored my mail and never let the connection to the home break. Without them such a tour would have been impossible.

 Private remarks

Private remarks

Private remarks